Rhubarb!

Tales of Survival on a Little Greek Island

David Fagan

Edited by

Jennifer Kelland Fagan

ISBN-13: 978-1482596137
ISBN-10: 148259613X

Cover painting courtesy William Pownall
Cover design by David and Jennifer Fagan

For information address:
David Fagan
Hydra, Greece

Or contact David through his website at www.davidfagan.org.

DEDICATION

For Jennifer—my love, my life, my very best friend, and my wife.

DEFINITION

Rhubarb: a heated dispute or controversy.*

* *Webster's Collegiate Dictionary,* 11th ed.

FEEDBACKLASH!

READERS' COMMENTS ON *RHUBARBS I*

Daaavid … I loved your book—the way you write is so full of colour I could actually see what you were writing about … the food strapped to the donkeys and sauce all over the place. —*Diane R. Williams Khalil*

I would have written back sooner, but have just been released from the hospital after a brief stay due to a bout of OPL—Outright Prolonged Laughter—brought on by reading *Rhubarbs from a Rock*. You really have the eye and ear for the funny foibles of our fellow man and woman, and I enjoyed it cover to cover. —*Craig Smith*

Glad to see that you are writing a new book with the same and very witty pen (keyboard), [*Rhubarbs from a Rock*] certainly was too short. —*Svanhild Sollos, Norway*

"Long time no laugh so loud so much" over printed words. … Truly enjoyed your ruminations relating Hydra's rocky rhubarbs. —*Myrto Liatis*

I've just finished reading your hilarious book *Rhubarbs from a Rock*. It has inspired me to visit Hydra on my next trip to Europe so I can see for myself such eminent locations as "Donkey Shit Lane" and perhaps meet with some of the wonderful and eccentric characters who appear in your book. Hope there's going to be a sequel. —*Astrid Roy, South Africa*

Not being the type to finish books overnight I have to admit *Rhubarbs* has been immensely difficult to put down. A really entertaining read which I give you credit for writing and for surviving on the Rock for so long. … As a by-the-way, you know the feeling when you've finished a good book and can't get into your next choice? … Well, I got that syndrome with *Rhubarbs* … so opted to read *Rhubarbs* again. I must say, it's a great second-time-round read, which cannot be said for a lot of books. —*Trevor Stokes*

Through your experiences, I felt I did travel to Hydra this year! Having been to many of the locations, as I read the *Rhubarbs*, I felt as if I could smell the scene in my head! I laughed out loud at the spider story, and "Leatherboy." The Rams head story was HYSTERICAL. It was a great read … having been to Hydra or not. —*Victoria Papale*

Elias has read *Rhubarbs from a Rock* as well and loooooved it: he had fun all the way through and was very sad when he came to the last page: he felt as if he had left the island. We are great fans (and believe me, we are also big readers, so we can compare). —*Isabelle & Elias Baltassis, France*

I was up until midnight reading the book and nearly fell out of bed when I read about Pan going down the cisterna to fetch a pair of glasses in the old Bahia Bar. I laughed out loud many times at the stories about Mardas, the Austrian Countess (her Barefootness), Bill Cunliffe, Captain Janis (God rest his soul), and Mikhaili the Boat Man. The next chapter is about sewage. I can't wait to read it. —*Kelly Shea*

These rhubarbs, these portraits are so vividly affectionate … I know the bone, flesh and muscle of our Hydra and you've, with truth and accuracy, been faithful to them. *Rhubarbs from a Rock* is intelligent, witty, and endlessly affectionate. Bravo!! —*Barbara Lapcek*

CONTENTS

WITH THANKS

To the cast, characters, and other fellow inmates of the Rock who provided the tales and inspiration for a multitude of unforgettable recollections.

Rhubarb! is the result of combining and rehashing tales from the first volume, *Rhubarbs from a Rock (Escaping the Rat Race)*, and what was going to be a sequel, titled *Rhubarbs Too (Sucker for a Pretty Place)*, into an all-in-one amalgamation of updated snippets of life and survival on this unique island.

Author's addendum: for those who may think I have deserted the mother tongue grammatically, my wife, editor, and publisher hails from the other side of the puddle and deemed it expedient to spell "colour," "favour," and such without the "u."

1

PIGEONHOLES

Whether we like it or not people like to pigeonhole, or assign labels, which some will then call nicknames. For instance, I was called "Fairy Fagan" in college once—just once. The fellow didn't know I was on crutches and avoiding physical sports because I was recuperating, with steel hip pins, from a rugby incident. Nor did he know a wooden walking stick could also double as a weapon—twit.

Anyway, to get to the point, I decided to unpigeonhole myself and leave the planet's first-world order for somewhere obscure. An island without cars seemed like a logical start.

What makes a bloke give up a promising career in advertising and move to a Greek island thirty years premature to his expected retirement date, trading golf clubs for fishing line and two cars and life insurance for sandals and a hand-to-mouth living?

I have masticated over this ad nauseam, eventually putting it down to fate—and one lunch in 1983.

I am gent who doesn't know which Zodiac sign goes with which month, unless it's mentioned with a specific date that's repeated annually. I wouldn't call myself a fatalist, but how I came to live for nearly thirty years on the Greek island of Hydra, a Rock in the Saronic Gulf, was decidedly fortuitous.

It was my first visit to the country, and my travelling companion was in the driver's seat. We package coached it on our first day to Delphi, our busload of cameras politely shepherded around ruins and oracles by a shrill guide. Time schedules were kept.

We scheduled ourselves down the coastline on another tour bus to visit the spectacular ruins at Sounion the next day. We also visited ancient ruins around the Plaka in Athens that night. I mentioned to my then girlfriend that I hoped our itinerary would include some beaches and islands—less tramping and more basking.

She returned to the hotel room from the info office with tickets to the islands for the following morning. A coach was picking us up at 7:00 a.m. to ferry us to the port, she explained.

Shortly after dawn I started packing.

"What are you doing?" she asked. "We're coming back tonight. You'll just need a towel and swimming costume for the beach."

Our island-hopping package included three islands in one day. "Back before dark," the receipt announced.

Aegina was delightful. I photographed a temple and a huge, brightly colored Cadillac that barely managed to squeeze down an alley. We reboarded the cruise ship an hour later.

At Poros, a dog caught the ship's rope, and the mixed bag of tourists bundled off to investigate the quayfront shops and photograph fishing caïques.

Everyone reembarked on schedule.

It was siesta time when we landed for our allotted sixty minutes on Hydra.

The Rock magnetized me immediately. Though beachless, it was also vehicleless, with mules languishing in a corner of the harbor, not a moped within hearing or even a bicycle in sight. Postcard picturesque, with a population of 2,500 according the guide pamphlet, it had a timelessness. Tranquility oozed from whitewashed walls and cobbled streets—an apparent paradise.

We didn't get back on the cruise ship.

Compulsion to investigate the island further led me to negotiate the price for a pension room at the back of the port. Next I called our hotel in Athens, which most obligingly agreed to pack our belongings and store our suitcases until we were "un-marooned." Island shops sold basic toiletries and so forth.

That evening, I saw a sign that rang a bell: "Bill's Bar," a place mentioned by a fellow I worked with who had been to Greece.

It was just opening when I asked for Bill.

"Anyone here know Bill?" asked the gent fidgeting behind the counter in surprisingly eloquent English. He turned a pair of early regulars who looked like part of the furniture.

"Give the boy a drink," they ragged, inviting me over to their table once the owner had poured me a "large one." I joined the fixtures in their corner for most of the evening, which led to a lunch invitation for the following day.

We putt-putted our way down the coast in a small caïque to a house accessible only by a rickety wooden jetty. Lunch overlooking the Saronic Gulf included waves of traditional Greek fare—bread with tzatziki and salads of eggplant and fish roe, octopus, squid, fried cheese, grilled lamb and pork, and of course, retsina—shared by sixteen guests of twelve different nationalities; conversation was sparkling and varied. It was the melting pot of my dreams set upon one of the most picturesque of Mediterranean islands. Lunch led to further sundowners and further rendezvous.

The hook was set. Without traffic, life slows down; with not a wheel to be seen, the fastest thing in the port was a scampering cat. The setting and community were intoxicating, and I decided to stay as long as I could.

Nearly three decades later on I am still "marooned."

* * *

"So what do you do?" is not a popular conversation opener on the island. People come here to get away from what they do. It's a question that I still have difficulty answering. While living on the Rock I have engaged in all manner of island industry. I even have trouble pigeonholing myself when it comes to background: Irish, African, and Greek influences have shaped my outlook and my inlook. In short I cheer for a lot of countries during world cups.

Anthony Kingsmill, one of the island's legendary artists, once succinctly advised me that you need never worry about how you subsist "as long as you justify your existence, old bean." I took heed and have resorted to all manner of activities over the year to justify mine.

After my initial sojourn on the Rock, having committed myself to a partnership in a bar and restaurant, I returned to Africa to quit my job, flog my belongings, and generally liquidate my life in the rat race. I returned permanently to Hydra in 1985 to live my dream come true. As it turned out, that life was nothing like my wildest dreams.

I quickly learned, within a year of opening the bar, that nothing about island living is simple. Indeed, failure to read the fine print translated into four potential years in the Greek courts in order to keep that venture going. So I abandoned inn keeping and opted for simpler, less complicated forms of labor. But even that wasn't straightforward; complication is the name of the game when it comes to this simple island life.

Over the last thirty years, I've met some wonderful people who have influenced my life in circumstances and places I could never have imagined had I stayed behind an office desk. I am genuinely surprised when people tell me they think it was brave to give up a secure life to dwell full-time on a Greek rock; I happen to regard facing ten traffic jams a week as courageous.

The island has acquired the nickname "the Rock" not just for its obvious geographical character but because it resembles Alcatraz in its power to captivate. Inmates often quote the Eagles lyric "You can check out any time you like, but you can never leave."

One of the complexities, when trying to write cohesively about the island, is that the cast fluctuates. Individuals are remembered in time capsules, pinpointed by where and when the events happened and which other players were on the scene. Places like Bill's Bar, Dirty Corner, Liako, Three Brothers, Moita, and Up 'n' High, to name a few, all invoke different memories. One picks up friendships where they left off, sometimes after many years; although the stage may have changed, the Rock generally hasn't. For many, their times on Hydra are among the best of their lives, and I am fortunate to have shared and witnessed a lot of these "good old days" in a long string of mini-eras.

These snippets of life on the Rock are my random "rhubarbs," illustrating aspects of an alternative way of life from one inmate's point of view. The word *rhubarb* has crept into my vocabulary as an expression for the shenanigans that accompany any activity. In the days of radio theater, two or three individuals standing around a live microphone "rhubarbing," or repeatedly muttering the word "rhubarb," gave the audio impression of a debating mob. When and if one obtains a license to work, nothing on Hydra happens without a rhubarb, even changing a light bulb.

To plagiarize someone else, "You can't make this shit up."

2

A CLEAN BILL OF WEALTH

It was like a something from the television series *The Amazing Race* or one of those popular treasure hunt episodes. The instructions seemed clear enough: Go to Athens for a physical examination. On issuance of a clean bill of health, collect your license from the EEC office to operate a public business.

In 1981 Greece had joined the European Economic Community, the forerunner of the current European Union. Membership supposedly entitled other EEC citizens to work legally and without hindrance in the land of Socrates and Onassis, much as many from Hellas worked hassle-free in the rest of Europe. One would have thought that by 1985, EEC legislation, rulings, and laws would be understood and functioning. But I was to learn the hard way, early on, that nothing in Greece is as it appears or is said to be.

The reasoning was fairly understandable: I was opening a bar and restaurant, and to ensure I was not infectious or contagious, I had to have a medical checkup. This sounded innocuous enough; little did I know that applicants for NASA lunar voyages underwent less physical scrutiny.

To be fair, the mid-eighties was a different era, one almost unimaginable today. You could smoke on airplanes and everywhere else on the planet with the possible exception of operating theaters. The Internet was still the stuff of science fiction, and only James Bond had a cell phone. Space shuttles and Russian nuclear power plants were infallible, and a single European currency a distant figment of some economist's imagination. The drachma as a coinage had no value anywhere else, but a dollar's worth would buy breakfast, beers, lunch, and cigarettes here.

So it wasn't as shocking as it would be now to receive instructions from a portly, mustachioed nurse with a cigarette in her mouth dangling a two-inch ash at the Piraeus general hospital. If one ignored the scorches on the tiled floor, the X-ray ward seemed up to scratch. A machine that hummed and clicked over one's chest while she took shelter behind an antiradiation bunker was pretty standard in those days. This was to ascertain that I was tuberculosis free.

It had taken sixteen inquiries on five floors to find the lung X-ray department, and I assumed that after traipsing up and down endless corridors for an hour, I had the lay of the land. I figured I'd find the next medical port of call, the blood-testing section, in some now familiar location. I had absolutely no objection to getting a health check as part of a policy that kept the food-and-beverage industry plague-free. It was a bit of a nuisance, however, that the monstrosity of this particular medical center only did the X-ray stuff; taking blood samples was beyond its capacity. Another hospital, a mere hour away by taxi, specifically catered to those wishing to have blood extracted.

Hailing a cab in the Big Olive is no easy feat for the feint of heart. Manners are not involved—relinquishing one's prime post to a grandmother dressed in black earns one nothing more than a half hour delay. The same queues of ailing, smoking casualties inhabited the next EEC-friendly hospital, and directions to the alien blood-removal unit were equally interesting; it was eventually found in the basement. This hospital was closer to the center of Athens and seemed to be the city's medical hub. I had a list of hieroglyphics to follow, issued by the local island constabulary, which I had been told required me to complete a couple of tests. A couple in my book was two—lungs and blood—and I assumed I was free to go.

Not so. Urine was next, presumably to confirm I was not pregnant or on crack.

"What floor?" I inquired, mime-like, drawing steps in the air with my hand.

Tutting and raising of eyebrows—I had quickly learned this is a negatory sign in Greece.

"*Allo nosokomeio*," the needle wielder said, then kindly wrote down the name and address of the next infirmary I was to visit.

Not surprisingly, this one was back in Piraeus, only on the opposite side of the main harbor. This time I got lucky; a helpful white coat told me to go the third floor after reading my police list and seemed to understand exactly why I was there—a pleasant change from what had so far been one continuous debate among staff about who I was and why I was wandering, apparently aimlessly, about the hallways of Greece's medical facilities.

At least when told to sit and wait in corridors, one could smoke freely (a habit that took years to kick), but in this case, I didn't have to wait for too long. As it was by then almost lunchtime, a nurse produced some plastic cups and handed them over.

"Come tomorrow," she said in broken English.

"Tomorrow?" I chirped. "But I live on the island of Hydra and have to get back today. Can't I just give you the samples now?"

She seemed a little surprised that I could muster up a dribble on call so instantly and guided me to a single loo, explaining that it was a staff ablution but I was welcome to make use of it.

Ten minutes later I dutifully showed up at the nurses' lounge with my specimens, hoping that the ordeal was finally at an end and that I had met the list's demands.

The gaggle of white starch burst into fits of giggles—not very professional, I thought, until my nurse explained, by way of pointing to her posterior, that I was not in the urine but the stool section. No wonder she thought it odd that I could come up with the goods so quickly.

By this time I established that there was no way I could complete my tasks and get home the same day; plus, I was grossly ill equipped to deal with the big, strange city and decided to call it day. Besides, foolishly thinking a full day would be more than adequate for the schedule set, I hadn't packed a toothbrush or change of clothes.

I would have to come back another day.

Soundly beaten into submission by the list, I paid my mate Pan, a gent who'd have been instantly cast as one the bearded shorter lead roles in *The Lord of the Rings*, a visit in his bar that evening and lamented my woes. A Vietnam veteran, Pan looked like a slightly stunted, hairy biker from the hard rock era. Without coercion he volunteered to guide me through the labyrinth of Greece's medical maze and accompany me on my return foray.

Two days later I reboarded the 6:50 a.m. hydrofoil to Athens with my bearded platoon leader at the helm.

The paperwork went on and on—more hospitals and testing … blah, blah … rhubarb … boring. Let's get on with the story.

Suffice it to say, I eventually got permission to turn on the lights for opening night. Now I just had to keep them working.

3

DIM AND DIMMER

I remember thinking that he was going to electrocute himself and that I should say something. But then I figured he was the qualified technician, and I was new to the island. Everything was new to me, including the fact that electrical wiring was supposed to look like spaghetti—bare unconnected wires protruding from weird places were the norm.

I let him throw the switch—

* * *

The bar had been closed for nearly a month for refurbishments, and I was re-opening that night. Yanni, the electrician, had finally turned up, his small donkey laden with toolboxes and coils of wire.

"I come before but they are painting," he shrugged, explaining the three-week delay.

I'd thought the idea of using a dimmer switch for the lights over the bar would be a simple affair—a switch with a knob that swiveled, allowing one to set the mood. It seemed like a grand idea, the final touch to the refurbishments.

I pointed to the light switch behind the bar and explained what I had in mind.

"Yes, I have, very good, German model," Yanni enthused.

Trouble was, the German model didn't fit in the hole, so a pneumatic drill and some hammers came off the donkey.

The area of wiring behind the beam above the little bar looked like a multiflex system that could have powered a car factory, with some wires so old and corroded they were black and others turning various shades of brown, depending on which decade they'd been installed. None of the old wiring appeared live, so more cable was unloaded.

I watched Yanni put a clean white cord on top of the old electrics, tap-tapping nails indiscriminately—a small hint of the pyrotechnics to follow.

It looked grand. I was impressed with how he had managed to work out the wiring and get the dimmer device flush. And I still had time to clean up the debris.

"Top job," he exclaimed triumphantly and turned the knob.

For a second I thought I heard oil boiling in the kitchen until I noticed the blue and green sparks fizzling up the wall in front of Yanni's nose.

There was a loud bang, some bottles fell over, and we were left standing in the gloom. Yanni's silhouette had perpendicular hair.

Immediate concern overwhelmed the urge to burst out laughing.

"Yanni, you okay?"

"There was a fault with the switch." He appeared more disturbed by the product's flaw. "I will get another."

I could only assume he was used to tests failing and had the heart of an ox.

Two hours later he returned. I had swept the rubble and cleaned the black scorch marks from the fresh paint as best I could.

"The German's is kaput, but I have Italian switch, very good," he said, brandishing a different dimmer. "Ees second hand, but ees very strong."

He readjusted the hole size again.

This time it appeared to work. We turned the wattage down and then up.

"Top job," said Yanni, in a satisfied voice, turning to go.

Then there was a pop and the light tinkle of glass on the counter, followed by another explosion in the wall. Gloom and silence.

"Well, Yanni?"

A hesitation before he replied. "I put the old switch back and order a Japanese switch."

I expressed my disappointment, suspecting this could mean weeks of delay.

"No worries, we fix it all today," he assured me.

He replaced the original on-off switch, taping it into the now enlarged hole so it didn't wobble.

It worked; at least I would have lights on re-opening night, albeit too bright.

"We will have dimmer, don't worry." He grabbed a tea towel and unscrewed a middle light bulb. It winked out leaving three of the five above the bar lit. He proceeded to unscrew a second, dimming the lighting even further.

"You see, everything works out in the end."

Top job indeed!

4

COLOR-BLIND

"You paint the bar? It smells fresh," asked Pavlos, settling onto his usual stool. "Good to have it open again. We missed you."

He was my first customer, regular as clockwork, and always sat on the same stool, drank the same drink, and played same game every night except Sundays.

He spoke some English, having served in the Greek merchant navy for years. Forced into early retirement by an illness that had left him almost totally blind, he navigated the island by brail.

He was keen to start a round of poker dice, as was our ritual. We would play while I polished glasses.

"Penta asses"—my first toss on re-opening night.

Five aces! Against a blind man with no witnesses.

"Penta asses?" he repeated mildly before throwing his dice. I remember wishing he would throw five aces too that night so I could reciprocate the call in his favor.

* * *

I had purchased the bar at the end of the previous season and decided to keep it open over the winter while I settled into island life. This had given me a marvelous opportunity to get to know the inhabitants and cut my teeth in the bar business before my first full summer.

My Bahia Bar became a local clubhouse. Those were the days before televisions invaded the island. Expats and locals would play chess, *tavli* (backgammon), cards, dice, dominoes, and the occasional game of charades. Spontaneous guitar playing periodically motivated oiled patrons to accompany with hand clapping, warbling, and spoon clacking.

Muleteers and fishermen would bundle in and order in quantity, sometimes taking a whole bottle of spirits to their table. The islanders were most convivial. They trickled in bellowing *yassou* (hello) or *kalispera* (good evening)—pleasant noises to a new innkeeper's ear.

The bar was small but had a couple of unique features: a 200-year-old plaster oven and an open cisterna, or well. Apart from the fresh appearance and novel wiring accomplished during the three weeks of refurbishments, I thought I'd come up with a great idea for resolving a rhubarb surrounding the cisterna opening. I was keen to see the reaction.

The problem with the cisterna had been that when the little bar filled up, or when the customers had consumed gill limits of alcohol, it became an ashtray—indeed, ashtrays often fell in. Some more sensitive noses had lobbied for its closure. Health concerns had been voiced too.

"Lord knows what's fermenting down there," a Swiss nose had twitched.

Another bunch said that the cisterna wellhead, situated almost bang in the middle of the room, gave the place unique character. To touch it would be sacrilege. Also, said others, by law one couldn't alter any building more than two centuries old. One had to live with the existing architecture or submit plans to the Department of Ecological Affairs for approval—a time-consuming procedure said to involve an exchange of thick brown envelopes if one wanted expedience.

One winter's evening prior to my ingenious refurbishment, a New York banker's upmarket pair of spectacles fell down the hole with a splash.

Flashlights reflected off the black water about four meters down. Cobwebs laced the tunneled rock face below broom level. A brave and nimble man was needed to enter the hole.

A runner was sent with a message for Pan at his bar. Pan held a reputation as the island's Rambo. No-nonsense-Pan was hailed whenever there was trouble. He promised to come by after work.

Short and stocky, with impressive beard and mane, he barely squeezed into opening.

"Pan, I'll be forever in your debt," said the Bank, squinting at the disappearing mop.

"There's fuggin' a lot of shit down here," Pan muttered, after which we heard splashing and grunting. A cobwebbed beard emerged, not unlike a creature from a black lagoon, glasses clenched in his teeth.

"*Efharisto para poli, Pan,*" the grateful Bank effused, holding out his hand.

"5,000 drachmas." A palm issued forth.

"But a new pair only costs 2,000," blurted Wall Street when confronted with a price tag for the service. Financial negotiations and basic economics were second nature to the bloke.

"Then go to Athens to buy some, you know whaddimean?" said Pan, not budging an inch.

"Okay, 3,000, and that's extremely generous," countered the Bank.

"Lions, tigers, sharks, okay, but fuggin' spiders—*oxi*," retorted Pan, making a point of brushing out his beard.

"I risk my life so you can see—5,500 drachmas."

"4,000!" Brave that banker.

"6,000," haggled the Beard, with a glance at the proprietor. "It's dangerous, you know whaddimean?"

A prolonged pause ensued while Wall Street processed the transaction mentally. Things were not going his way. The cost of a trip to Athens and hours wasted carried the day—just.

"Done," grumbled the Bank.

* * *

This incident had sparked the idea, which I thought was a decent compromise, satisfying all arguments and benefitting Hydra's wildlife, the cats.

During the renovations, I blocked the cisterna off inside the wellhead at ground level and made it watertight. Then I installed a small kitchen plug so it could be drained and cleaned.

Just before Pavlos came in on re-opening night, I had filled it with a few inches of water and thrown in a few coins. A wishing well for Hydra's cats!

Apart from Pavlos, the locals tended to come later, with the expats arriving first. Some threw a couple of coins in for luck and complimented me on the bar's new color scheme.

Françoise, a Parisian fashion designer and animal lover, went straight over to the well for a look. "Zees is a good idea," she said, throwing in a 500-drachma note.

When the first bushy moustache arrived, the usual jovial banter was missing.

He peered disapprovingly into the well.

"*Tee naf toe*" (what is this)? he asked, twisting his right hand and giving a little shake of his head, indicating incomprehension.

"For the cats," I said, showing him the little sign I had made saying as much in both Greek and English.

He shrugged and sat down. He didn't want anything to drink and mimed that he was waiting for his mates. Not a comment about the new décor.

Perhaps I had broken protocol by sealing the cisterna, so Pavlos asked him what he thought about the wishing well idea for me. The moustache said he thought I was a little crazy, but sealed or not, it was of no concern to him. A couple of his mates turned up, and their response was similar, or perhaps I should say, they had no response. The wishing well was ignored.

Pavlos smelled disapproval and suddenly asked me, "What color you paint the bar?"

"White with green trimming."

"Why?"

I explained that green is the Irish color as well as my favorite.

"Ahhh—so you no passock?"

I couldn't figure out what he was trying to say.

"What's that?"

"PASOK, a socialist. This island is mostly Nea Democratia—blue and white."

"And green, I take it, is the opposition?"

"Yes, PASOK, the socialists."

Pavlos informed the bunch huddled in the corner that I had taken no political stance and the green was for Irish luck.

"*Ahh, Eirlandos*," they exclaimed. There were guffaws, thumps on the back, and drinks all round.

With that, Captain Yanni, who was often called the island mascot, came in and worked up quite a fuss about the sealed-off cisterna.

Yanni had disabilities; his speech wasn't coherent but animations clarified his point.

"*Oxi!*" on the cisterna job.

Everyone loved Yanni; he caught fish for the cats and yacht ropes for cigars. He never accepted money unless he could reciprocate by buying one's newspaper. He had much pride, many morals, and nothing on his feet.

The locals explained to Yanni that the well was for making wishes and that the change would go toward feeding the cats.

At this his face lit up. He gave me a smelly hug, rolled up his sleeve, and fished out all the cash, including Françoise's 500 note, which was pegged to the metal arch above the well, drying.

"What's he doing?" I asked Pavlos.

"He is going to buy food for the cats with it," he explained.

"*Bravo re*, Yanni," I encouraged.

"*Etsi*," echoed the bushy moustaches in the corner.

Yanni would regularly empty the well at the end of the evening thereafter.

Anthony, a permanent island inmate, would saunter in every night to holler down, "Are you well?" then chuckle to himself at his silly joke.

"I see Yanni's been at you again," he'd say, before sidling up to the bar. His chilled glass of house wine would be waiting in front of a stool adjacent to wherever the poker game had progressed to.

"Beat me to it," he'd wink. "It was supposed to buy me into a round of dice."

I know some cats did well for a while too.

* * *

Postpublication of the first edition, response from the Banker:

Subject: The Gods of Hydra Lore from Michael Kelland
Just finished your tome, quite enjoyable. Publisher delivered within 5 days of ordering. HOWEVER, your inaccuracies will be punished by several, if not a multitude, of the myth keepers of the rock. I got Pan down to 2000 drachmas within two days of retrieval and 6 1/2 hours prior to departure. He finally realized the concept of a vanishing asset. It is true that in the 48 hours till success was finalized, bruising did occur from walking at night with sunglasses. I trust subsequent editions will correct the above-cited inaccuracy, and my attorneys request a correction in the local newspaper of record. Regards and Happy New Year to you and yours and other familiar denizens.

Reply
Dear Mr. Kelland,
Sorry to hear that your spectacles were also a victim of the hole and Mr. Pan's extortion. The Bank recorded in the "historical documents" was not a gent prone to behavior associated with boozy bruising or wearing shades at night, and he obviously did not have your tenacity in negotiating. A decent, clean-cut fellow.

Any similarity to yourself and the bloke in [chapter 4] is therefore pure coincidence, and we will alert the media as such.

Your reputation, I assure you, is intact.

5

IT'S ALL GREEK—FOR GOOD REASON

It is no coincidence that the cliché "It's all Greek to me" denotes incomprehension. Notoriously tough to master, Greek poses difficulties with an unusual twist on the island. There are about a dozen subdialects of the mother tongue, which can be confusing to the untrained ear.

A fairly common sublingo is Bar Greek, a dialect devoted to obtaining service, ordering rounds, and calculating the tab.

By uttering "*Parakalo, mia beira, ke ena boukali pagomeni aspro krasie meh tessera vouteria*," an inmate can politely specify his or her exact wishes: a beer and a bottle of chilled white wine with four glasses. Impressive ensuing bar banter may include requests for ashtrays and directions to the loo.

Once, a year or so after my arrival, having spent an enjoyable afternoon with one old timer on the port, I stopped a muleteer and asked my companion if he could explain about keys and the whereabouts of a house booked for shortly arriving guests.

After introductions and a brief discussion about the weather, my translator ran dry.

"My dear fellow, I don't understand a word he is saying."

He went on to explain that he was fluent in taverna and cafe Greek, but when it came to other matters, the language became a blur.

One local Aussie skipper, marooned for more than four decades on the Rock, admits that he will never get his tongue entirely around the language—but he speaks fluent Nautical Greek. He knows the words for obscure things like grappling hooks, and his tongue skips lightly over complicated phrases like, "Your anchor is laying port side of my chain, so be cautious when raising yours, as our respective yachts could become entangled." On land the man needs a translator.

Similarly, other versions of Greek could leave one with the impression that all participants were fully conversant. Expatriates who have dabbled in the building trade appear to have full command of the language but are in fact only partially bilingual. Cement we can order, ink no.

My pidgin has a broader base due to the selection of tasks I have undertaken, but the reality is that no matter how many new words you learn, some will trip you up. A misplaced vowel can elicit an excited response.

Early on I learned the word for soft, *malako*, so that I could explain to the chef at the Breakfast Club that I preferred runny rather than rubber-fried eggs with my bacon.

"*Parakalo, thelo avga ke baycon—malaka*," I said, emphasizing my new word.

"*Tea!!??*" The volume of the cook's response indicated that he was not asking me what beverage I wanted with breakfast, and, anyway, I knew *tea* in Greek meant "what."

"*Malaka eemay? Essee ena malaka!*" The animated chef, not amused by my order, was calling me "soft" back?

"You know you just called the guy a wanker?" interjected a nearby inmate, coming to my rescue.

It was explained that a twisted vowel had been the culprit and that I had indeed being trying to impress the bloke with my newly honed linguistic skills.

Greeks are used to foreigners making a hash of their language. He laughed, and I never got yokes my fork could bounce on after that either.

Another trick to expanding one's vocabulary is to fiddle with an English word by adding a vowel or two.

A mate and I were in Four Corners minimarket searching for mustard. I explained in pidgin what we were after.

"Mustard. You eat it with meat. It's hot on the tongue. A kind of paste."

Shopkeeper Dimitri's eyebrows jerked in the negative with each additional in description.

I was running out of vocabulary when he proudly produced a bottle of tomato sauce.

"Not tomato sauce, mustard," I repeated.

"*Neh*, *ketzup*, sauce for food," he explained.

"Ketchup aye? You say potato and I say—that's another word to learn—but *oxi*, that's not the right sauce. The one I want is yellow," I said, offering another clue.

Dimitri scratched his head, muttering, and we gave up. As we walked out the door his voice boomed, "*Ahh, moustardo! Ella, egho.*"

On another occasion we spent an interesting morning going through the chaotic piles of stock at the Plastic Man. The Plastic Man sold everything and sported the largest selection of plastic kitchen utensils and furniture. So through description of his store, he had inherited the nickname. Many shops on the island acquired monikers similarly—the Frozen Man, not surprisingly, sold frozen victuals, the Video and Gunpowder Man sold pyrotechnics next to videos for rent, and so on.

* * *

Not all nicknames originate from an obvious source—take, for instance, a fellow who became known as Chicken George, not because of a cowardly streak or, indeed, a special secret poultry recipe but because of the brave ferocity of his pet rooster.

Swedish Anita, a head-turning statuesque blonde who years later married my HydraNet partner Michael, was a friend of George. A shortish fellow with thinning hair who worked in one of the islands' favorite tavernas, he was fluent in English and a popular character—especially with female tourists.

Anyway, one afternoon Anita had popped into George's house, situated just past Four Corners, for a glass of his vintage barrel. George had apparently begged off because of an errand in the port and invited Anita to stay and finish her wine at leisure, simply asking her to close the front door behind her when she left.

When that time come, however, Anita suddenly confronted George's pet poultry, who refused to allow her to depart. The brave little bantam attacked her with wings flapping, pecking at her shins and shrieking like a banshee.

Anita retreated to the safety of the kitchen and had another glass, summoning the courage to get past the feathered sentry. Again the enraged pet thwarted her escape, jumping at her with claws extended.

This apparently happened several times, and eventually the now humiliated and slightly intoxicated Swede decided, with George showing no sign of returning to her rescue and the jug empty, to flee out the kitchen window onto a little balcony, which was a floor up from the spring garden lush with greenery. Climbing over the railing and hanging down to lessen the fall, she dropped into the garden, much to the amused curiosity of the neighborhood.

The soft green landing turned out to be a bed of stinging nettles, which promoted a slew of Scandinavian curses. In foul mood, with Viking blood boiling, Anita steamed down to the harbor front, only to spot her host lounging at Antonio's Café, with an attractive American tourist under each arm.

Now, Anita, while fluent in English, did not always understand the nuances of the language. She stormed up to the busy café, legs red with rash and cheeks flushed with anger, and yelled, "George! GEORGE!"

She had the attention of everyone enjoying the tranquil afternoon sun.

"Your f***ing cock has been hunting me for hours. I had to escape out the kitchen window, and now I sting everywhere!!"

It doesn't take much imagination to see why the audience burst into laughter and the new nickname was born.

Anyway, I digress. Back to Greek …

* * *

As we ventured into the Plastic Man's shop in search of a kitchen utensil, we thought the word for egg, *avga*, accompanied by some miming would do the trick, an egg flipper being a common-enough cooking device.

In our search for said item, the Plastic Man unearthed a 1950s East German eggbeater, pans, whisks, poachers, anything connected to cooking an egg.

"Everything except a spatula," said my mate, shaking his head in awe at the selection.

"Ahh, *spatoula*," beamed the Plastic Man, who made a beeline an exact spot in the mountain of paraphernalia.

For one inmate emphasizing the wrong vowel resulted in a delivery delay of over a year. Once every so often she would go to the local courier and inquire about when her parcel would arrive.

The words for "never" and "when" are so similar that it is easy to see how confusion and time lapses can occur. Saying *poté*, emphasis on *e*, and *póte*, emphasis on *o*, can make the difference between an immanent package and one marked "never." My friend had been walking up to the baffled but disinterested postmistress and exclaiming, "Never does my package arrive!"

Another tip for increasing one's vocabulary on the fly is to consider the object under discussion in terms of time period. If it was built or invented in the last century or so, then the word often will often have an Anglicized base: airplane/*aeroplano*, television/*tellyorasie*, computer/*komputer*, etc.

A lot of Greek words form the basic foundation for similar words in many major languages: *democrasia*, *philosophia*, *catastrophia*, *klistophobia*. Even thinking about an English word's root can assist the linguistically handicapped, like myself. An earthquake is a *seismos* (seismic) and to steal is to *klepsie* (kleptomania)—both great words that one tends to adopt in time.

Some words just look the same: "difficult" is *disscolo*. Others simply seem impossible: a toothpick is an *othontaglyffeetha*.

It's a question of mixing and matching words and associations. Another few *thekahdes* and I reckon I'll have this *glossa* down pat. (Greek for tongue and/or language, no doubt the source of our word "glossary").

Easy, this language stuff, really.

6

DOGS, DONKEYS, AND DO-GOODERS

Territorial disputes, especially in a small community, tend to get up-close and personal.

Mike didn't like the look of me, and there was nothing I could do about it. Simply put, he was a bully. The more I encountered him, the more our mutual dislike intensified, and as ours is a little island, avoidance was almost impossible.

He made me nervous, and he knew it.

His self-proclaimed territory included the local supermarket entrance; the closest alternative shop was a good walk downhill to the port.

The trouble with Mike was his unpredictability. Most of the time he lounged passively in the sun, but every now and again, he felt the need to get upright and macho. One ran a daily mental gauntlet—to risk Mike's mood at the local shop or to take the hike.

Mike was a mean dog—black as his mood and built like a mastiff. His gene pool probably included every known form of large canine breed in the Med.

Even basking in the Saronic sun, he would grumble and hoist half an upper lip to show you his ivory, just in case you had forgotten whose turf you were on. It was only a matter of time before some incident occurred, and when it did, the ensuing riot was amazing.

Mike's self proclaimed no-walk zone was about 100 meters either side of a scruffy little shack situated just off the street known to expats as Donkeyshit Lane, the main route from Hydra Town to Kamini. The shack's inhabitants included the many offspring of a local fisherman and his large, unkempt wife, who appeared to produce an additional family member every year. They had earned the nickname "the Barefoot Tribe," an uncouth mob that did nothing to discourage Mike's inhospitable disposition.

Most of the time I took my chances, praying I'd escape the dog's wrath, rather than take the long route home.

I'd had a bad day—the third consecutive spent in fruitless waiting for an elusive plumber, and I had nothing to eat at home. When Mike started rumbling his disapproval at my incursion into his district, I flicked my cigarette butt in his general direction.

Perhaps Mike thought it was a peace offering, some tasty morsel. Whatever his motive, I watched in fascination as he gave a little jump and deftly caught the glowing ember in the back of his throat. His jaws snapped shut like a rattrap. I suppose if he had swallowed a nest of hornets, the result might have been the same.

Mike went nuts, and I, the perpetrator of his discomfort, was still standing right in front of him. Extraordinary sounds issued forth as he launched himself at me. Instinctively, in self-defense, I whacked the animal on the side of his ear-flattened head with my leather satchel.

My bag was a rather clumsy saddlebag affair that I always lugged about with me. It contained sundry possessions of varying daily and occasional use: an outdated Filofax, cigs, lighter, wallet, bunches of keys, my lucky Chinese musical ball, a Swiss army knife, some fishing tackle, and a few screws and nails for emergencies. The contents were all loosely covered by a flap, which, because of constant opening and the lack of pickpockets on the island, I never buckled shut.

The bag exploded on impact, raining noise on the cobblestones, which in turn attracted the attention of the Barefoot Tribe, all of whom emerged from their dwelling to investigate the commotion. The enraged Mike, emboldened by the arrival of reinforcements, redoubled his efforts at trying to extinguish his smoldering tonsils on some soft, cool part of my anatomy.

Too shocked by this sudden turn of events to act rationally, I added to the cacophony by yelling incoherently at the dog. At this particular instant, a donkey train hove into view around a corner.

Laden with plastic rubbish bags stuffed into two large baskets on either side of its wooden saddle, the lead animal was having none of this excitement and turned to escape. In its haste to flee, it caught the plastic liners on a nail sticking out of the wall, spewing trash onto the street.

The muleteer had obviously also taken the brunt of Mike's disfavor in the past and came to my rescue. Wielding a large stick he entered the fray with enthusiasm and a yell, his donkeys braying for backup.

Then the owner of an adjacent house, a quite, retired expatriate who valued his serene surroundings, put in an appearance. He already had an ongoing feud with the unruly shoeless clan about their constant littering, lack of decorum, and window-rattling indigenous rock music blasting from the dot of six each evening after siesta. The developing scene on his doorstep obviously merited some law enforcement. I suspect it was he who summoned the local constabulary.

In the meantime the size of this animated debate grew as neighborhood *yayas*, or grandmothers, another dog, and some builders got involved. Even Kyria Maria, an elephantiasis-suffering, stick-wielding terrorizer of children, managed to waddle up with an important, vocal point of view.

The sight of two uniformed police did nothing to dampen the spirit of the occasion. Indeed, their arrival seemed to encourage more chaos, with all the contenders voicing their version of the story. Each was convinced that he who shouted loudest and gesticulated most would get heard first and therefore earn the sympathetic ear of the law—and thus, most importantly, not be charged as responsible for cleaning up the now trampled mess.

The smaller cop, newly posted to the island, decided to settle the matter and laid down the law: the offending dog was henceforth to be tied up.

That should have been the end of it, but the unfortunate policeman had no idea of the can of judicial worms he was opening with this declaration. The Barefoot Tribe had already been called to the carpet for tying up a canine, and now they were being ordered reschackle Mike!

They had previously owned an enormous Great Dane crossbreed, which they had dutifully tied up because it too had acquired the habit of terrorizing passers-by. Local pedestrians and tourists alike had complained, so a restraining order had been placed on the family hound.

The trouble was, they'd gone to the other extreme. The animal had been tied up with a two-foot rope and left to roast in the summer sun, often without water—an unhappy specimen to behold.

A flamboyant Austrian countess and part-time island resident had taken pity and had gone to the local law to report the family's cruelty to animals. She too walked around shoeless, the difference being that her toenails were brightly manicured and ornaments dangled from a chain around her ankle.

The police had then ruled that the Barefoot Tribe must not tie up their pet in future, which of course left it free, once again, to persecute passers-by. This particular quandary had been resolved when her Barefootness adopted said huge dog. She eventually took it home to her *Schloss*, where it could chase rabbits to its heart's content.

The tribe members ungraciously informed the unsuspecting policeman, unaware of the previous events and history, of the ruling and told him if he wanted to amend the existing corpus juris, then they wanted to see a court order stating as much—signed by the minister of domestic affairs himself.

The incident had now been elevated to a matter requiring judicial hearings and future court dates. As the instigator of this situation, would I be prepared to mobilize a team of legal troops to take this matter further, the smaller cop inquired of me.

The entire affair had now been tossed into my innocent pedestrian lap.

I declined to take official action. Shopping downtown was by far the cheaper and easier option. I would wait for word that Mike had been moved or manacled.

7

A VARIOUS SELECTION OF SHORTCUTS

An exhausted hiker once described a gentle walk in the country with Jeannette as a forced march and foraging expedition. The unsuspecting stroller following one of her recommended shortcuts faces thorns, stings, wildlife, seized muscles, and life-threatening heights. She herself appears impervious to pain, regularly grasping clusters of stinging nettles en route and stuffing them into a bag for *mezes*, or snacks.

Jeannette had come to live in Greece as a young woman and spent her life accumulating rural survival tactics. One couldn't deny the exotic flavor of her nettle soup, purple *loulouthi* (flower) pâte, or wild asparagus dishes. Multilingual, with a talent for project management, she'd won the locals' high regard, having worked with and among them for over three decades.

"I need a hand on my next trip to Othonis," Jeannette announced.

I hadn't heard of the place and asked for details.

"It's a small island, half the size of Hydra, situated between Greece, Albania, and Italy, with fewer than 100 inhabitants; the census age would be about sixty-five, and no one speaks English," she enthused. "Untouched, very lush, wonderful diving and great fishing."

Having spent a substantial part of my youth in Africa, this sounded like the makings of a decent safari, so I grabbed the opportunity.

"Martienne will pick us up in Piraeus, and we'll drive to Patras over the Corinth Canal with her." Jeannette had the whole trip planned. "We'll catch the night ferry to Corfu and stay in the Astron Hotel, run by friends of mine who won't mind us getting in very late."

"In the morning after breakfast," she continued, "we can take a scenic drive up to the northern port of Corfu and catch a fishing caïque to Othonis. We should get into port before it gets dark, and the pony can take us up the hill and home for sunset!"

It sounded idyllic—and organized.

"Leon is coming with us"—apparently she couldn't find a suitable dog sitter—"so he'll have to share the back seat."

I had no problem with that. I had a soft spot for the old guy. We had shared food and fire together the previous winter, when I'd house-sat while Jeannette was visiting the UK, and we knew each other well. Leon at the time had probably been 125 in doggie years and suffered from memory loss. She'd phoned during her trip to see how we were doing.

"And how's the old man?"

I was on the phone downstairs and heard the click-click of Leon's long toenails on the wooden floor above me.

"We're both fine, sitting in front of the fire upstairs, watching videos," I replied.

Staying in Jeannette's house was a luxury. A cupboard full of videos to watch beside an open log fire on an island with no cinema and almost nonexistent television was the height of decadence.

While we were talking, Leon had stopped directly above me and paused.

"I'm becoming a Cordon Blue at cooking spaghetti Bolognese," I said cheerfully. Jeannette had left ample mince and pasta in the house for us to eat.

"How's Blighty—" I'd started to inquire, when I realized what the small drilling sound above me was, and by then it was too late. Leon had ambled over to cock his leg against the grand piano, and the stream he produced had seeped straight through a crack in the floorboards.

"Swine dog," I'd squawked into Jeannette ear. She roared.

* * *

So I was well acquainted with Leon and had some idea of what travelling with him would be like.

The expeditioners assembled. Leon, Martienne, Jeannette, a chainsaw, and I managed to squeeze between the luggage. What Martienne lacked in city-driving skills—almost resulting in two fender benders as she wended her way through congested traffic—she made up for in speed on the open road.

Martienne was French and apparently did not like being overtaken.

"An Alfa Romeo can't beat my Golf," exclaimed the Gallic art dealer, displaying surprising enthusiasm for motorized competition as she put her foot down. A burst of horsepower and a hair-raising overtake on a bend put us back in the lead shortly before we reached the Corinth Canal.

Minutes later, the designer stubble in the red Alfa took up the challenge and reclaimed the lead. A gentle scenic drive through the country had become a matter of death-defying speed and defense of honor.

It was my first car ride in many moons. After prolonged periods on the Rock, it takes a little time to get reacquainted with traffic. As a perpetual pedestrian on Hydra, one rarely moves faster than a brisk walk. Even mopeds seem to pass at warp speed for a while when one returns to the mainland.

I inquired, hinting hopefully, about the existence of speed traps.

"Oui, but zay never uze zem ziss time." The right foot remained flat.

Needless to say, Martienne put us on the ferry at Patras well ahead of schedule. The old dog and I hadn't leaked much, and I think we beat the Alfa.

The next day, by the time we had scoured Corfu's market for "basic necessities" and arrived at Sidari on the northern tip of the island, it was early afternoon. Our accumulated luggage looked like the trappings for a farmhouse.

The caïque turned out to be a sixteen-foot fishing boat. Dog, plants, bags, and a various selection of forest-clearing equipment were loaded on to the deck.

"We sail for about four or five hours—if the weather's okay," announced the fisherman.

It wasn't.

The presence of cloud made our sunset spectacular, and escalating winds gave everything movement. Leon was getting seasick, and eventually we had to tack into the waves.

Soon after dark, a speck of light on the horizon beckoned, and we spent the next hour carefully navigating our way through the reef to the quay.

The promised pony revealed itself to be a four-wheeled Citroen; I was grateful. Jeannette, knowing the joke worked in her favor, chuckled while we loaded.

"*I batteria pethane.*" A helpful moustache informed us that the battery was dead when we tried to start the dust-covered jeep.

"How long since she was driven?" I asked.

"Months. But not to worry—there are a couple of other vehicles on the island—mainly tractors—but someone's bound to have jumper cables."

The town of Othonis consisted of a dozen buildings and a church, with two tavernas serving as the hub. One doubled as the post office and magistrates' court, the other as a supermarket. The rest of the island's inhabitants were scattered on farms.

Finding jumper cables took time and a lot of walking. Along the way, Jeannette said, "It's lobster season. Let's get up before sunrise and lay some traps—I've got a boat and a new outboard."

Leaving Leon behind the next morning, we marched for ten minutes by flashlight through the bush to where the recharged pony was parked on the peninsula road. This, in reality, was a dirt track running through the center of the hilly island, connecting the town to the island's northern attraction, the lighthouse.

Fog rolled in as we headed down the mountain in the predawn light.

"It's only a bit of morning mist. It'll evaporate when the sun comes up," said Jeannette glibly when she caught my sideways glance.

Our vessel wasn't much bigger than a bathtub, but the motor was brand-new, and I optimistically put my faith in the skipper.

"Pass me the instruction book behind you," she said, as we wobbled in the middle of the small harbor. "How does one start these things?"

That should have been a clue.

We managed to thread our way out of the reef, with me peering into the gloom for marker beacons. The sea carried swell but was a smooth as glass—tranquil but eerie.

We motored out to sea. The mist got slightly brighter but showed no sign of dissipating as time went by. Skiers call the effect snow blindness.

"Jeannette, do you have a compass?"

"We don't need one. I know exactly where we are," she answered confidently. "Just start looking for fisherman buoys. We must be getting close to the catchment area."

It was difficult to guess knots or direction when swaddled in a light grey blanket, but I judged the captain to have maintained a steady hand on the tiller—meaning that we could be miles out to sea, in a tiny dingy, without a compass, in a fog.

Eventually Jeannette cut the engine and pronounced the spot perfect. We dropped our traps and broke out the flask.

Guenda, guenda, guenda—a large, throbbing diesel engine sounded through the mist, growing in intensity.

"Have we got any flares?"

"What for? We don't need help."

"So we can alert the ship to our presence," I suggested, figuring the flare might exit the cloud and be visible from the elevated bridge of an inbound tanker.

"You're being silly. That boat's miles away," said my captain with solid conviction. "Don't worry."

Ten minutes later, the deep throb had become deafening. I was convinced a giant prow would shortly emerge from the mist; visibility wasn't more than forty feet.

"*Kalimera*," shouted Jeannette, through cupped hands, over my shoulder, nearly sending me into the drink. Her voice carried across the water.

"*Yassouooo*," came the reply. An alert crewman had heard Jeannette's call. At least the ship was now aware of another vessel in the vicinity. A large shadow, belonging to an oceangoing fishing vessel, chugged by moments later. We exchanged a few shouts, pleasantries, and bearings. Afterward, it dawned on me that the freighter would have had radar and known of our presence all along.

When the mist finally lifted, we found ourselves well northeast of the island. Leaving our traps marked with a buoy, we headed for the nearest beach.

"The house is just up there, a three-minute shortcut," said Jeannette pointing up. "We can leave the boat here and go home for lunch."

Getting off the deserted sandy beach proved the first obstacle.

"The path used to start here," said my adventurous companion, "but it seems the rough winter seas have washed it away."

Indeed, exiting the shoreline appeared impossible as a small cliff that ran its entire perimeter hindered access to the jungle behind it. Erosion had cleared away any means of heading inland.

"Give me a hand with this driftwood—it might make the top of the overhang, and we can crawl up it to breach the overhand." Jeannette had found a twenty-foot, washed-up plank. "I know where the path starts."

The makeshift bridge reached the root systems protruding from the eroded lip, and we crawled up onto the "path" to face an impenetrable wall of bramble bush; the path was indistinguishable.

"Othonis is also called *Fithi Nisi* in this region," she announced, as we struggled, ear-deep, through thorny foliage. "Snake Island. So it's advisable to make noise and carry a stick."

True to the nickname, we encountered many vipers on our slow advance through the dense brush. I was just happy the place wasn't called Spider Island, as eight-legged wildlife gave me the jitters. Rescue helicopters were out of the question.

After three hours of bushwhacking up an incline, which often required the use of all four limbs, we emerged onto Jeannette's plateau, scratched and weary—more precisely, I did, as my indefatigable leader seemed to have the hide of another species.

Even she admitted that clambering back down to collect the boat seemed a little rash. With the boat inaccessible and the pony in town at the bottom of the mountain, we had no choice but to opt for another march, mercifully on the cleared tractor track.

In the little harbor, we hitched a lift from a local fisherman, who drove us around the island to collect our boat. Then we headed out to sea again in search of the buoy and hopefully dinner.

Three lobster of acceptable length, half a dozen colorful, but unpronounceable, bony fish, and an *octopothi*, or octopus, went on the grill that night—a feast fit for exhausted adventurers.

During the next two weeks, I learned to wield a chain saw to some effect and even picked up a smattering of outdoor baking skills. There were no bakers on the island, so locals made their own bread. I developed a taste for wild greens and weird fish.

"I think we will take the pony back to Ermioni," said Jeannette, referring to the little town on the Peloponnese opposite Hydra, where we could leave the car.

"Leon can have the back all to himself," I said, as Martina had returned to Athens a week earlier.

The little pony was laboring up the steep winding roads of northern Greece when we spotted a tortoise trying to cross the road. Suggesting that the little reptile might get run over, I insisted we stop.

"The poor thing has already been run over," I exclaimed. The tortoise's shell was blemished, scratched, and appeared slightly flattened. "He seems fine though. Perhaps we should take him back to Hydra and give him a good home."

I thought he would make an excellent companion for Felix, a tortoise I'd nurtured back to health after Bluebell, my donkey of the period, trod on it, reinforcing my perception that a tortoise's armor can withstand heavy punishment.

So, with the best of intentions, we put the flattened little tortoise in the back of the pony with Leon. That night we stayed in a small hotel outside Patras, and I left some fruit and lettuce in the back of the car for my new pet.

I was a little disturbed to note in the morning that the tortoise hadn't touched the offerings and put it down to motion sickness. "He'll be alright once he has a garden to play in," I enthused as we continued motoring down through the Peloponnese.

We stopped to stretch on a panoramic bend a few miles from our destination.

"I think I'll give Felix's mate a walk too," I said, lifting the little animal out of the back.

A recent thunderstorm had left a very large puddle on the side of the road, and the reptile hotfooted it for the water, obviously thirsty. On reaching the edge of the pond, it carried straight on in and disappeared under the murky brown water.

"Do you think maybe your tortoise is a turtle," said Jeannette, laughing.

"It didn't appear to have webbed feet," I spluttered. "Poor little thing, and now we have taken it hundreds of kilometers from its home."

Concerned that it would be left high and dry once the puddle evaporated, I felt bad.

"Listen, there is a stream down there," consoled Jeannette. "Remember that we found him far from water, and he seems to have a nose for it, so he'll be okay."

My reputation as a zoologist, however, was not.

8

DEANS AND DYNAMITE

"Don't you get bored living full-time on the Rock?" island hoppers and other travellers frequently ask.

Some folks get twitchy even a few hours after being marooned. "Not even a tennis court? How do you keep yourself entertained?"

My answer has always been simple: "The theater."

All the island is a stage, the actors constantly twisting the plot and always full of surprises. The cast and setting are award-winning stuff. Two- and four-legged, alien and local, new players flit and rotate constantly through the script of life on the island. One never knows what's around the corner ... or on a neighboring rooftop.

"Quick, come in! Did he see you?" The door opened before I had a chance to knock.

Leonard had been awaiting my arrival so we could plot the day's chores. He seemed wider-awake than usual and tugged me inside.

"On the taverna roof. Waving a stick of dynamite—threatening to blow up his brother's restaurant." Leonard turned the key, locking us in. This in itself was an unusual act as people rarely locked their doors, even when they left town.

"What? Who?" I had seen nothing—nobody, in fact—when I came into the village.

I knew Leonard to have an active imagination, but it was eight o'clock in the morning, and he appeared genuinely distressed, suggesting that this apparition may have some tangibility.

I asked for more information.

"Ouzo mixed with about a barrel of retsina will impede logic. This is the worst bender I've seen him on." Leonard was by then peeling back a blind in the lounge at the rear of the little cottage, peering at the adjacent tavern. "He's been at it all night. The man's capable of serious mischief."

"Who? And is he after you?" I solicited specifics in order of priority.

"He's done it before, rampaged through the village waving his shotgun, but this time he is really off his rocker. He's been warned to go easy on the hooch," Leonard spilled. "Seven brothers, none talk to each other, all big brutes, but Barbajanis and Jorgo have a rivalry stronger than the others."

A sibling rhubarb had apparently been simmering for decades between seven moustaches, who hadn't exchanged a single greeting during that time, according to Leonard. Individually nicer blokes you couldn't wish meet, however.

Jorgo and Barbajanis owned the village's tavernas, named Martina's and Marina's after their respective wives. Both families were charming, and the villagers alternated tavernas so as not to offend one or the other.

Leonard's cottage was bang in the middle, and with two barrels of his finest plonk on offer, he attracted his share of visitors. A most generous host, Leonard generated a little hub of his own. He and guests would diplomatically, and prudently, rotate their custom between the two tavernas.

As both establishments competed in every aspect, including menu and price, there was little difference between them anyway. Rumor had it that Martina's did better fresh fish, whereas Marina's oven dishes were slightly superior.

I doubted Leonard had a rhubarb with anyone in the village or had inadvertently gotten himself involved in an outbreak of intertaverna warfare—caused, it turned out, by the alleged theft of a dozen eggs from Barbajanis's chicken coup.

Barbajanis had interrogated the neighborhood all the previous afternoon, trying to establish where his eggs had gone. Denials had confirmed his suspicion that brother Jorgo's establishment would be serving *omelettas* that day—with Barbajanis's produce.

Barbajanis took his complaint to the retsina barrel, and the more he talked to the barrel, the more it convinced him that his prime suspect was indeed the thief. His one-way discussion in the corner about fresh eggs and justice got louder with time. No one loitered about that evening, and he sat alone with his echo. By dusk he was on the roof of the taverna with TNT and a box of matches, demanding retribution.

"He is as unstable as his ordinance, and dynamite is not as selective as a shotgun." Leonard's little cottage stood in no-man's-land, and considering the lubricated state of the catapult, we stood a probable chance of becoming the unintended targets of a muddled gunpowder plot.

"Worked himself into a right old paddy. You should have heard the noise, and the vocabulary! Outdid the roosters at dawn, he did." Leonard, a scholar who loved Greece, had left his position as the dean of Cambridge Collage to become a Vlichioti—with a tranquil retirement in mind, no doubt.

Vlichos consists, population-wise, of a handful of families. If living on Hydra is like living under a magnifying glass, then living in Vlichos would be like living under a microscope. Everything is noted, down to the egg.

"Everyone is hiding or has fled, including Jorgo in his caïque. Nobody can reason with him." The Dean was peeping outside again. "Bugger and blast, there he is. At least he's managed to get down without falling off or blowing himself up."

On cue there was a shout from the front garden. "*Olla malakas*." Barbajanis followed this general curse of the land with some gruff, incomprehensible Greek.

"I think he is looking for more to drink," whispered Leonard, "and of course he knows I have wine in the house. Let's hope he forgets about it."

"*Leonardeh!*" Pane-rattling thumps on the kitchen door dashed the Dean's hopes of remaining undetected.

"What do we do?" Leonard was seriously perturbed. "He knows I'm here."

"*Leonardeh!*" The bellow alone rattled panes. "*File mou!*"

"If we don't answer, we could antagonize him. His wife ran away, and everyone is steering well clear of him. Even the police want the family matter settled domestically before they'll come."

Leonard filled me in on the intricacies of Hydriot policing.

"Unless the caller is prepared to lodge a formal complaint himself, the constabulary generally only interfere when a crime has been committed, particularly this far out of town."

Apparently it's not a crime to wave a stick of dynamite about. Only if the fuse was lit, and the incendiary was then utilized, in unfriendly fashion, would it constitute a civil disturbance.

Involving the police by filing a formal complaint can lead to years in court. In this case, one suspected, it would invite another conversation with the barrel and attention from the retsina and dynamite show. Understandably, folk were reluctant to lay a nemesis on a neighbor with such exciting pyrotechnic tendencies.

"*Leonardeh! File mou, thelo leego kokkinelli sou!*" The pounding fist demanded a glass of the house rosé. It was like being in a sixties movie, with Anthony Quinn and real props.

"So he remembers not just your wine but your special distillation." The Dean's expression cautioned me to add quickly, "But look on the bright side—he is still calling you a friend."

"Just let him in, Leonard." I advised. "Perhaps if we encourage him, he'll pass out. According to your observations, the man should be drowning from the inside already."

I had a feeling the day's work schedule had gone out the window by then, as Leonard would be in no mood to conduct operations after this. I had been Leonard's right-hand man on a number of maritime, gardening, moving, painting, and carpentry projects over the years, so I knew the fellow well.

Working with the Dean was entertaining and normally safe. He had a tool for all occasions; one wore protective goggles and gloves when engaged in industry at Leonard's. A tool room, complete with spare wine barrel, stood adjacent to the kitchen.

A careful man with humor and a big heart, he was a popular host accustomed to visitors who appreciated his vintage.

"Don't worry. He hardly speaks any English." The Dean was doing his best to look unworried, sitting opposite me at the kitchen table, with Barbajanis in the middle.

"What do we do now? I don't want to be guzzling wine at this time of the day," Leonard added.

Our guest, stick of dynamite protruding from top pocket, had insisted that he couldn't drink alone and poured three glasses.

"*Yamas!*" The baritone stubble clinked glasses with us a second time, not sloshing too much. We toasted.

I have been encouraged to drink in my time, but never under threat of instant dismemberment shortly after dawn. As the company was gruff but convivial, however, I quickly discarded any thoughts of grabbing the stick and legging it. And because Leonard was portly and no longer the fine scrum half he'd been in former days, capture was highly probable. Our best option was to join in, and our guest had a full barrel start on us.

"*Yamas!*" Clink. "*Oraya kokkinelli, file mou.*" Barbajanis, a big bloke, complimented the host on his fine wine, followed by a friendly whack on the back—dentures almost evicted.

Conversation with Barbajanis fluctuated between egg thievery, honesty, and the art of making good wine. Our visitor thrust an empty glass forward with regularity.

We sipped as Barbajanis, in no hurry to go anywhere, gulped. Gossip exchanged, we agreed with all his views. One does not disagree with bomb-wielding morning callers.

Three jugs later, Leonard gawked at me and hiccupped. "Rasputin reincarnate, the bastard appears rejuvenated. Any passing out might be achieved by me. The man is an ox."

Indeed, Leonard was looking far less athletic than our visitor. A while later, Leonard announced that his precious barrel of blush was sounding awfully hollow.

Kokkinelli is resonated wine made from red grapes, and Leonard's was particularly notorious. I never did have the heart to tell him the truth about that season's wine, as neither he nor any of his multitude of guests had ever suspected anything was awry. Jorgo, the allegedly thieving brother and owner of the sunset taverna on the Dean's starboard—our visitor's intended target—had sublet the cottage to Leonard. When the Dean went back to Blighty periodically, Jorgo's family would keep and eye on the house, garden, and their tenant's basic affairs. This year he had asked them to order his year's supply of *musta* while he was abroad.

"*Kai, tee kanees me to kokkinelli mou?*" Leonard had asked over the phone, curious to know that status of his annual wine supply. Jorgo was about to explain to Leonard that the blush had been unobtainable, and they had gotten him standard white retsina instead, when wife Marina wagged a finger under his nose, commanding silence.

"*Olla endaxi, Leonardeh,*" assured Jorgo, frowning at his spouse in confusion.

Jorgo had told me conspiratorially that his wife had poured some red food coloring into the white grape base. "*Kai, san kokkinelli,*" he said, holding a sample glass up to the light to show that it indeed had the correct rose tint. Nobody was the wiser, and revelers had sampled and admired the contents all summer long.

"Knock the barrel. Show him its empty, and maybe he'll go home," I suggested.

Leonard was old-school, manners, etiquette, and sense of fair play part of his fiber—a middle-aged Boy Scout who did things by the book.

Once, when we were planting sunflower seeds he had bought from a reputed English gardening faculty, experience confirmed value of this by-the-book philosophy. We were following the instructions on the back of the envelope exactly: pointy end down, an inch and a half deep in loose soil, eighteen inches apart, goat shit and stuff, planted in a neat row, in the second week of March …

"*Tee kanete etho?*" A black shawl had come to investigate. Leaning over the garden wall, she pointed at our efforts. I had yet to learn the art of plowing ahead regardless of helpful interruption, and with the aid of the photo on the packet, I explained.

"*Oxi, oxi!*" she tutted adamantly. A lot of wrist tapping amid the subsequent burbling indicated we had our calendar wrong. Leonard came over. She told him we were starting too early and not planting the bulbs far enough apart. The *yaya* waddled off, leaving us to contemplate the back of the packet.

"*Tee symveni?*" A fisherman stuck his head over the wall to inquire what the matter was. Leonard explained the dilemma posed by such contradictory guidance.

"*Oxi, oxi!*" Bushy eyebrows jerked in sympathy. "They must be much closer, and you are too late."

"But the packet says … " Leonard flicked the side of the envelope. "Written by experts—"

"In you country, yes, but ess different in Greece. Very hot." Convincingly dismissive of alien horticulturists, he left us pondering. Three additional conflicting opinions from others in the village within the next half hour made up our minds.

We decided to stick with the written instructions.

A bumper crop proved to Leonard why one always stuck to the book. I learned not to explain myself to interested parties: it only invited rhubarb.

"I'm a belts-and-braces man myself. One can't be too careful," Leonard announced with regularity. One could hardly plan for the contingency of Barbajanis inviting himself into the kitchen with a stick of dynamite for a liquid breakfast. Leonard looked stumped.

In fact, we were both almost as befuddled as our guest, who by then had revived to the point where he was demanding "Greek musik," his fingers clicking to an imaginary tune. Leonard and I were in no condition to dance, and it wasn't even ten o'clock.

Barbajanis also had it in his head that my name was Steve, and he'd been calling me Steve for years. I had corrected him once, then let it slide.

"*Ella*, Steve, dance, live." The seated stubble, both arms extended in a Zorba-like stance, was about to get upright, and the room was small with lots of breakables. "You get music."

We had shared enough *kokkinelli* by this stage to establish comradeship, and both to avoid waltzing with a weaving moustache and to settle the Steve matter once and for all, I employed a distraction tactic.

"*Eemay o David. Oxi Steve.*" I held him down with one hand on his shoulder, passing a glass with the other.

We toasted my new name with gusto several times, and dancing was forgotten.

The chances of our succumbing before the guest drowned were looking likely … which would leave our guest singularly perpendicular within range of an as yet undiscovered second barrel and still sporting an unlit bomb.

I suggested filling a plastic bottle from the blush dribble, giving it to our guest as a "nightcap," and pointing him toward home. The gift was well received.

"*Endaxi, efharisto! Yassou, Leonardeh! Yassou, Davie.*" Far less belligerent than when he arrived, he carried the bottle contentedly home, about twenty yards to Leonard's portside.

Peace reigned, and nothing got blown up. Plus, we had this name business sorted out.

Leonard made my legs a mug of strong black coffee, and I made it home two hours before lunch for an uncharacteristic midday kip—the day's work done.

I saw Barbajanis sitting in his taverna sipping a cup of Greek coffee on my way past the next morning, a cat on his lap, locals at adjacent tables, the dynamite episode apparently forgotten.

"*Kalimera, Keerios Barbajanis,*" I piped.

"*Yassou, Steve! Tee khanees?*"

A clean slate all round, in fact—the incident might never have happened.

Both brothers have since sublet their establishments and taken to fishing—in separate boats, of course—on different sides of the gulf.

9

FOSSILS AND FOIBLES

A couple of the younger artists had found a bleached skull on the beach, two feet long (including the beak) and nearly a foot wide. They had waded back out to the caïque, brandishing it with glee and puzzlement.

We had taken a group of Bostonian artists to the sandy beach on the mainland opposite Hydra in our usual caïque, captained by old man Mikhali. Everyone was left to his or her own devices once we dropped anchor about fifty feet offshore.

Mikhali, wizened and weathered brown, sported jet-black dyed hair and a pencil-thin moustache. Rumored had it that he was still skippering several decades past the legal retirement age. He was our favorite, and his wide-beamed boat accommodated two-dozen picnickers in comfort. Her Barefootness, the dog-rescuing countess, generally commanded such outings and adorned the picnic table onboard with exotic dishes. Mikhali, suspicious of anything not produced in a Greek kitchen, was not to be seduced by guacamole and curried chicken salad and the like.

He had panache; with a white Panama hat pulled down over his nose, he would quietly siesta between sips of retsina and *tiropita* (cheese pie). He looked and played the part of the wise, experienced old man of the sea.

He got up to inspect the find.

"It belong to a big bird from *Afriki*," he explained authoritatively to the gathered group of attentive students.

I thought he was taking the piss.

I glanced at the students, a mixed bag of housewives, teenagers and under graduates, who, to my surprise, were nodding in awe.

Clearly this bunch was not remotely ornithological.

"A long flight for such a large bird," I chipped in, curious about what Mikhali really thought they'd found.

"Very old," he hedged his bets, flapping a hand back over his shoulder to emphasize generations. "Not now, before."

More nodding. He had just convinced a dozen American East Coast urbanites, in few words, that we now had in our possession a pteridactalorosourous find of magnitude.

I couldn't let him get away with it. Morally it would be wrong to let these guys to leg it back to their professors with such an "antiquity."

"What about the hole in its head?" I asked, offering him an out.

"It has been shot," said the pencil moustache—as any fool could see, his tone implied.

Boston's creative minds appeared to favor intrigue and bobbed even more.

"Perhaps it swims?" I thought that would induce the captain to reevaluate his position.

"*Oxi, oxi*," wagged a brown finger. "*Palio*, very old bird from *Afriki*."

"Okay then—what's the biggest bird in the world?" I could see that the Panama hat's authoritative tone still held more audience appeal.

Debate ensued, and when the condor seemed the winning choice, I suggested an ostrich, crooking my arm and making a loose fist.

"A skull about this size. Seconded by an emu, which also doesn't fly."

An atmosphere of "so?" permeated the silence; Mikhali peered at me over his shades, unconvinced.

"All right then, if skulls contain brains, and bigger brains go into bigger skulls, which is the most intelligent species of flying bird?"

More debate ended with my idea of perhaps the parrot.

"The biggest of which is a macaw."

Again, my fist demonstrated a close approximate size.

"The biggest flying bird around here's a seagull, right Mikhali?"

Mikhali's lined forehead crinkled, eyebrows elevated skeptically.

"*Poli paleo*," he insisted. We were back on the flying dinosaur kick.

Turned the head over, I noted that dental apertures lined the "beak."

"Birds don't have teeth, right?" I asked the inspectors, genuinely intrigued to see how far removed from the wild these big-city dwellers were.

"Dinosaurs did," said some diehards, still preferring Mikhali's version, so I persevered.

"Fossils weigh a ton."

I held the skull out to them.

"Feel the weight of this—hardly petrified."

I watched a few nods turn into frowns of doubt.

"It's a dolphin skull, chaps."

Silence, including from the Panama pencil.

"To fly, this bird would need a wing span of ninety feet."

More silence.

"The hole isn't a bullet hole but blowhole, for breathing, and we know dolphins are extremely smart, hence the large cranium."

I could see the flying-dinosaur theory was vanishing.

"It's been washed up on a sandy beach in a gulf known to have schools pass through."

I looked around for Mikhali, wishing to ask him what year he thought firearms had come into use.

His horizontal, tilted Panama was already snoring.

On the way back to the Rock, I took the helm for him, as I sometimes did, and he patted me on the shoulder approvingly.

"We had fun today," he said in Greek, squinting at my course and clenching an oval cigarette. "We nearly had them, my friend."

Old man Mikhali died of throat cancer a couple of years later, and I never found out if ultimately I had been the one who was had. The "fossil" still adorns the entrance hall of her Barefootness's mansion, a fond reminder that the question remains unanswered.

Was the old sea dog having me on, or did he himself learn a new trick?

10

WRIGGLY BUTTS

Smokers at sea in sailing boats quickly adapt to using empty beverage cans as ashtrays. Conventional ashtrays seem to lie in wait for a well-timed gust to blow an accumulated mouthful of cinders in the direction of a yawning non-smoker. I myself have used cans ever since I was halfway through my first smoke break as a new navel crewman up-wind of a burly, health-conscious helmsman.

As we left the harbor on our first day of a scheduled ten-day sailing cruise, I thought I would share this wisdom with my new shipmates. I highlighted the benefits of drinking from a can as opposed to glassware as it saved sloshing, and you could then convert the vessel into a no-mess cigarette dispenser.

The trick is to partially crush the can, indicating that its contents are finished and thereby differentiating it from those still containing refreshment resting in the poop deck glass holders. The potential hazards of drinking from glass on a seesawing surface served as further recommendation for using cans only. Not all new sailors know this handy advice.

We were but a few nautical miles from port when I took a swig from my half-full can. A cigarette end floated against my teeth, and I instantly blew it back into can with disgust, assuming someone had not yet mastered the intricate courtesies of partaking in vices on the upper deck of a yacht.

I was temporarily perplexed as to why the butt remained lodged in the front of my mouth, when it suddenly grabbed my lower lip and started to wriggle enthusiastically.

Nostril hairs froze, eyebrows levitated, and vigorous spitting dislodged the grapple, attracting the attention of fellow passengers.

"What's the matter?" they asked.

"A wriggly butt"—I nodded at the garish insect emerging from the can's drinking hole—"of the sinister persuasion, not the kind one had in mind."

We nickname them B-52s, huge brown-and-yellow hornets, that mercifully are not aggressive, unless they think you are going to bite their head off. They carry a sting that can hospitalize a child. I briefly wondered about the effect it could have on a soft lower lip. What a start to the voyage that would have been.

Fortunately the creature droned off laboriously without taking revenge and, in so doing, taught me not to think I have all the answers. No one else wanted to meet a wriggly butt on that trip, and everyone converted back to drinking out of glasses. It no longer mattered what shape a can was in for the unwriggly kind.

11

STRIKES AND STALEMATES

Before the Berlin Wall came down, huge chunks of EU financial support flowed into Greece, and some of it trickled down as far as the Rock. It was decided that Kamini merited a bigger harbor.

With the increase in yacht traffic, the main port was becoming too crowded in high season. Another dock, the reasoning went, would allow some fishing caïques to moor in the suburb, alleviating main harbor congestion.

The single Kamini pier, used for summer inflatables and embarking only, offered no protected anchorage. Nothing permanent bobbed there. Turning it into a year-round harbor entailed building second convex seawall about thirty meters out. The plan sounded modest enough, but at about that distance the seafloor drops into dark fathoms, necessitating construction of a wall of some multistory depth—a major project.

The proposal was approved and tenders submitted.

The municipality decided to blow up Palameetha, a village several furlongs south of Vlichos and the island's boat repair yard, for the raw material. For weeks floating cranes hoisted massive boulders and dropped them just off Kamini by the ton.

Like all grants, these finances came with an expiration date. Brussels would eventually ask to see tangible evidence of its investment.

I would not be the first to observe that Greeks tend to lull one into the belief that they cannot possibly meet a deadline. Then, in a last minute blur of activity, they get the job done against all odds. Generally the finished product is up to snuff on opening night, but sometimes this haste leaves a fly or two in the ointment.

Eventually an EU suit announced he was arriving on Monday at noon to inspect the new harbor. It was Friday.

The pile of jutting boulders did not quite comply with the section of the approved project proposal that promised an "access road with bollards and a navigation harbor-entrance light."

A special license for a cement truck materialized with unusual bureaucratic speed. As the whole island is a national monument, obtaining a license to import any form of vehicle is normally next to impossible. New, with a tinted-glass cabin set above the right front wheel and a small ladder up, it was an impressive machine, it must be said.

I walked back from Vlichos after helping Leonard with some gardening around seven o'clock in the evening on that Friday, and builders were still hard at it, the enormous, mechanized yellow barrel churning at their heels.

"They've got an inspector coming, haven't they," Don said, leaning out of his window, which overlooked the little port. Nothing escaped his view from this vantage, and the construction of a new harbor on the island had historical implications.

Don is an extraordinary fellow, an Englishman who hasn't budged from the Rock since he landed more than five decades ago. He is purported to have written 628 books, mostly by candlelight, as he has steadfastly denied any advantage to electrifying his various dwellings—this one a ramshackle stone cottage with a concave roof, an outhouse, and a selection of gypsy-like cages, containing chickens and ducks, scattered in an unkempt adjacent garden.

He likes the simple life and suffers from "remote-control-o-phobia," a severe handicap in this day and age. In the early nineties, push-button phones still made him nervous.

"I dunno," he would tut, shaking his head. "I like the ones that go round, a real dial, you know what I mean?"

Explaining why the phone didn't work in a house he was watching for a friend, he'd described replacing the hand piece upside down and perpendicular to the cradle.

But building stuff he knew about, and the construction noise had now disturbed his peaceful surroundings.

"All this time, good as gold, they were," he tutted some more. "And this afternoon they didn't even stop for siesta." Siesta was a serious part of Greek culture: one did not phone in the afternoon; even dogs kept quiet.

On Monday morning, Don was up as I passed on the path to Vlichos, which meanders up out of the little port.

"It's nearly done. At it until dark all weekend, they were."

The builders and their mates, with the aid of the four-wheeled monster, had slaved on the wharf nonstop.

At lunch, as I was returning to town, I could hear the rhubarb from halfway along the cliff road. A lot of people with vocal opinions had congregated around the building site.

"Nearly drowned, didn't he," Don told me, leaning on elbows in the window. "Now how are they going to get that bloody thing out of there. It was full, you know, tons o' the stuff."

It took me a second to take it all in. A lot of gesticulating and noise surrounded what appeared to be a bomb blast in the middle of the new structure.

"Someone said a fishing boat may be underneath it," said the Bard behind me on the window ledge. "Maybe with a bloke in it."

A rectangle of four huge tires, about a meter below the surface, gazed skyward from the middle of the new port.

"The driver was trapped in the cabin. He only just managed to get out," Don went on. "Hadn't set, had it. Drove the thing on, and half way down, the wet cement sagged and collapsed. Quite a splash, I can tell you."

The EU suit, who had arrived just in time to witness the resuscitation of a semi-drowned driver, was greeted by municipal officials with an affidavit swearing that the structural slump would be repaired ASAP.

And it was—as soon as the salvage operation had been completed, and the surviving cement and stones were dry a couple of weeks later.

* * *

Shortly afterward, an even bigger rhubarb developed surrounding the sudden appearance of another vehicle. A bulldozer had landed in Vlichos and started munching a road for itself along the coastal path to Kamini. Civil wars have erupted with less emotion.

As I've mentioned, all vehicles, other than two or three small garbage trucks and a golf cart that serves as an ambulance, are banned on the Rock, and permission to import anything on wheels is extremely rare. This vehicle seemed to be carving a path for its brethren in the future.

The demand for information grew loud. Where had the beast obtained its papers?

Eventually an official statement clarified that the bulldozer was cutting a firebreak, in the light of two big fires in 1985 and 1987. Three locals had perished in the first, attempting to rescue icons from a church when the flames had surrounded them. The second had almost incinerated a monastery, so the fire-hazard card had strong support.

The excavation was a fire-prevention measure, and some parts of this firebreak would provide access for a fire engine, the municipality explained.

A fire engine!

Conversation on the port rippled; currents formed.

"The thin end of the wedge, I say. Next it'll be a bus," stated one inmate, invoking a hearty rhubarb among the debates.

"What fire engine? Authorization for more vehicles is not written into the island's constitution."

"Anyway, what good would an engine do when 99 percent of the Rock would be topographically inaccessible. The only way to fight these fires is from the air—as we've always done," a pragmatist voiced.

"Prevention is better than cure. They should build a reservoir near the dump, where the fires always start. That would be more effective and cheaper than a road," advised the table behind.

"What's the harm of one little minibus? It's their island. Who are we to tell them what to do," piped a Californian.

"So the Brazilians can chop down the earth's last natural rain forest, asphyxiating all life because it's theirs!" A tree hugger with a different perspective elevated the controversial road to an international issue.

"One bus is hardly a rain forest," defended the Valley.

Someone hinted that hitching a ride to Vlichos would be lazy, another that felling a forest always starts with one tree.

"Don't they realize that the absence of vehicles is the only thing that makes this place special?" rallied another anticonstruction voice. "One little moped, and this place is over. It becomes just like Poros, Spetses, or any other island for that matter."

"Where else in the world is there a town so close to a major capital that still runs on just donkeys," agreed another. "If there were cars, what would be the point of coming? Motors would ruin it."

Debate flowed and ebbed, with only decibels increasing.

As the bulldozer progressed along the coast, getting closer to making Vlichos accessible from Kamini by car, concerned parties fired a lot of rhubarbs off to the press. Some entertained picketing the cliff road. "Human sit-down barricades!" enthused California, who had swapped sides. The "thin end of the wedge" brigade threatened night raids with bags of sugar to halt the monster. A kilo or two in the petrol tank would do the trick.

Eventually, the societies for the preservation of Hydra won, and the dozer came to a stop—within sight of the new harbor.

* * *

The rhubarbs generated by Kamini harbor itself didn't stop with its completion. Indeed, they became the cause of further civil unrest.

The dynamiting for the new Kamini harbor wall had created a deeper entrance at Palameetha, which until then had been a semi-accessible beach used mainly for boat repairs.

"Palameetha is now an ideal place for unloading building materials," said a gold shop owner.

The merchant lobby had long complained that, particularly in winter, Hydra Town's elegant, picturesque harbor front looked more like a construction site, often hazardous to ambulant locals and tourists alike. A construction boat, the *Agios Nikalous*, would dump tons of building material on the port every so often. When it rained, mud soiled everything.

The Muleteers' Union got wind of the proposition to use Palameetha as an unloading point and lodged a complaint. Walking an extra third of the island to collect building materials would overburden their beasts and jack up delivery times and costs.

"Preserve Hydra" types sided with the gold shops, and the municipality decided that building activity must be conducted out of town.

The muleteers took quick action. The following day, donkeys and mules stood in idle groups outside the town hall and cathedral with placards attached to saddles in two languages: "Donkey on strike! No fair, Palameetha!"

Bemused Asian cameras clicked, and locals postponed heavy shopping. The muleteers sat in a mid-port taverna sipping beer, and the island's sole transport system ground to a halt. Check.

But then the merchants countered the muleteer union's victory strike by targeting the boat bringing in the building supplies. Its crane, after all, unloaded the piles of material—so if it couldn't enter the harbor, it couldn't dump anything on the port front. No building supplies on the port meant no donkeys either. Countercheck.

Some paperwork arrived, and a couple of uniforms went out to enforce the banishment of the *Agios Nikalous*, cargo and crane vessel, from the port of Hydra. It would henceforth be diverted to Palameetha.

Gold shop doorways grinned as the small, still-laden ship chugged out of the harbor. The very next morning, the same merchants watched amazed as the scruffy cargo boat pulled back into harbor at daybreak—bold as brass.

"*Oxi! Oxi!*" A walkie-talkie in a peaked cap wagged a finger at the mooring ship.

The moustache at the helm stepped out of the bridge, waving an official-looking paper in one hand, and continued to issue docking instructions with the other, ignoring the port authority.

A couple of reinforcing uniforms were summoned; some gathered gold merchants egged them on.

The captain explained to the walkie-talkies on the quay that the boat no longer belonged to him and that they should speak to his brother.

"*Vlepete*," he said, pointing to the bow of the ship.

We looked. In rough letters painted over the old name were the words *Agios Takis*.

Preventing the boat from docking would require issuance of a new court order and initiation of a new round of legal proceedings against the newly christened ship, which now bore the name of the owner's brother.

Moons of red tape. Stalemate.

"Perhaps if we applied for another grant, then we could build another pier right in the middle of the harbor exclusively for donkeys and Takis?" someone suggested.

A rhubarbless solution to the quandary, it was accepted unanimously. The motion was submitted, money raised, and the extra quay finished without the aid of yellow four-wheeled monsters or bulldozers long before any suit was due to inspect.

And so, it turns out, compromise can be reached and cooperation achieved even here.

12

DIRTY CORNERS AND CLEAN SLATES

The name stuck like melted chewing gum to the sole of a hot summer sandal: Dirty Corner, one of the island's favorite little watering holes.

"'Ambrosia.' Nectar of the gods," announced Christos, proudly surveying the newly erected sign outside the hole-in-the-wall cafe just back from the tourist-infested port front. "That should fix it."

Appalled to discover that his freshly acquired snack bar had such an unappealing nickname, he had been determined to shake the association. He refurbished and decorated, added designer cushions and candles, and even put a seat on the single loo. The establishment's only ablution facilities were more like a broom cupboard housing a bare-rimmed bowl.

"Pretty sign," said I, "but a waste of time. This place has had a dozen names and twice as many owners over the past few years, but the locals have always called it Dirty Corner. Blame Jimmy."

Ouzo Jimmy, a regular fixture, had dubbed the joint when it first opened. He worked as the cockney butler for one of the grand dames of Greece, Madam Paouri. Rumored to have been, as well as the richest, the most beautiful woman in Greece and to have funded the resistance during the Greek Civil War, she was pictured on the back of the 1,000-drachma note with Hydra as the backdrop.

If you sat in Dirty Corner, you got to know Jimmy, a slender gent with a vowel-heavy accent who dwelled most of the year in the madam's "key house" on the port front, even though his butlering stretches rarely lasted more than a week or so. The blue door of his quarters, situated between Antonio's and the Liako, right on the docking quay, was the lowest in a string of blue entrances to the madam's rambling estate on the east side of the harbor.

"I'm the only person on the island who doesn't even 'ave to climb one step to get 'ome," he would regularly brag, finishing his "roader." Indeed, Ouzo Jimmy was one of the most visible characters on the harbor front during the eighties; he would emerge, creased from the previous night, park in his doorway, and watch the morning activity nursing a milky aperitif.

A gentleman who had mastered the art of Greek island retirement, he was a known and likable suspect. His day's exercise consisted of at least two laps around the port's popular watering holes.

"So, what do you do here?" a nosey newcomer inquired of Jimmy one evening, having overheard that he was a longtime inmate of the Rock.

"Nuffing," Jimmy fobbed. Like all lifers, he considered such an opening line a breach of etiquette, an island taboo.

"You can't do nothing. You must do something with your time," said the Nose, not getting the hint. "I mean what do you do when you get up in the morning?"

"I brush my teeff, don' I," the dry Cockney dripped.

"Okay, but I mean, how do you occupy your time?" insisted the Nose. "What do you do after you have brushed your teeth?"

"Well, I open the door, and sit outside the house with a little ooouzo, waiting for Willy." Jimmy had watery blue eyes and a deceptive hangdog expression. His accent added more vowels to the aperitif than one could believe possible.

"And when Willy comes?" The Nose was determined to get to the bottom of Jimmy's career.

"Well, I fix him and me a little ooouzo, don' I," Jimmy answered, sucking noisily on fag. German Willy was Jimmy's chief partner in crime. A burly blond bloke with a Bavarian thirst who sometimes painted, he owned a small house right at the top of the hill behind the village and periodically crashed in Jimmy's pad when the long climb seemed too daunting for equilibrium-handicapped ambulance.

"Okay, so what do you and Willy do after the ouzo?" The Nose wouldn't give up.

"Then we go to the Liako for a little ooouzo—and Eva's eggs," sucked the fag.

"Okay, but surely you don't sit there all day?" The conversation had attracted the interest of other punter's; regulars grinned.

"'Course not. Then we go to the Loolaki Bar and have a little ooouzo." Jimmy looked around with "doesn't everyone" inferment.

"And?" The Nose belonged to a social terrier, it seemed.

"And then it's time for lunch, so we go to the Free Brovers for a little ooouzo—and chicken." Jimmy decided to give her the blow-by-blow.

"Then we go back to the Liako for a little ooouzo—" The rest of the itinerary followed in the same deadpan tone:

Pan's Bar, the Bahia Bar, "and then 'ere, Dirty Corner, and after a couple more, it's 'ome for a little nightcap of—ooouzo."

The Nose, agog, peered over her spectacles in disbelief, a question brewing. Jimmy decided to nip any further interrogation by continuing.

"And then I go to bed, and in the morning I wake, brush me teeff, open the doors, and have a little ooouzo."

The Nose sensed that the piss was being taken by the time Jimmy got back to the part about going to the Loolaki Bar for a little ooouzo and decided to cut to the chase. Terminating Jimmy's repetitive ramble in a decisive tone, she demanded, "Alright then, where do you get your money?"

Jimmy paused for a second, sucking noisily on his cigarette; it seemed to spend more time dangling from the center of his lower lip than in his hand. He blinked before answering.

"From a bank, don' I, like everyone else?" Bushy eyebrows and shoulders hoisted in feigned surprise at the stupidity of the Nose's question.

"Ja, and he is also ze boyfriend of ze richest woman in Greece, Ja Jimmy?" his burly sidekick elbowed, flicking the back of a 1,000-drachma note. "On the money, Ja Jimmy?" Willy chortled at his own in-house joke.

The interrogator gave up in bewilderment, convinced that normality was not to be found at the local hangout. She was right.

Dirty Corner was one of those rare establishments where millionaires and muleteers sat side by side with one goal in common: escape from the bustle on the port front in summer or shelter in winter, when it was about the only establishment open.

Because it was open year-round, the nucleus of clientele remained faithful. Jimmy once described the mix of patrons as "Rockefeller's and other feller's." It served as an offbeat hub, a mini-theater.

German Willy and Jimmy were perhaps the most contradictory fixtures to occupy the same table in most watering holes, and Dirty Corner was on their agenda at least twice a day. Jimmy was skinny and jowled with an accent as strong as his liver, a gent who remembered the London Blitz. Willy was big and broad in attitude and size, not quite old enough to have served in the Luftwaffe, but "the war" was still just cause for much debate between them.

They made an odd duo, a comedy act in the port-front theater of life. They generally staged their closing performance at the prime table outside Dirty Corner around midnight.

The management of Dirty Corner changed with regularity; their table and routine didn't. Dirty Corner had such a long and popular existence in part because its pricing and hygiene standards were more in line with the rural Greece of an earlier era. The proprietor was not the draw, because in the decade Dirty Corner was open, it enjoyed two dozen managers that I can recall, myself included.

"Caprice? What the hell is that? Its always going to be Dirty Corner." Her Barefootness, another frequent member, commented on a new sign over the establishment's door. "It was Dirty Corner even when my son Shteffie ran it. Just look at it—no pretentious name is going to fix this."

She pointed at the freshly asvestied (whitewashed) steps where Manolis had painted over a lump of kitty-doo.

Mavro Manolis was another regular who lived at Dirty Corner, season in, staff out. He resided in the little house directly across the narrow alley and used the place like his lounge.

He looked like a suntanned, hairier Jack Lemmon and often brought platters of fried fish from his own kitchen for the punters to sample. With his infectious chuckle and light banter, Mavro was an added attraction—no one complained. Sometimes he even lent a hand.

"I painted in the middle of night," Mavro chirped from behind the mosquito grill on his front door. "The streetlight doesn't show these things."

Manolis claimed the only reason he wasn't a war vet like Pan was because during the early seventies, when both of them were caught jumping ship in New York, abandoning the merchant vessel they crewed on, he turned down the offer to become a US citizen by joining the army.

"Not stupeed," said Mavro, tapping the side is his head. Fellow seaman, mates, and rivals, he and Pan had grown up together on the island, competing for fish in all ponds.

Pan had his own bar to run and rarely ventured to the west side of the port. He lived up to his Rambo reputation and was always in the thick of things. News from his bar would filter across to Dirty Corner within a few seconds.

"Pan got bitten by a shark," puffed Ouzo Jimmy one night as he parked in his corner.

"Yeah, right," Mavro scoffed. "He probably cut himself opening a bottle."

"I'm telling you, I've just come from his bar. Got a right gash, he 'as. Lucky he didn't loose a thumb," Jimmy insisted. "Off Mandraki Bay this afternoon, maybe fifteen foot long."

Others verified the story, which indeed involved a large shark sighted, hunted, and caught just off Mandraki. Pan had been bitten while trying to remove the hook.

"So, it isn't a hero story but a stupeed one—getting bitten when the thing is already on board," Mavro tutted, unimpressed with Jimmy's Pan-and-the-shark tale.

"Ja, but zees is nussing. I remember when a giant octopus attacked Pan underwater and nearly killed him," German Willy piped.

"You always got to go one better, 'aven't you," said Jimmy. "Suppose I 'ad said ee 'ad lost a limb to a barracuda; you'd 'ave said he'd got eaten whole by a great white."

Someone else interrupted and claimed to have heard about the killer-octopus incident. A local piscatory expert said that *octopothia* couldn't grow that large in these waters, so somebody was blowing smoke—enough smoke, however, to investigate the matter further, at least a match worth.

One becomes accustomed to double-checking any rhubarb, and I asked Pan himself the following day.

"What's this about you and a giant octopus, Pan?"

"A fuggin shark man, not an octopus," he held out his unbandaged hand, pointing to a nasty-looking wound at the base of his palm as proof.

"The shark we know, but there is a debate about another incident with a different monster from the deep."

"A couple of years ago. The thing left marks as big as my hand for weeks all across my back. Must have been forty-fifty kilograms," chuckled the beard with round shades. "I saw a little tentacle sticking out from under a rock and thought, maybe lunch, youknowhaddimean."

"I'm lucky it grabbed me with all its legs because if it had held onto the rock with one, I would have been finished, youknowhaddimean." He tugged his facial mop, apparently emotionless at the memory of a huge slimy beast attaching itself to his torso in the depths of Mandraki Bay.

"His own fault, I mean who pulls the pointy end of something hidden that can grow into a monster. *Malaka!*" Mavro was still unimpressed with his rival's antics when I confirmed German Willy's tale the next evening.

"I know he saved a dolphin once," quipped Ouzo Jimmy.

"Yeah, right, like we have loads of dying dolphins around here." Mavro knew the waters better than anyone.

"And about sixty people," Jimmy added.

"*Malaka!*" Mavro extended an open palm, an explicit hand sign denoting disbelief, associated with sending someone to the devil or something.

"That's why he has a lifetime ticket for free travel." Jimmy dropped his punch line. "A flying dolphin, the hydrofoil service, one of which was floundering in the harbor when Pan came to the rescue."

"*Malaka*," chuckled Mavro at no one in particular.

"Suppose your going to come up with a sinking cruise ship full of people now, aye?" Jimmy dared Willy.

"There you start again—bringing up the U-boats." Willy could give as good as he got. "I sink we should have a toast to all drowned sailors. Jimmy it's your turn to order."

Like I said, one didn't go to Dirty Corner for the view.

The world has changed dramatically in a few short years, and even Hydra no longer has room for the likes of Dirty Corner. The cost of ablutions, for starters, would prohibit its existence. There are rules these days against the urinating in broom cupboards; hot and cold running water are no longer a luxury but a requirement in island washrooms. EU currencies and regulations and all that stuff.

We did our time, and it was grand while it lasted.

Dirty Corner is now a little hole-in-the-wall tourist shop that doesn't run a tab. Ask for Dirty Corner when you go in, and the proprietor will probably smile. No doubt he will have heard about the good old days and may even offer you a serious discount on a trinket. But he won't serve ooouzo.

13

AN ARTIST IN ANY CURRENCY

"Artists have always been attracted to Hydra's light, like moths to a flame," German Willy said philosophically, admiring the beginnings of a golden sunset from the Liako after a long lunch. The island is world renowned for its list of associated creative names, and Willy counted himself as a full-fledged citizen of the island's "artist colony."

"Wot sort of artists then, aye Willy?" Ouzo Jimmy's fag wobbled in the center of his face. "Like you then? When did you last pick up a brush, aye?"

"Ja, but you don't understand, Jimmy. An artist needs inspiration to see with his own eyes and absorb the beauty." German Willy's appearance belied the gentle words. He was a fellow unlikely to get mugged in a dark alley.

"The only thing I've seen you pick up in the past week is that glass, mate." Ouzo Jimmy nodded at Willy's pint. "Absorbing alright—piss artist more like."

The exchange initiated banter on the types of artists inhabiting the Rock and whether heavy-drinking painters fell into both the aforementioned categories. Piss artists progressed to con artists.

"What about ze police chief?" German Willy opened. "Is he an artist or a con?"

The newly posted young chief had taken up watercolor painting in his spare time. A likable fellow with some talent, he was every bit as accomplished as regular art students.

He had held an exhibition of his work at an exclusive show at the popular Up 'n' High cafe above the port. Eighty pieces depicted an abundance of bougainvillea and white-washed houses. Seventy-three enthusiastically priced works sold before half the snacks had been consumed. The fellow had broken all opening-night records.

"Ja, but that had nothing to do with his work," Willy pointed out. "This was to win favor with the police chief, nothing but a case of blind customers buying paintings for a blind eye in return."

Punters had indeed included plumbers and other tradesmen not usually seen at such arty gatherings.

The Chief had subsequently invested in an elevated chunk of land overlooking the harbor—and a billionaire Texan's estate.

It was suspected that the land was above the line delimiting the zone of permitted building, but Tex didn't mind the idea of having the Chief as a neighbor and was prepared to turn a blind eye too. He was a nice cop and seemed like a potentially good neighbor—until workers started dynamiting rock to lay the foundations.

Pebble rain splashed into the pool.

Billionaires have influential phone numbers. When last we heard, the Chief was studying landscapes on a distant Balkan border.

* * *

Debate drifted into compromise: the ex-cop was a bit of both, neither total con nor real artist.

"At least the locals were getting something. Usually brown envelopes don't purchase anything tangible"—Jimmy knew the system—"so it wasn't a complete con."

I only knew of one such incident that could be classified as a dinkum con.

"It started with a phone call," I began.

"Mister Devid, sorry to bother you so early, but you are the only one from last night whose number I know, and we are looking for the one with the black hat," announced an unfamiliar female voice.

"*Signomee?*" I checked my watch: 8:30 a.m. If it hadn't been for the fact the caller knew my identity, I would have hung up—wrong number, wrong day.

"The German's are here, and they want to go home, but cannot until they see the one with the black hat," said the voice in a tone that suggested this detail would clarify the issue.

The hour was normally acceptable, but this was not an acceptable morning, following as it did Jimbo's stag party. I had co-organized a bachelor train starting with sundowners at the Hydranetta sunset bar—a grand tour of the island's watering holes for a dozen blokes, stopping at all stations. I seemed to recall a rhubarb involving the borrowing of an ornamental anchor shortly before dawn at the final stop and Jesse leaving Disco Heaven with a one-ton trophy.

But no black hats or Huns popped into the replay banks.

"Mister Devid? Are you there? Remember the party you brought here last night; well, we are looking for the one with the black hat. I don't know his name, but you know him. I am Anigira from Mavromatis Taverna." The voice had identified itself and yielded further clues.

"Which Germans and what black hat?" The room seemed awfully bright.

We'd had lots of nationalities in our party but no Germans; perhaps she meant Dutch or Swedish.

"*Oxi*, German tourists who were at another table here last night. And the black hat, who only shaves sometimes, drinks a lot of beer, English, lives here—he was with your table last night."

Mark! I didn't recall the hat, but she definitely meant Mark. We had left him at Mavromatis.

"The German's want to go and cannot leave until they see him. He must come here today." She sounded serious. "Sorry to disturb, but we must find him. Where he is?"

Mark shifted digs with the wind. It was anybody's guess, but tracing the bloke wouldn't be difficult, I assured her. I inquired as to the nature of the summons so that I could leave word for him.

The black hat, it seemed, had some *pragmata* (things) of theirs that they desperately needed back. No further details were offered. I left word in town.

By the following morning the German couple were muttering about going to the police when Anigira called. I told her that Mark must not have been to the port yet; otherwise, he would have received word. But promised I would put out a serious APB on the chap. We both knew that on Hydra people don't just vanish without someone seeing them go; he was obviously holed up somewhere. Stuttgart had a connection to make and was most keen to talk to the black hat. Last chance.

I told Georgo at the Three Brothers, Mark's favorite haunt, that Brummy was to make immediate contact with

Mavromatis on pain of the German's visiting the police. Mark failed to surface on day two.

"There wasn't much money. They care only about getting their cards, licenses, and tickets back. Just tell the black hat to bring it back. We know he had it, and it hasn't been turned in at the police station."

She gathered I was a bit lost and went onto explain that a German couple had left their wallet behind, and my friend in the black hat had kindly taken it, saying he would catch up and return it to them.

* * *

Sometimes talent is highly disguised. By the looks of him, Mark was just a lout in need of a bath and shave, a gent of the road—or on the run.

Mark was all of the above when he hit Hydra, and his entrance into the community was nothing short of spectacular.

A private in the British military, he had been caught trying to sell dope to the general's daughter and opted not to face a tribunal. A nonconformist with a gravelly Brummy accent (Birmingham) that even I had trouble translating to other English speakers, he'd try anything that came his way. An event to do with nonconformity with an Israeli Kibbutz's rules had encouraged him to take to the road. A long stint travelling culminated in a room at Douglas's Pension, situated right on the harbor front, near one of the island's favorite watering holes, The Pirate.

He celebrated his escape to the Rock, not suspecting, as he introduced himself with rounds of drink to all and sundry, that the Rock would mark a turning point in his life. Mark was generous when he was flush.

To him Hydra seemed like a sanctuary with inmates who loitered in cafes, a place to park for a bit.

Travel weary and sea legged from substantial quantities of balance-inhibiting refreshments, he decided to call it a night at about 3 a.m., leaving the party to continue without him. He didn't wish to make a complete spectacle of himself on his first night, as he had already made up his mind to look for a job the next morning. The few shekels he had left over from his Eastern Mediterranean adventure would only last a couple of days.

He fell out of his jeans and onto the bed.

Douglas, the proprietor, was asleep in the room above. He had retired to Hydra and ran his boarding establishment like a marine barracks. Tenants were "not allowed" to play "jungle music"—ever! Jungle music in this case meant anything involving a drum or electric instrument, including Elvis. But his place was immaculate, with bleached, starched sheets and scrubbed ablutions—without doubt the cleanest on the island.

* * *

"A workaholic he was," Ouzo Jimmy interjected, referring to Douglas. "I mean wots the point of retiring to a Greek island to work yerself to death? He would sit over 'ere with his binoculars, I tell you, watching for custom like an 'awk."

Douglas's used the spyglasses to keep an eye on his pension entrance from the Liako on the opposite side of the harbor. The door displayed a permanent note reading, "I will return in fifteen minutes"—a clever ploy. Folk seeking a room would assume the proprietor's return was imman-ent. Twenty-five minutes' delay, Douglas figured, was a tad too long as they would probably look elsewhere or go for tea and possibly get side-tracked. Five minutes wasn't long enough for Douglas to finish his beer, pay up, and amble round to meet the backpackers parked on his doorstep.

Douglas polished his shoes before going out at night and wore an RAF tie in winter. He was as rigid with himself as he was about all matters in life. Guests were expected to behave to the same standard. He had a dozen clean, reasonably priced rooms for rent for the purpose of sleeping in only. He was full most of the season.

The smoke woke Douglas, and he went to investigate. Clouds of white billowed out from under Mark's door, the light still on inside.

All the folks at the Pirate Bar heard was a gruff "Out! Get out, now!" echoing across the little port, followed by loud thumping down the steep wooden staircase that was the pension's entrance.

The door crashed open and a smoldering mattress landed on the quay. Sparks flew. A bleary stubble in underpants appeared seconds later.

"Oi, Douglass, I'm sorry man, but can I at least 'ave me trawzers?" The door slammed shut.

He banged on the door awhile. "Douglass, please, juss me trawzers! Me money's in the pocket."

The door swung open, sucking in smoke from the billowing mattress, and a bucket of cold water hit Mark full on the torso, some of it dousing the smolder behind him.

"And if you don't shut up … " a gnarled fist shook through the opening. "I said no smoking in bed. Be thankful I didn't leave you to burn." Slam.

Such entertainment did not go unnoticed by late-night revelers congregated outside the Pirate. The Up 'n' High cafe above had closed, and the overflow had refilled the bar. Mark was invited over to the party—the night's instant star attraction.

The next day he had a job, semi-permanent digs, and enough money to replace the mattress and obtain his belongings, if not forgiveness from the old Barrack Master.

Mark's appearance belied a talent he denied, his rough accent and slang disguising the razor sharp synapses that lay behind darting, dark eyes. Kind to animals and generous to a fault, even if it was with someone else's purse at times, Mark could turn his hand to anything.

He was frustratingly skillful—I say frustratingly because he appeared so unimpressed with his abilities. Within a few days he spoke Greek better than many long-term expats, adding it to the other languages he had absorbed along the road—all spoken with a gruff midland accent.

Mark, a lovable, Indiana Jones–type rogue, had charm. He drifted into all sorts of activity during his stay on the Rock and was generally in the thick of any rhubarbs going on. He would work like a Trojan when he turned up, but often something else would turn his head, and he would resort to flexible hours, perhaps days.

In no time he figured out the island's electrical wiring, which the blokes at NASA would have found challenging; yet despite obvious instant demand, could not see himself top-jobbing it for serious. His easygoing manner and quick calculating mind made waiting tables a doddle, and he was rugged enough to work building sites.

Any income generated he then invested in more PR in the port, his expense account lavishly distributed. After some reciprocal sponsoring, he would find another source of industry. He read and would come out with amazing quotes and arcane knowledge, backed up by debate if need be: Tolstoy, Nietzsche, astronomy, theology, anthropology, how to hot-wire a car.

Once, when we were walking past an open gallery with a baby grand piano, he sauntered over, took a seat, and opened the lid.

"Oi wonder if Oi can remember anything. It's bin a while." A pirate with a delicate instrument, he cracked his knuckles.

I seem to recall it was Beethoven's Eighth, played flawlessly, attracting passing tourists. I was moved and aghast—Brummy Mark was a Ludwig in disguise. He randomly picked another couple of classics and closed with *Piano Man*, to applause from the doorway.

"My dear boy," I enthused, "what the hell are you lugging cement around a building site for. You'd knock the spots off any of the other live entertainment around here, for starters."

"Nah, not my scene. I'd rather be in the party than playing for it," he fobbed. I never heard him play again; not many people knew Mark had this skill.

Mark's fortunes yo-yoed; the concept of budgeting beyond the moment was alien to him. Apparently Mark was low on dosh the night of Jimbo's stag.

About two-thirds of the way through the evening, the party found us toasting the groom at Mavromatis, a taverna on the ground floor of an ancient red-and-yellow building in the little port of Kamini. Mark had started the stag party a little earlier than the rest of us and begged off the final lap, staying at the tavern while we took the coast road back to town.

The third morning after, Anigira called again, most apologetic, asking if I had managed to track down my friend yet. The German couple wanted to leave—today.

I had been spreading the word and asking around, but there was still no sign of Mark—unusual as the man had the recuperating abilities of an ox and was rarely absent from the watering holes long.

"They don't care about the money. They just want their documents and tickets," said Anigira. "It must come back today, or they will go to the police. We know he picked the *portofoli* up after they left."

I left urgent instruction with the Three Brothers to collar Mark and get him to call me before he went anywhere; otherwise, he could be in a lot of trouble.

"Don't move!" I ordered when he phoned rather sheepishly later.

A repentant expression sat in the back corner of the Three Brothers nursing a pint.

"It sort of juss 'appened like. These geezers left their purse behind, and Oi was going to go after them an' give it to them," Mark explained remorsefully. "But Oi met some-one on the way past Petroleka's ouzoria and borrowed a little, like."

"They don't care about the cash. The plastic and licenses are a real hassle to replace, and they can't go until they get their stuff. They've already stayed two days longer than they had planned, got it?"

"Yeah, but Oi can't give it back without replacing the money, which is going to be difficult." The gravel stroked his stubble.

"They don't care about the money, mate! They just want their cards and stuff. You have the wallet, right?"

"Yeah—yeah, man, of course." His head bobbed in the affirmative. "But it not the money, like; it's a matter of honor. Oi must replace what Oi took, and how am Oi going to find deutsche marks? Oi exchanged theirs for drachmas."

Bolstered by my assurance that he could avoid another future court marshal if he set matters straight, he left to call Anigira immediately.

"I'll make a plan about the money," he said bustling out the door. "Thanks mate."

I called Anigira the next day to see if things had worked out with the black hat.

"*Neh, neh! Olla endaxi*," she enthused. Everyone was happy.

I inquired as to the cash aspect.

"*Neh, neh. Meh kati paraxeni*." Money yes, but something strange had occurred.

"*Xrimata apo Polandia eetaneh mesa*." Polish zlotys had appeared in the wallet in place of deutsche marks.

The Berlin Wall was still standing, and Poland lay behind it. One couldn't buy much in the West with a Polish zloty. I went to find the stubble.

"Ah, the honorable Shylock," I said as I joined Mark at the Three Brothers later.

"Wha'?" said the dead pan.

"Mugged any Poles recently?"

"Wha' you on about?" Not a flicker from Cool Hand Luke.

"Wonder how many zlotys a cuppa tea costs at the airport."

He lit a cigarette before answering in a cloud.

"Look, I searched the whole port looking for someone with deutsche marks. Germans everywhere, except when you need one." He paused. "The geezer I got them from told me that they were worth about the same, neighboring countries and all."

"So, you found a Pole and swapped your drachmas for zlotys?"

"Yeah, man. I figured any money other than drachmas would be good. Why—were they upset?"

"No, they were happy to get their things back, just a little perplexed as to how their cash changed color—and value."

"The bastard con artist." He took a drag and exhaled in a smoke screen. "I was robbed. He told me they would be happy with zlotys."

* * *

"And so, everyone lived happily ever after," I concluded.

"About time too," interjected Anthony Kingsmill, sitting at an adjacent table at the Liako. "The sun is about to set, and I always make it a rule at my table to have ten minute's silence during each sunset, a time to contemplate the beauty in peace and quiet."

"Now he's a real artist, he is," wagged Jimmy's fag in a hushed voice. "They say he's good, that Anthony."

"Ja, and he works even harder at getting inspiration than me," Willy retorted, getting his oar in.

"Ten minutes silence," said Bill from the table behind, seconding the motion. Anthony smiled.

"Zat must have been the longest Jimmy has shut up in his life," Willy quipped on the dot of the ten-minute mark.

Jimmy had been thinking about Mark and claimed to remember the chap. "Once tried to swap me quid for rubles saying that Soviet money would be worth something one day, Chernobyl or no," Jimmy jested. "Wot ever 'appened to him?"

Moved to Australia was the common consensus among those within earshot. German Willy proposed a toast to all Australians—for their bravery and patronage of artists.

* * *

Years later, Mark came back to make amends for any misdemeanors past, beginning with a bottle of Drambuie for Douglas. He wanted a fresh start; his mission, to set up a home for his new family—and find a career to support them.

"I know how it works: down to the port, do a little PR, meet some people, and put the word about." Mark had shaved and changed into a clean shirted. "Won't find any work sitting at home, will I? Need anything from the bar, mate?"

Seeking employment was thirsty work: stubble grew, weeks passed, pockets grew holes.

Rhubarbs accumulated. Eventually crocodile wrestling Down Under was deemed safer, his second attempt to become a permanent inmate having bogged down in the brew of port life.

"This Rock has beaten me again. It's a real trap, dat port. Never seem to get away from the table conversation. Suddenly the day is gone, and its sunset chitchat. Oi guess the only way to survive here is to be a real artist, and Oi wouldn't know what to do with a brush and canvas." Mark packed his bags and caught a one-way to Sydney.

Last we heard, Mark had two daughters and was living clean and gainfully employed Down Under—rumored to have taken up painting.

14

WAKES AND WHISPERS

If rumors and rhubarbs abound in life on the Rock, then in the event of death, they positively leap.

"He was murdered by the police," a distraught voice on the phone informed me just as I was about to head down to the port.

The news, to say the least, was shocking. Mavro Manolis, without doubt one of Hydra's most beloved characters, had given up the ghost—in what sounded like a haunting manner.

"What, in his hospital bed?" I was a little perplexed, having seen Mavro only two days previously, sitting on the balcony outside his ward in Piraeus. I had popped past the hospital during a day trip to the Big Olive and was therefore probably one of the last islanders to see him alive. He had sounded and looked to be in fine health, just waiting for a "simple" operation, and he expected to be back in Dirty Corner within a week.

"No, here on Hydra, in the police station," the snivel explained. "Made it to hospital in Athens and died there."

"But he left Hydra two weeks ago." I couldn't let Manolis's passing turn into a memory about a murderous scuffle with the law without double-checking the facts. Here lies Mavro, victim of oppression—it just wasn't him. A romantic of *Shirley Valentine* ilk, this likeable, sun-tanned rogue deserved a better epitaph—the truth.

But finding the truth in rumorville isn't easy, as many absolute versions of it exist, depending on whom you ask and where that person heard it first.

Dirty Corner was subdued that day. Patrons sat silently with their thoughts; Manolis favorite stool stood empty with an untouched beer in front of it—one traditionally poured for the gods.

Mavro's premature death smacked of Greek tragedy, a tale of the good guy verses the fascist police—if one believed a few of the murmurs at the gathering.

Circumstances were clouded, but three solid facts stood undisputed: First, Mavro had been involved in a party at Dirty Corner the night before he went into Athens. Second, he went to the police station sometime well after midnight. Third, he left on the first hydrofoil for an Athenian hospital.

The speculation that filled in these points varied substantially. A Dutch contingent of the militant left-wing tree-hugger variety rooted keenly for the fascist police theory. Manolis had gone to make a legitimate complaint and been viciously clubbed to death in the hallway of the precinct.

"One goes to the police for protection, not to be taken away on a stretcher. He only asked them to control the noise." Said with conviction, this dramatic version had conversational appeal and held some sway among the Left.

The middle-of-the-road accident theory seemed palatable to most, but even that had variations—from Mavro slipping and falling down the stairs to a policemen pushing him out the door. Greek arguments rarely turn violent, but when they do, things can get most enthusiastic.

"That's what I heard—that it was self-defense," said Christo on the other side, whose cousin was a cop. "Manolis was drunk, in a foul mood, and picked a fight."

"Greeks don't brawl. They make a lot of noise if they are upset, maybe poke a finger to emphasize a point, but that's all," said a moderate voice. "Our police station doesn't even posses a cell. They are not like big-city cops, and even in Athens one doesn't hear of suspects being murdered, never mind an ordinary citizen going in with a complaint."

"There is no motivation for murder, so I think we should drop that word for starters," added the Middle.

"Okay, how about manslaughter, negligence in the face of duty." The Left didn't give up that easily.

"Manolis started it," said the Right.

Gradually the facts unfolded.

There was nothing unusual about the night in question. A group of jolly folk had stuck around at Dirty Corner. Spontaneous guitar strumming, utensil drumming, and out-of-key sing-alongs grew louder and louder with time. Manolis, a prime instigator of the revelry, decided to call it a night, stumbled the five feet home, and fell straight onto his bed. The jolliness didn't abate for more than a few seconds after he yelled at the merrymakers to turn it down a notch—twice.

He got up, emerged, and met with more jolliness that showed no sign of loosing steam, so he stormed off to get the cops. What happened next became everybody's guess.

It was a confirmed fact that Manolis was not his usual jovial self when he went to the law and that an argument had been heard in the police station. That he was taken off on the first dolphin with an internal pain was not in dispute either.

Woollier facts included that he had come back from the precinct complaining that they had thrown him out and wouldn't have anything to do with him until the next day.

The Law's defense sounded solid enough. The constabulary was of the opinion that as Manolis had started the party and got it going, he was responsible for shutting it down too. It was not a reasonable basis for the long arm of the law to yank out its handcuffs; nor would it be until such stage as someone laid a formal nemesis, or complaint, against the offenders.

Manolis had wanted to throw the book. The Law suggested that he return in the bright light of day with a clearer head. Putting his name on paper and committing himself to years in court might not seem so appealing after a good sleep. Besides, wasn't Manolis under doctor's orders not too drink?

About two years previously he'd had a kidney removed, and doctors had warned that he must take it easy on his surviving one. In short, he'd have to change his lifestyle or die.

"One plus one equals eleven, right?" I felt the Law was getting a bum rap. The island police had always been, to my knowledge, too laid-back, if anything. Nice, helpful blokes, they rarely worried about uniforms and such formalities.

I suggested perhaps that the culprit and the victim were one and the same.

"Had Mavro been tapping the barrel?" I started on the basics.

"Let's just say he was an enthusiastic participant at the party. You know what he was like at parties," a voice sobbed.

I suggested that if we were able to ask Mavro in person, he would agree that he himself was the primary felon. He knew that going against doctor's orders was playing with fire. The removal of a kidney is warning enough for any mortal.

Even those favoring the murder conspiracy had to agree that the victim had to share some of the blame. Mavro's liver had played up on occasion too. The man was on notice.

"Manolis would have submitted himself as chief culprit for his undoing were he at this hearing, don't you agree?" Nods from the Dirty Corner jury seemed to indicate his ending could be laid to rest without pressing the police-brutality angle.

It happened because he refused to compromise a lifestyle that was his essence. People do not die two weeks after an alleged assault, when they have subsequently been seen walking around chatting up nurses.

Finally, it came out that Manolis had developed complications under surgery and been rushed to an emergency facility where ten hours later the medical team eventually admitted defeat.

"Medical neglect! The doctors should be sued," began the Left, starting a new fire with which to build verbal smoke screens.

"Nope," said I, "ultimately still Manolis, and if he were here, he would agree. A party too far put him in the clinic in the first place."

Mavro Manolis was a gent who knew how to live. He wasn't the type to go quietly into the night, and he didn't—his exiting rhubarb made sure of that.

Even his funeral had a "Mavro" touch to it. A Swedish damsel of long acquaintance, Charlotte, turned up late and found that the service for Mavro had begun punctually. Already on the brink of tears, she broke down at the sight of so many gathered in the church to remember him and slipped into a back pew, sobbing quietly.

She stood clutching a wet tissue in respect as the mourning procession traipsed past, then noticed a lot of happy, smiling faces—trailing a one-year-old infant with wet hair being carried at the head.

"I swear, I could hear Manolis chuckling. He would have appreciated that," she said, explaining that she had misread the service schedule. "No wonder they were giving me strange looks."

* * *

Sometimes bad news spreads even faster than wildfire in a gale and gets ahead of itself—stoking confusion.

I hadn't begun to start down Donkeyshit Lane one morning when Georgo and his mules passed me with some somber news.

"O Douglass died yesterday."

Douglas! Dead? I couldn't believe it. I was holding the key to his flat while he was away on holiday. We were known mates—surely I would have been among the first to receive a phone call in such a tragic event. I preferred to dismiss the news as a myth, a mistaken rhubarb involving someone else.

By the time I had reached the clock tower in the port, half a dozen people had informed me of his passing, and I began to fear there was too much smoke for there not to be fire. Details were vague and contrary, but the common factor in all cases was that he was definitely an ex-Douglas.

The cafe airwaves carried the sad news all that morning. Two-dozen sources had confirmed the old curmudgeon's expiry by noon.

The following day a few surprised faces greeted Douglas as he ambled off the ferryboat. The old guy was perplexed to be greeted by an excess of welcome hugs and pats on the back.

"Dead? Who said I was dead?" Douglas chuckled as he plonked himself in his usual spot at the Liako.

"Mister Colin say so," Eva piped up, bringing him his usual pint.

"I never said he was dead," claimed Old Colin, a Canadian veteran with a pipe.

"Yes, you did! When I ask you where is Mister Douglas, you say he has gone," Eva explained. "I say, 'Gone? Like *pethane*?' You say, '*Neh*.'"

It would be a compliment to call Colin's Greek rudimentary. People who say yes a lot in a foreign language give the impression they understand far more than actually computes.

"Again I say, 'Gone, like *pethane*?' and you say, '*Neh*.'" Eva was adamant she had it straight. "You didn't see I look like shock?"

"*Neh*," puffed the old pipe.

"You know what it means, *pethane*?" Eva asked quite loudly.

"*Neh*." Colin was a little hard of hearing in one ear due to an incident with a Japanese grenade, it was said.

"What it mean?" Eva, hands on hips, was not convinced, having just served the living Douglas a pint, that the old pipe clearly understood the Greek word for "he died."

"*Neh*, uh … holiday," he exhaled proudly.

Eva laughed. "Where you learn Greek, aye?"

"It's all Greek to me." Colin attempted to cover his faux pas with a cliché and a shrug.

"More like Chinese whispers around this place." Douglas was good at getting the last word in. One couldn't argue with that.

* * *

In memory of Manolis, Douglas, and Colin.

15

THE ODDS

One ripple of gas was all it took to start a cavalry charge and nearly wipe out half the island's seven-year-olds.

I had offered to stand in and help Chris with the school's annual Christmas party.

"Simple," he drawled. Chris, an English teacher at the local language school, hailed from North Carolina.

"Their lesson can be writing cards and letters in English, and then we'll have a Christmas party for the class."

We assembled music, refreshments, crisps, cheese pies, cake, sweets, and balloons on the front desk.

The lesson part went well, apart from a small debate among the "teachers" about whether the kids should address their "wish lists" to a North American "Santa" or an English "Father Christmas."

No sooner had the class been dismissed than a food fight began brewing among the children at the tutor's table. I grabbed a packet of balloons and drew the disturbance outside, where it could do less damage.

The school was not too far up Donkeyshit Lane, just before it got steeper, at a section flat enough for donkeys to move quickly and for balls to materialize and games to develop.

A mule train came clip-clopping down the steps. It was unusually long, sixteen animals, interspersed with four muleteers, returning single-file from a building site on the hill.

"*Yassou, Vangelimou,*" I greeted the first sidesaddle.

"*Yassou, pethia.*" He beamed down at the children completing the happy village Christmas scene.

I was standing in the school doorway, surrounded by eager faces waiting for me to inflate and tie more balloons. As the last mule plodded lazily past, a large red balloon escaped as I was tying the knot. Pffrrrr—

This flying fart spun around insanely for a few moments, gaining velocity, and then with its dying burst, went straight up the last mule's raised tail.

Big ears shot upwards, and the surprised animal suddenly broke into a full gallop—straight into the mule in front of it, which in turn—

"*Malaka!*" yelled the muleteer, bouncing about as he struggled unsuccessfully to contain the stampede of his four into the squad ahead.

As with all good swear words, inflection dictates meaning, and this time the *M*-word wasn't used endearingly. Similar shouts echoed down Donkeyshit as the entire train took flight, bobbing moustaches hanging on.

Island kids are as instinctive around donkeys as city kids are around traffic; all had the good sense to stand against a wall.

Grateful that nobody got hurt in the stampede, I went to make peace with the drivers, who were under the impression that I could manifest such perfectly accurate flight from a flying balloon at will.

"*Oxi, oxi!* Think of it like the lotto," I told them later in Dirty Corner, "a million to one. I couldn't do that again, and it's doubly lucky that no one got hurt."

Nods and orders—it was indeed an against-the-odds luck of sorts.

Now, would I help them with their lottery picks?

16

THINGS JUST 'APPEN

It sounded as though a donkey had just stampeded through the taverna kitchen. The crash of breaking glass and crockery drowned out strumming bazookas. Then silence.

It was opening night at the beginning of the season in The Garden, one of the island's biggest and most popular dining establishments—and it was packed. We had the added incentive to book a table because it was Lydia's first night as a waitress there, and her boyfriend Jeff had promised we would come for moral support.

"Lydia!" was our table said at once during the lull.

Lydia, a young, French primary school teacher had hooked up with Jeff the previous summer and stayed. We had come to know her well over the winter.

Jeff had already extended his writing sabbatical four years beyond its original six months. An expat from San Francisco entrenched on the port, he was one of many suspects in the late eighties who resided on the Rock.

"That was what, three hours on the job?" said Jeff, shaking his head.

"Nearly a record!"

Lydia had tried her hand at a number of tasks. She was willing, bright, and good-natured but one of those few unfortunates whose life was a series of "things just happening" to them. "Accident-prone" is a popular description of this syndrome.

If we were sitting inside the Liako playing cards on a blustery winter day and there was a domino-like shatter of cascading beer bottles, then it was because Lydia's anorak toggle had snagged the prime skittle.

As one's *logariasmos* (bill) was tallied at the end of the day by counting the number of empties amassed, the bottles could fall for a while. Once, after an earth tremor, someone immediately suspected Lydia.

In short, a bet that the crash in the taverna involved the new employee wouldn't have gotten long odds.

Lydia emerged from the kitchen looking forlorn, her night's wages in hand.

"Ze tray jus sleeped."

"How many plates?"

"I don't know, forty, maybe fifty."

Jeff added a few to counter underexaggeration and still figured the restaurant was coming off worse financially, even including our still-to-be-paid dinner bill.

"You were lucky to get any wages," he admonished. "Now cheer up."

"Hey, three hours in a new vocation isn't bad, Lydia," quipped a second spoon. Her history of minor disasters and short careers was semi-legendary.

"Eet wuzn't my fault," she stomped. "Eeet could 'appen to anyone."

As first-hand witnesses to a few previous 'appenings, we were somewhat skeptical.

It must be said that her accidents weren't all the result of clumsiness. Some people, I have come to believe, are especially selected to have machinery die on them; some devices may even hang in there just until a Lydia flicks the switch. Pipes about to burst wait until she's in the head, cassette tapes get munched, and so on. But sometimes she had a hand in her own bad luck.

Lydia was helping me to prepare a house for the general manager of the Intercontinental and his wife, when this hand played a part. The couple were affluent part-timers, Germans who drank designer water and had decided to make the island their weekend bolt hole.

They donkeyed bottled water up to the house, when most of us were content with the *glyko* (sweet) rainwater from the cisternas. Mrs. Intercon had an aversion to microbes and owned a pet dachshund called Fritz.

"You clean up here, and I'll take the downstairs and fireplace." I knew not to leave Lydia in an area that might contain glowing embers.

"Just don't throw anything chemical down the loo as it'll affect the ecology in the septic tank." Even those accustomed to using a bin for toilet paper sometimes forgot this aspect of island plumbing.

When I came up, the floors were wet, and the smell of *chlorini* (bleach) would have put mortuaries to shame. The house gleamed, so we started putting the cleaning gear away.

"Where did you throw the dirty, chlorinated water?" I asked, noticing a general absence of puddles outside and dry flowerbeds.

"Down ze 'ole," she said, in an "obviously" tone, and catching my glance, she added, "I didn't want to kill ze flowers."

"What hole?" I smelled a rat.

"Zees one wiz ze lid. Why?" She pointed at the fresh-water cisterna wellhead.

"How many buckets?"

"Maybe five or six."

At an average of fifteen liters each, this meant at least 100 liters of detergent dumped into the drinking well—not well.

"Just as well they are microphobic and drink bottled *nero*," I said, hoping it would still be okay for showering.

Lydia and Jeff were my immediate neighbors. Our apartments shared a kitchen wall and a large terrace. As I returned one afternoon, I noticed a small pall of smoke hanging over the house.

I found landlord Lefteris and a couple of neighborhood moustaches standing, hands on hips, surveying the smoldering remains of a double-sprung mattress.

Apparently Lydia's bed had caught fire in the middle of siesta, while she was still asleep on it. The source of combustion had yet to be established, but had the neighbors not been attracted by the billowing smoke and broken in to rescue her, she—not to mention the entire four-apartment block—might have been flambéed.

"She okay. Very lucky. She go very quickly," they said.

The suspect had apparently made a marvelous recovery and escaped up the hill to a friend's house, not wishing to face Jeff without a satisfactory explanation as to why his newly imported orthopedic mattress was toast.

Jeff reckoned she was an insurance man's nightmare, and he would regale us over breakfast.

"You guys won't believe what happened last night," he'd start. "She can't just have an ordinary flood like anyone else.

No, she has to almost electrocute herself and blow up the building as well."

"Ze washer macheen door eez leaking," Jeff mimicked.

"Yeah, and it happened to overflow down the hall, across to the center of the bedroom to where a hairdryer lay, still plugged in."

Some pyrotechnics and shrieking had ensued as the house blacked out with a bang.

Like she said, it could 'appen to anyone.

During her stay she added color to our society, and she certainly did 'appen to us. She had a heart of gold and a way with kids—all of whom fortunately had their own guardian angels.

17

CAVIAR AND MOUSSAKA

The donkey looked as though it had been shotgunned in the flank.

"*Po-po-po*, look my donkeys." The muleteer's right palm flicked up and down as he gazed on his animals.

Indeed, all six beasts looked like abattoir survivors. I knew from experience that this could be the opening for re-negotiation in our transportation costs. The cleaning of half a dozen donkeys covered in red oil had not been factored into the deal.

"*Po-po-po*," I retaliated, gesticulating at the red splashes all over the carefully whitewashed entrance, from which eager hands had helped to carry the still dripping trays upstairs. I had just begun a new career as majordomo for a local ty-coon, and my carefully manicured steps and arches, in pre-paration for what was supposed to be the island's party of the season, looked like carnage.

This gesture of solidarity put the moustache and myself in the same boat, and we gave each other a shrug that said *tee nah kanomay* (whose silly idea was this anyway).

"Tasty stuff in red oil" is how a gourmet friend of mine describes Hellenic cuisine. Imagine dozens of traditional

Greek dishes, metal oven pans loosely covered in foil, strapped onto planks like stacked bricks and anchored to a wooden saddle, wobbling up steep inclines—a recipe for disaster.

The damage looked collateral, and guests were due to start arriving in ten minutes. Blood pressure surged. I briefly considered fleeing and reflected on how I had come to be in this ghastly predicament.

"Joan would like to have traditional Greek food for her birthday party," the Sixth Beatle had announced a week earlier. Presumably Miss Collins was trying to be accommodating—when in Greece and all that.

"It's her fifty-fifth," he had added conspiratorially.

The guest list for her birthday bash was to include anybody who was somebody on the island's social roster. Joan accumulated a hundred new friends in no time, and invitations had been sent: Alexis Mardas cordially invites you to Joan Collins's birthday party. RSVP at The White Mansion. Phone, fax, or send a runner. Yours, etc.

Alexi had approached me a couple of months earlier to say that Miss Collins was coming to stay in his mansion for a few weeks and asked if I'd be interested in a summer job.

Mr. Mardas had befriended John Lennon back in the days when the Fab Four were at the height of their fame and is referred to in Paul McCartney's biography as Magic Alex on account of his skill with electronics.

On occasion Alexi would bring out a pair of glasses, a guitar, and other miscellaneous Beatle memorabilia.*

"John wore these when we were in India together," he would say, always a crowd pleaser when table conversation

* The BBC and other world media reported on May 19, 2013, that in 2004 Mardas had sold the guitar, given to him by John Lennon on his twenty-fifth birthday. It resold at auction in 2013 for $408,000.

dribbled—hence his acquired nickname among the expats: the Sixth Beatle.

So there I stood on steps splattered with moussaka and tzatziki, waiting for a ton of immanent, well-dressed guests, wondering whether we could still pull it off.

There was no way young William, the resident chef, even with my assistance, could have catered for so many in a house that sported forty-two phones (before the days of mobiles), a pool, Jacuzzi, sauna, games room, and five enormous bedrooms, but only a shoe box for a kitchen.

The Sixth was a self-appointed tycoon whose preference lay in obvious opulence. His house had been featured in numerous, illustrious *House & Garden*–type magazines but not in any *Kitchens & Cuisine* supplements, if you get my drift.

So the solution had been to cater out.

Invitations said 7:30 p.m., so if the donkeys arrived by 7:15, we'd figured we could be squared away and serving cocktails and caviar to the first arrivals right on time. It was neither the done nor practical thing to have the food arrive during the event.

Delivery of a various selection of a taverna traditionals in vast quantities on an island with no wheels represented a considerable logistical transport problem.

Tupperware was not an option, as the dishes had to be served warm and conveyed in their heated oven pots. Lamb, mince, chicken, keftethis, kalamari, beef—all had been generously basted in spiced red oil, covered in foil, and then semi-perpendicularly attached to each mule with rope. I doubted there could be much sauce left.

I surveyed the entrance hallway in horror. The Sixth, being of nervous disposition and critical eye at the best of times, would have apoplexy if he saw the chaos unfolding in the candlelit foyer.

Frantic activity ensued once the muleteer had departed: feverish, partially futile cleaning, extinguishing of more than half the candles to dim the lighting, and strategic placement of pot plants over stubborn smears camouflaged the worst.

We were just putting the finishing touches on the buffet when the first group arrived. Still dripping, we greeted the troupes with champagne in hand. None commented on the dimly lit foyer or reported slipping in any oily residue.

Apart from one almost catastrophic incident, the party went off without a hitch. The food was tasty, just served with a gallon or two less sauce then the chef had originally intended. The Sixth had insisted that three-foot, crystal, hourglass-shaped candle covers be placed at regular intervals along the hip-high walls of the main terrace.

A reveler during a "rock 'n' roll" demonstration bumped into one of these heavy glass ornaments. Naturally, it happened to be the one on the bridged arch above the mansion's entrance. Just a few seconds sooner, and it could have decapitated a departing Dutch poet. For the rest, the night went well.

It was gone 3:00 a.m. by the time Willy and I had cleared up.

"Hey, mate, I have a bottle of vodka on ice," said my exhausted colleague. "What say we have a nightcap or two. I think we deserve to unwind."

In dribs and drabs family members and entourage would wander in for a morning bite. We thought that on this particular morning we'd have time to recover with some strong filtered coffee first, as we suspected most guests would have a lie in.

Joan was always the first to rise in the morning. Fresh as a daisy, she'd do her aerobics on the terrace while sipping several cups of sweetened black coffee. Three or four teaspoons of sugar and lashings of caffeine might have had something to do with her early-morning vigor.

Willy and I were normally in better shape, but the morning after the party, we were suffering from a lack of, shall we say, energy. An empty bottle and sleep deprivation were major contributing factors. We were hopeful that Joan would sleep in for a change.

Oxi—fit as a fiddle, there stood Miss Collins in the breakfast room before a drop had percolated.

"Morning, boys! Thank you for last night's party. You were wonderful. May I have my usual on the terrace, please," she said with a dazzling smile, as she swirled through the veranda doors.

A few minutes later, young William appeared on the bright, panoramic terrace, carrying morning coffee. He had morning-after DTs, and the cup rattled alarmingly in its saucer—noisily enough for Joan to notice his palsy.

"Willy, that's disgusting!"

William replied without skipping a beat. "Yes, it is disgusting, Miss Collins. You would think that Mr. Mardas, with all his money, could afford crockery that didn't rattle."

18

PINCHES OF SALT AND BUCKETS OF CASH

Any majordomo worth his salt discloses the movements of neither his employer nor his employer's guests—particularly in a small society that is prone to gossip. The island may enjoy a reputation for handling the rich and famous discretely, but "what the butler saw" stuff is always of interest to less-rich idlers.

As it is, speculation about which celebrity will be visiting and why has on occasion been elevated to fact status.

"Nicholas Cage, Robert De Niro, and Julia Roberts are coming to make a film here this summer." The fact that a few movies with big stars have been shot on the island adds credibility to such murmurs.

"The script is based on *The Sleepwalker* written about Hydra—Bill's Bar days," quoted one authority.

"And I'm going to play myself," added Bill from an adjacent table. Bill Cunliffe's little black phone book included many household names, contributing further plausibility to the report.

That story took about two seasons to die.

In the meantime Roger Moore did turn up with Cuba Gooding Jr. for a couple of days. The filming—for something to do with a Swedish netball team in hot pants—attracted at least as many onlookers as Cage playing Cunliffe would have done.

The truly famous have erected infrastructures to avoid the paparazzi wherever they go, and their visits usually don't hit the cafe airwaves until after they've gone.

A part-time resident and high-ranking English diplomat once arrived at the Up 'n' High and informed us of an extraordinary encounter.

"Guess who I bumped into on Donkeyshit Lane last night," he said a matter-of-factly. "Rather took me by surprise, what with the boat picnic and numerous sundowners we had with you chaps yesterday. Suddenly, out of the gloom, a voice says, 'Is that you, Sir D? Fancy meeting you here. How are you?'"

The hand extended belonged to Prince Charles himself.

"Didn't know you knew the Prince of Wales, dear boy?" quipped Bill. "Playing ambassadorial polo in the Saudi desert or New Delhi, perhaps?"

The future king of England had just popped in for a day, and his visit would have gone unnoticed had he not bumped into an old school chum on Donkeyshit.

A few times the island's tom-tom's have gotten it nearly right—helped no doubt by red herrings cast into the chatter—but not quite.

The Sixth Beatle's chef William and I were walking down to the port one morning, when we were collared by a speculist.

"Hey guys, I hear Liz Taylor is staying at the Sixth's. What's she like?"

I was about to deny all knowledge as usual, when Willy piped up.

"Yeah, she's great fun. Michael Jackson is coming next week." It was known that Liz had been on the Sixth's guest list, and by association with that friendship and the Sixth's history with pop stars, the MJ rumor was quite a plausible fish to float.

"That's not a red herring mate," I said to Willy as we continued. "That's a red whale. Now the tom-tom's will really get banging. Lucky the Sixth's guest is leaving tomorrow."

"It would appear that you are here under the pseudonym of Liz Taylor," I told our guest later that afternoon.

"That's okay. It's a lot better than some names I have been called," she smiled back.

"Look here. It says Jane Seymour is staying with friends on Spetses," said someone at the Liako cafe the following day, quoting the *Athens News*.

"Yeah, but she is not as famous as our Liz." Willy winked at me; we knew the pitfalls of discussing The White Mansion's visitor book and kept our council.

However, folk definitely knew when Madam Paouri was coming to the island because Ouzo Jimmy would switch to Amstel a couple of days before she landed. And we knew exactly which day she'd arrive when he emerged from the key house in an ironed shirt. Further clues were provided when German Willy passed the blue door and headed straight to the Liako cafe.

There was an unspoken rule when Madam was in town not to approach Jimmy's table when he was in the company of an elderly lady. Madam may have looked like a frail little *yaya* (grandmother), but she was as tough as an old boot.

Rumored to be worth billions, she commanded the respect of royalty on the port front. Waiters would positively fawn.

"Guess its because she drops huge tips, aye Jimmy," one inmate had inquired.

"You know 'ow the rich get rich and stay rich?" said Jimmy in confidential cockney. "They don't give money away, and they always do business, no matter wot, when, why, or how old."

"Last time she was 'ere, we were 'aving lunch at the Free Brovers, and she asks me to put the salt and pepper shaker in me pocket. I can't do that Madam, says I. What do you want these for? They are only common cheap shakers."

Apparently she liked the simple style and, as Jimmy wasn't prepared to pilfer them, asked him to ask the proprietor if he would sell them.

"Fifty drachmas, Madam," said Jimmy returning to the table. Nico, brother number two, had thought the request unusual, stating that such items were available everywhere. But as it was for the Grande Dame herself, he was prepared to make an exception and sell the salt and pepper cellar.

"Fifty drachmas!" she exclaimed. "Piracy. Tell them I'm not paying that amount."

Jimmy went back inside and related the objection to Nico. He laughed and said, okay, she could have the pair for ten drachmas.

"Excellent," said the eccentric old dear. "Tell him we will take a dozen sets."

"*Oxi!*" wagged Nico's large, adamant forefinger. "I pay twenty drachmas each. For one I make *dora* (gift) price—but from all my tables, *oxi*."

Jimmy explained these economics to Madam.

"See," she said. "I told you they were not worth fifty."

Madam's fame and fortune were literally evident on the backside of the country's largest bank note of the time, the 1,000-drachma bill. When I asked the locals why she had been elevated to currency figurine status, the answers, in true village fashion, were diverse. One contingent went so far as to say that it wasn't Madam Paouri at all but a substitute model. She was an associate of Onassis, said another, as though oodles of cash automatically merited representation on a bank note. One old timer said the image was indeed of Madam, who'd been selected not because of her billions but because her family had connections to the underground liberation movement during the Greek Civil War.

"But she hadn't led some revolutionary cause herself, like Boubalina?" I said, seeking the specifics. Boubalina is the patron heroine of neighboring Spetses, revered for her fearless leadership during the 1821 War of Independence from Turkey.

The *oxi!* was unanimous, so it is safe to say she was awarded fame in perpetuity on charm and wealth.

We also knew when Madam had left the island—always the same day Ouzo Jimmy, a raconteur with the staying power of a walking liver, reemerged. His boss provided loads of amusing material for his tale-telling talent.

"She 'ad a big party for all the rich and famous this time, didn't she. 'Ad 'em all sign a fancy guest book." Jimmy sucked on his fag. "Next morning after breakfast she was going through the list and commentary when she suddenly exclaimed, 'Jimmy, look at this! Someone has scribbled all over a page—the vandal!" He mimicked her squeak.

She had passed the book over. "Tear it out immediately, Jimmy."

"I wouldn't if I were you, Madam," he had advised upon inspection.

"It's a drawing one of your guests has done for you—signed 'ere, Marc Chagall."

19

HELICOPTERS AND MODEL BOATS

"Goddamn chaos," a bloke on his way to Hydra had drawled as he pushed his way back out of the mass of hopeful passengers, waving what appeared to be a flying dolphin ticket.

"This thing will take nearly two hours," he grumbled to no one in particular as he headed in the direction of a waiting stretch limousine. "I can't handle this crap—I'm hiring a helicopter."

My ears pricked, and I followed him back to the long black car. Perhaps I could assist the bloke and convert my nonsecured return ticket into his booked seat. I wasn't sure what I had in mind, only that he appeared to have confirmed steerage on the next hydrofoil and wasn't going to use it. I hadn't a drachma left in my pocket and didn't relish the thought of being forced, hobo-like, to reside on a bench near on the dock for the night, because my next option for getting home was the morning boat.

I tapped on the tinted window, which slid down an inch. Suspicion emanated from within.

"I couldn't help overhearing that you plan to take a helicopter to Hydra." I was pleased to be dressed in travel attire and looked semi-respectable for a change. Island garb—T-shirt, shorts, and beach sandals—would have been less helpful in visual introduction.

"Yeah?" grunted the drawl impatiently.

He sounded Texan. I guessed oil money, judging by the size of the limo and youthful, white Stetson.

"Who are you guys staying with?" I asked, figuring that I might know their hosts and have good opening credentials.

"Ain't stayin' with no one."

"I assume you have donkeys arranged. The helicopter lands at the cemetery, on top of the hill, and there are no cars."

My tinted reflection remained motionless as this statement was digested.

"Yer joshing, right?"

"Absolutely not!" I said, in my best upper-class inflection.

"Y'all from around here?" Blonde hair and mascara loomed into the crack.

"Yes, actually, I am a full-time resident of the island." I decided to lay it on a bit. "I've just flown in after a few days break in Venice. I'm getting my return ticket endorsed now, as a matter of fact."

Y'all loved the accent, and I was invited into the cool leather cabin. We got to talking, and I explained that I had been self-marooned on the isle for some years.

It turned out that the Drawl and Y'all, his bride, were headed for Mykonos ultimately, having just flown in from Dallas on honeymoon.

"Why Hydra?" I inquired.

"I remember someone saying it was also cool and was told to come here for a hi-dra-foal."

"Not in mid-summer," I quipped. It was sweltering outside.

They had come straight through customs and hoped to grab the next flight to Mykonos.

"Is full," the domestic flight desk had told them, "all flights, until *avrio* (tomorrow)."

Clearly not folk accustomed to hanging about, they had decided on Hydra instead and had taken their long cab to the hydrofoils, only to be confronted by a Greek rugby scrum at the ticket office.

"One really should check the availability and book in advance for a helicopter. It will help with the hordes there as well. I could make a quick call if you like. It could save you going all the way back to the airport and finding them fully booked too," I added.

"See, Honey," Y'all enthused. "I told you we were lucky. This fella is just what we need."

They gave me a name in case I was able to secure a helicopter; finances were not a consideration.

He could have been related to a southern politician for all I knew; the vehicle certainly looked the diplomatic part.

"I need to order a *helicoptero* to Hydra for the American ambassador," I fibbed, squeezing my way to the front of a mob of folk determined to get back to the island that day.

Queuing is not a phenomenon known in Greek culture. In circumstances where there are only a dozen tickets left, with a hundred punters bidding, matters tend to get loud. The only way to jump this lot was to pull rank, albeit using a virtual stranger's fictitious credentials.

Pointing to the stretch limo with tinted windows behind the boisterous throng, I explained to the harassed cashier that my client simply had to get to the island that afternoon. So could she please phone Olympic Airways and see if a *helicoptero* was available, as this crowding didn't suit the *keerios* (mister), and he was seeking alternative transportation. It should be noted that cell phones had not been invented back then and requesting to use a phone, never mind that someone make a call, was a asking for tall favor.

They obligingly booked a flight, which, I was told, would be ready to go by the time the *keerios ambassador* got back to the *aerodromio* (airport). I optimistically reckoned that I had secured myself a seat on the last dolphin of the day for my trouble.

I returned with the good news and inquired whether they would like me to call a donkey for them.

"It takes half an hour from the port for one to get up there." I had gathered these folk were used to first-world clockwork. "Longer than the flight itself."

I said I could arrange for a mule to meet them when they landed, offered advice on accommodation—few hotels were air-conditioned then—and gave them the general introduction rhubarb.

"Why don't ya come with us? There is room on the helicopter, right?" Y'all glanced at her new hubby.

An exhausted travel fund could leave one in an embarrassing situation, even if only minor expense was involved—for example, I couldn't offer a reciprocal lunch—but I saw my opportunity.

"No, no, you guys are on your honeymoon, but I would be awfully grateful if you would give me your dolphin seat in exchange for mine, which is for a later boat."

Perhaps I was going to sleep in my own bed after all.

"I could cash my ticket in and leave the amount at your hotel."

"Absolutely not!" Y'all mimicked my accent. "Come as our guest. We're paying for the heli anyways."

"Ya saved our baycon! It's the least we can do," the Drawl insisted.

In those days, there were few standard phones on Hydra, so ordering a donkey was a palaver. One needed contacts. I called from the airport.

"Davey, I thought you were in Amsterdam! You aren't due back for another week." Her Barefootness doesn't siesta, so it was safe to phone her mid-afternoon.

Everyone on the island knows each other's movements. It's part of the charm and, at the same time, one of the drawbacks of living in a small community. One doesn't need to lock doors, but privacy isn't an option either.

"What happened? We were wondering whether you would survive a trip with those two."

I told her Barefootness that it was a long story and I would explain when I landed, but could she call for a donkey and send it up to the cemetery for me in about three-quarters an hour.

"You're coming by helicopter? I've got to hear this," she chirped. "Consider it done. I'll send Miltiades and his mules up."

The helicopter's rotors drowned conversation.

As we flew in over the gulf toward the picturesque little harbor, a toy town from such heights, I counted my blessings: home by a whisker—in style!

Another safari behind me, I thought back to how it had begun.

Tina had approached me the previous month and wanted to know if I would accompany her on a drive up to northern Europe. Her vehicle's visa had expired, and a trip abroad was required to renew or extend its Greek parking permit or something.

"I know you don't drife in years. I just need a nafigator." Being half Israeli and part Dutch she had a distinctive, if unplaceable, accent.

I accepted the offer to copilot a drive through Europe, when she insisted a flight home for me was worth the security of travelling with a companion and would be part of the deal.

"I am going anyway, so it will cost nothing. We visit some friends along the way, and you can fly back from Holland. I can drive back down later" she enthused. "Tree weeks maximum."

She possessed a pair of exotic little villas on Hydra overlooking the harbor entrance. Tina regularly flitted in and out of the island community and was a distinctive presence in the port-front social scene.

We decided to delay our departure so that Willy could put in his notice at the White Mansion and come with us. He had a job offer in Amsterdam and saw this as his chance to escape the Rock for bigger pastures.

The Sixth had not been keen to see his prize young chef hotfoot to the bright lights of Amsterdam. A rhubarb ensued, ending with our young chef packing in a blur, garbage bags stuffed with pots and shampoo.

Willy turned up breathless at my place in the middle of the night. "We don't have to wait, mate. Alexi said I could bugger off—like, immediately. Call Tina and tell her we can leave tomorrow."

William and I, not responsible for driving, celebrated our parole along the Corinth highway to Patras with a couple of refreshments.

The customs officials took particular interest in Tina's car with its Dutch number plates and late dates. They then commandeered her passport; Willy's and mine were quickly checked and handed back.

A stream of large trucks flowed past into the massive hold of the ferry. If we were allowed on, it looked as though our fellow passengers would be mainly Italian and Greek truck drivers with only a smattering of tourists.

"Look all these bic trucks going on." The chauffeur was beginning to show signs of impatience.

"No matter, we will be first off in Italy." I tried to inject a positive.

The uniforms stuck long poles with mirrors under the car and laid every stitch of luggage in a row on the quay. The hatchback was crammed with Willy's life and Tina's travel wardrobe. Several large, designer suitcases and miscellaneous paraphernalia she wanted taken to her Holland home stood in single file next to the road, where truckers drove slowly and inquisitively past.

Another uniform had gone in search of a sniffer dog. Willy and I chatted and joked with guards.

"Why you talking to the them?" she growled at us, when they were out of earshot, clearly uptight at the delay.

"We only offered them a drink."

"What?"

"They're friendly blokes, it's Friday afternoon, and this is their last shift."

"Are you crazy?" she hissed. "Now they will think we are trying to cover something."

Clearly our tactics differed. The mention that our passports hadn't been the ones impounded caused our shares to plummet even further. Not a grand start.

The dog eventually declared us free to embark shortly before sailing. Ours was one of the last vehicles to board the boat for the two-day voyage to Italy.

The ferry was a luxurious affair, complete with restaurants, shops, bars, a disco, and a casino. We were sitting in the restaurant after dinner on the second evening, when I pulled three twenty-drachma coins out of my pocket.

"Might as well get rid of the change—I think I'll go and pop them in a fruit machine."

The slot machines were in the entrance room to the main casino. A single cashier in a teller's cage manned the entrance.

The smallest acceptable coin to play was a fifty-drachma piece, it turned out, so I went to the exchange box.

"Give me one fifty-drachma coin, *parakalo*," I said, placing my shrapnel down. "And keep the change."

"*Oxi*." The trimmed moustache behind bars wasn't very helpful.

"I just want to play once for luck, one coin. I don't even want a ten back."

"*Oxi*, only paper money." The fellow didn't bother glancing up.

"For fun, *parakalo poli*—"

An adamant "*Oxi!*"

There wasn't another punter in the room so he didn't appear swamped.

I decided to see if I had any Greek money left in my wallet. I found a single fifty-drachma note—no longer in mint as they were dwindling out of circulation, but still legal tender.

"*Ena peninta coin*, *parakalo*, with paper money," I requested, pocketing my three smaller coins.

He seemed hesitant to proceed with the transaction, and I reminded him that he had stipulated paper money only. Clearly this wasn't the size note he had in mind. Not exactly a high-rolling afternoon, one could concede, but still, a punter with little was better than no punter at all.

I walked over to the one-arm bandits and randomly selected a machine. Aware of the watching pencil moustache, I inserted the coin. One coin, one pull—that's all I had.

Bar—Bar—Bar, the spinning objects showed.

Lights flashed, jingling ensued, and a passer-by or two stopped to investigate.

I took a coin from the pile and fed it back to machine, as one would tip a croupier, then dumped my winnings—two pockets and a handful's worth of coins—into the cashier's stainless steel bowl, a mechanism that whizzed around, using centrifugal force to count large numbers of coins in a few seconds.

"Careful, there might be three smaller twenties in there somewhere."

The mute moustache didn't twitch and rummaged humorlessly through the change.

Willy was most impressed when I returned with a re-upholstered wallet five minutes later.

William had come to Hydra as a teenager on holiday the same year I moved to the island. I had just opened the bar, and he had shown a keen interest in returning the following year to work. One gets used to hearing that on holiday islands.

The following season young William turned up on my doorstep early one morning with a girlfriend in tow. I hadn't heard a thing from him since the previous summer.

"My dear fellow, all the positions have been nabbed over the winter by locals," I explained as I brought them into the bar for tea. Indeed, I had acquired a staff of seven composed of half a dozen nationalities.

"Who cleans this mess up?" Willy asked, indicating the bar, which was littered with ashtrays and dirty glasses, the floor still tacky from the previous night.

"I do." It was only a little bar.

"Well, we can do that."

And so, William joined the island's expat community. He and his girlfriend understandably didn't stick to the floor-swabbing career for long and moved up to house sitting before he slotted himself in as a house cook with the Sixth.

It had taken five years to extract himself from the Rock, so our trip with Tina was a significant move for him.

As we sat down for breakfast on the last morning, the ship's intercom announced in three languages that we were docking in Ancona. Disembarking passengers were to have their papers and passports to hand.

Tina gave the disembarkation cards to Willy and told him to go hand them in while we went to the cabin to collect all our overnight bags (the main luggage had obviously remained in the car), saying that we would meet him in the departure zone.

There was no sign of Willy as we stood in the customs queue. The customs disembarkation booth was trying to move human traffic, and fingers clicked impatiently.

"Disembarkation card, *parakalo*."

"Did a young English boy give you our cards?" Tina asked.

"What?"

"English man, about twenty-three years old, brown hair, average build and height, was supposed to meet us here—"

"*Oxi*, no card, no get off ship. We leave one hour." The uniform was impatiently emphatic. We lost our place in line and went in search of our passport holder; already the departure area was thinning.

"Go find him." Tina was beginning to acquire an angry hue.

There were few people about, and I asked every employee I could find if they had seen my friend as I searched up and down long, similarly lit gangways and decks. Soon I was asking for directions out of the maze myself.

By the time I got back to customs, half the ship's crew had been pressed into the search for Willy, and Tina was again being detained. She was by then nearly purple, and who could blame her. Thus far, she'd found the help from the "nafigator and mate" a tad shy in both the assistance and direction-finding departments.

Eventually young William was spotted ashore, sitting on an Italian bollard having a cigarette, unaware that he was the center of a major manhunt. A sailor was dispatched to bring him back on board.

Willy had given the documents to the waiter at breakfast apparently.

"Why?" Tina asked through clenched teeth.

"I thought they were breakfast tokens—I even said to the bloke he could have them as we were not going to use them. No wonder he gave me a strange look."

When asked how he had managed to enter Italy without this card, he shrugged, "I showed my passport and—nothing, I just walked off."

More troops went in search of the waiter in question.

The steward never materialized. A further delay followed, as new forms were found and filled out, before we were allowed to go ashore. We were by far the last departing passengers left on ship.

"Willy, you carry the bags to the car meantime," said Tina icily. There was no doubt as to who would be issuing orders for the remainder of the expedition.

I waited until we got final clearance and then headed down the pedestrian ramp to meet young William. Tina went down to the cargo deck to collect the hatchback.

"I think there's going to be a bit of a rhubarb, mate," he said, looking sheepish.

"Why, Willy?"

"You remember all those truck drivers who were chatting her up in the bar last night?"

Willy had appeared on the cargo deck with the bags to be greeted with much enthusiasm—fists, fingers, and foul language out of windows—from exasperated drivers. A small Honda, parked at the front of the unloading queue, was causing major traffic congestion. Remember, we had been last on back in Greece and now blocked an entire row the length of the ferry.

Even for Tina, this was going to be a tough one to weather. Truckers kept to strict time schedules.

Sure enough, we heard a host of angry klaxons erupt from the bowels of the ferry, presumably greeting the driver of the small obstructing vehicle. The little car came scooting off the ship chased by a convoy of huge honking lorries.

Her dark eyes were almost cartoon-like, blazing with embarrassment and fury, knuckles white on the steering wheel. If thunder had a color, that would have described her tint.

As predicted, we were indeed the first ones to be let off on that row.

Willy slithered silently into the unoccupied half of the back seat, I into the front.

Wheels spun, and then the brake was suddenly stomped.

"What the fok is that?" Clearly something else had touched a nerve. She turned around and pointed to a large box blocking the back window.

"I got it in duty free. It's a radio-controlled speed boat, and I thought because Amsterdam has canals, it might be a fun thing … " his voiced dwindled into inaudibility.

"Well, I can't see out the back window—there is no room. It will have to go." She got out, opened the back, and yanked the model boat off the parcel shelf. She then marched over to a little family sitting on their suitcases and handed Willy's boat to a girl of no more than four.

"*Prego*, take. Is for you. Keep it," she said, then came steaming back, leaving a perplexed mother and toddler clutching a big box.

"Be happy I still keep you in the car," she spat, glowering into the rearview mirror.

Tina was silent all the way to Venice, where she decided we would stop for the night. But by the time we went out for pizza that evening, conversation had begun to flicker again.

Enter Carlos, a Venetian waiter of charm who took us under his wing. Carlos was a keen fellow and most hospitable, showing us local haunts down back canals away from the usual tourist traps. In the days that followed, Willy and I packed ourselves off to see glass-blowing factories, museums, galleries—

Nearly two weeks later, Tina was talking about a real estate purchase in the city and had decided to halt any northerly advance while these negotiations were in progress. Venice is a costly place, and our funds dwindled rapidly. Stranded, nearly penniless, in one of Europe's most expensive cities with no escape date on the immediate horizon, we opted to take matters into our own hands.

Willy had barely enough cash left for a third-class train ticket to Amsterdam. I packed him and a couple of arms full of paraphernalia off; we wished each other *kalo taxithi* (bon voyage) on Venice's station platform.

Then I explained to Tina that at this rate of travel, we would be lucky to make Holland by Christmas. As my wallet was depleted save for a few drachmas for the taxi from the airport to the flying dolphins, I would be more financial burden than help to the trip from there on.

Carlos, I was sure, would agree that accommodation for three was unnecessary.

It was decided to put me on the next plane back to Athens. I spent my last night in Saint Marco Square, ticket in hand, waiting for the first water taxi to the airport, and was saved a second night on the *dromo* (road) at the Athens end, by the fortuitous arrival of the long black car on the home stretch.

I left Tina contemplating Venetian real estate, having learned the risks of leaving the Rock with a one-way ticket.

Four months later I bumped into her in the port, the day after she arrived back on the island. The car was still parked on the outskirts of Venice. Carlos hadn't worked out; nor had suitable real estate been found.

"Do you want to come with me to pick the car up?" she asked. "That was quite an adventure we had—maybe we should do it again and go to visit Willy in his new job?"

"Via where this time, the Ukraine? Or maybe Poros would be the final destination?"

I pulled her leg, but I'm not sure she got the dry.

20

ROYAL RHUBARBS

"The king's brother and the princess of Rhubarb are coming to stay at the Sixth's mansion, and our chef has legged it to Amsterdam," I implored Jesse. "And you're a great cook, mate—"

I had been given carte blanche to find a cook for the royal visit.

As my culinary skills didn't extend past breakfast, never mind to three weeks, we were in a bit of a stew since Willy's escape. Skilled, unemployed gourmets were thin on the island at the height of season.

So I'd approached my old comrade Jesse, a gent of girth and generosity in all matters. A fellow soul who liked variety in occupation, he also had flair in the kitchen.

"But the wife has her heart set on Rome-Paris-London, and we're booked to go."

Jesse's extended vacation time had expired after eighteen months. His wife and baby daughter had reached their threshold of life on the Rock and were keen to see some other European sights before heading back to Miami.

"Come on, mate. The princess's sister is fantastic fun—I know her. Plus, you'll be handsomely reimbursed for the experience." I needed a mate I could trust for moral support as much as the production of menu.

"They are dinkum dynasty royals," I added. He knew I'd had fun catering to a dinkum *Dynasty* soap star earlier that summer. "How often in life do you get to meet blue bloods? The Coliseum and Eiffel Tower will still be there."

The deal was cemented when Jesse saw that, although the White Mansion had a disproportionately small kitchen space, the Sixth had acquired every conceivable cooking gadget, some still unpacked.

"New toys!" he beamed.

The Sixth, as host, would get extra twitchy the day "special" guests arrived and would nervously fidget his way through the White Mansion alone—looking for lint.

Then we would walk through the premises together, as he pointed out things for me to tell the maid, gardener, or pool man.

Sparkling wasn't sufficient. Unattended details sometimes lurked in the closet.

"This is a tremendous embarrassment," he grumbled while inspecting the royal clothing cupboard.

I ran a finger over the top shelf and bottom corners: spotless. The princess's cupboard looked perfect, so I was curious as to what the flaw was.

To avoid future "tremendous embarrassment," clothes hangers from this point forward were to be aligned. And the radio aerial compressed.

Alexi was a gent with a discerning eye, so I had enough on my plate, without having to worry about what was going on other people's, and I was glad to have Jesse handling the *carte du jour*. He had scoured the island's markets, used every cookery toy, and carefully prepared his introductory dinner—a meal fit for a king's brother.

Our guests had spent a long day travelling and grown an appetite to match. Dinner was served on the white marble table outside under a lush, green overhanging vine. There were green-trim designer cushions, green candles, and white china.

I took the first course out: a chilled cucumber soup, produced in a various selection of high-speed processors and garnished with a sprinkle of fresh basil.

Jesse was keen to know if anyone had commented on his first attempt as chef royale.

"Excellent! Delicious! And can one of them have the recipe, please," I assured him, the finest compliment one can pay a cook, I thought.

He had worked hard to impress the regal stomachs with the second course too: chicken breast poached in a green grape sauce over rice, with a lightly sautéed zucchini dish and a fresh green salad, artistically displayed on individual hexagonal white plates.

"Oh man, there's no color!" exclaimed Jesse. "Everyone knows a plate should have balanced color, at least a couple of carrots—too late now."

It had to be said that the only item not green or white associated with the banquet thus far was the silver cutlery.

"Compliments to the chef again," I said to Jesse, as I went down to the storeroom to get desert: champagne and fresh honeydew melon sorbet in crystal goblets, garnished with a sprig of mint, made in the sorbet-making machine and served on a frozen white tray.

"They're going to think I am taking the piss."

"Stick a cherry on it," I suggested.

He looked at me incredulously.

"You mean as in "a cherry on top"? You're kidding, right?"

"Okay, if they mention anything, I could say you're color-blind."

He looked over his spectacles in disbelief.

"Or I could blame the Sixth—say that he told us green was their lucky color."

I took the final course out, not really as convinced as Jesse that anyone had noticed.

"In keeping with the color theme throughout," said the princess, as I placed the emerald desert in front of her. "How clever."

Jesse and I were to repeat our double act with the royal family in London and the Caribbean, where their appetites appreciated dishes incorporating a variety of hues.

21

DONKEYS AND TORTOISES

The Sixth returned from the port one afternoon with a solution to my transport problem.

"*Ella*, Devid, I have brought you a present."

Alexi was standing outside the mansion's archway with a classic little brown and white donkey on the end of a rope.

"Somebody was selling her, and I know you need help with the shopping."

Indeed, most would think a donkey on an island devoid of motorized transport an asset, something to be envied, especially when one was the majordomo for a tycoon with a flare for ordering in bulk.

"Where are we going to keep her?" inquired my horrified girlfriend, Paula, when I came home and tied the animal up to the front door of our little rented apartment.

Tortoises and snakes she had learned to cope with, but an animal of this magnitude required serious housing. Ours was a small flat below the landlord's, and we shared a small portion of his family's garden. A rabbit would have been crowding.

"What's her name?"

"That's up to us," I replied. "She's ours, a gift from Alexi. He didn't know her name."

"Lunatic," she snorted. I presumed she meant the Sixth.

"Where, how, who is going to house and feed her."

An animal lover experienced with large quadrupeds, having once served as a groom at the stables of the duke of Marlborough, Paula was more aware of the accommodation logistics than I.

"You shouldn't have accepted her."

Still, big brown eyes and pointed ears won the day. The donkey came with a traditional wooden saddle, complete with hooks for tying on paraphernalia, and a corroded bell around her neck.

"Bluebell," Paula said with instant inspiration.

And so, we negotiated a trial period with the landlord. Bluebell could inhabit the uncultivated area below our terrace, but we would have to find alternative accommodation in winter, when she would need a roof. That gave us about six months to find her a suitable stable.

Unlike snakes and tortoises, donkeys need daily exercise, watering, feeding, brushing, and some attention. A bored donkey can kick up an awful racket at any hour, including, we discovered, the much observed siesta hour.

The muleteer union quickly got wind of the fact that Bluebell had cut into their weekly paycheck for grocery deliveries. The White Mansion at the top of the hill had been a source of regular custom for many.

I'd had Bluebell about a week, when a large moustache purchased me an ale at the local, sat down, and asked about my intent.

I knew it was prudent to assure them that Bluebell was a pet, for personal use only. No, I would not be meeting Mr. Mardas's or anyone else's guests off incoming ferries. Neither Bluebell nor I intended to carry baggage—in fact, I would continue to steer arriving guests and any other transport jobs the muleteers' way. Another ale and a pat on the back secured the agreement.

The muleteers observe a strict code of conduct. They had taken one fellow to court for using his multilingual wife to lure tourists into rides, claiming unfair advantage and breach of union rules.

Bluebell proved more difficult to park than one would imagine. Even as a full-time inmate of the island, I has no idea what was in store.

Tying her up to the nearest lamp pole was quickly discouraged. Some trinket shop or taverna owner would get vocal as soon as Bluebell dumped on the cobblestones.

She also became adept at untying her knot and finding her own way to the local vegetable market. Irate grocers on the phone became a regularity.

"You donkey eat all my fruits outside. Come get it. Now." Most embarrassing.

Donkeys are not allowed on the port after dark, unless for the express purpose of meeting a suitcase off a boat. So night "walks" were off the agenda too.

The White Mansion was too well groomed and had no appropriate place to keep the animal during work hours, so she was returned to the garden after each shopping trip.

Bluebell decided that she didn't intend to carry humans either. One is supposed to sit sidesaddle and indicate direction by gently pulling the chin rope. In Bluebell's case, you could yank her head perpendicular, and she would still drag your legs against a wall.

So Bluebell spent most of her time prancing around the enclosed patch of land, which she shared with Felix the tortoise and at least one grass snake, reptiles that had found their way home with me during walks in the hills. Felix loved scraps of apple and lettuce and would wander up to the front door a couple of times a week for a snack. An endearing little fellow, about the size of an oval grapefruit, he walked, fed, and amused himself.

Long before Bluebell's arrival I noticed one day that Felix hadn't appeared for his treat and searched the garden. I eventually found the poor animal, his geodesic shell cracked and crawling with wriggling white maggots. A chip, the shape of a donkey's hoof, had caved the center of the tortoise's shell inwards. Surprisingly he was alive as I carried him up to Paula—but only just.

Felix made an amazing recovery. After we had picked the visible parasites out with tweezers, the chemist advised us to swab the cracked shell with bicarbonate of soda. Felix would then prop himself against the wall to catch the maximum of restorative spring sun. We made sure he had plenty of mashed fruit and henceforth barricaded him into the safety of our little patch.

* * *

I reported Bluebell's accommodation problems to the Sixth—a wonderful pet, we loved her dearly, but not a practical tenant in our circumstances, thanks all the same.

"Take her to the stables in Molos. She will be happy there," he suggested, understanding our predicament.

Indeed, Molos had acres of space and proper stables. The trouble was that as a secluded bay halfway down the west side of the island, it was easily accessible only by sea.

The little donkey was ceremoniously saddled up for the long hike, Walkman strapped to the front of the saddle, an ice chest with hiking fluids and picnic gear tied to the pommel. Jesse and I took the day off. Getting Bluebell down the goat paths to Molos bay was not quite as precarious as I had anticipated, and we left her happy in her retirement paddock.

The next time I saw the large moustache, I reciprocated a pint.

"*Po-po-po*," I exclaimed, sitting down next to him.

"*Mularia enai poli thoulia*," I said, explaining that after so much work and *fassaria* (fuss), we packed Bluebell off to live in the country.

"*Bravo sou*," he said, grinning. I was lucky to be rid of her—too much trouble, he agreed.

* * *

Twelve years later, I moved back to the same neighborhood into a house below the patch of unused land where we had kept the menagerie.

At the Four Corners shop one afternoon, I bumped into Rebetika Ed, a gent I knew from my days running an Internet shop in town. He was still in need of cyberassistance, so I invited him home to check his e-mail.

I was leading him back to the house when I saw, walking directly toward us in the middle of the lane, a tortoise about the size of a rugby ball. His shell was missing a chunk in the shape of a half moon.

Ed followed me onto the terrace, somewhat bemused by my enthusiasm over a tortoise.

"Sorry, Ed! Felix and I go back a long way. I probably saved this guy's life back in the eighties, and I haven't seen him since."

"Girls, come and meet Felix," I bubbled, as soon as I got in the door.

"Hello, Felix, nice to meet you," said my ex-wife, extending a hand to Ed.

"Not him! Here, Felix, still alive after all these years," I said, indicating the large, healthy tortoise walking across our terrace.

22

KINGS AND PAWNS PLAY POKER TOO

Even with three kings in my paw, I knew I was way out of my league when, without looking at his cards, the Sixth bulldozed a mountain of chips into the center of the table.

"Eighty thousand," he pronounced, not even looking in my direction.

The pot suddenly represented a full month's wages, and the Sixth knew it. After all, he paid me. What had started out as a friendly poker game with low stakes so as to include the less-heeled player—me—had turned into a game for real money.

As majordomo for Alexi Mardas, host to the rich and famous currently seated around the table, I was the only salaried person there. A film star, a pair of royals-in-exile, a fellow who owned some Caribbean islands, and another whose fleets traded in the four corners made up the rest.

I had been lucky during the earlier rounds, so I was able to keep pace with the gentle rise in stakes. But 80,000 drachmas would wipe me out, and we hadn't even called for second cards.

The trio of kings stared back at me, daring me to take up the challenge. I counted my chips: 83,000 (then the equivalent of about US$ 450). Without hesitation I pushed out all but three and prayed he stayed.

The others folded, and Alexi finally glanced at his hand; we each drew two cards.

With barely a pause after glancing at his cards, he shoveled the rest of his pile forward, nonchalantly flipping a few notes on the top. "The rest and another 50,000."

I gingerly turned the corners of my cards. A pair of ladies smiled up.

A full house, high royals, kings on roof. But it didn't beat aces and a flush or four of a kind, any kind. If I folded I would leave with my shirt and some dignity; if I went on and lost, I could find myself working for the fellow for a decade wage-free.

"That's not fair. Can't we just do all or nothing. I mean, if I had the cash to play with, I would be all in." I tried appealing to his sense of benevolence.

"Sorry, but the rules of poker are very strict. If you want to play at this table, you must play by its rules." The Sixth knew he had me beat.

"Come on, Alexi. Be fair. You let Anthony play for paintings." Mr. Kingsmill, an artist of some repute not known for his liquidity, was a well-known character at high-rolling games. One of his paintings was said to have passed through four owners before returning to its original purchaser for the same outstanding poker debt or some gambling rhubarb that was never made quite clear.

"Anthony was an exception," Alexi replied curtly, sensing by then that perhaps I was holding a good hand.

"Can't you make an exception for me?" I begged.

"Anthony's paintings may be of some value one day," was all he had to say.

At this point the princess, whose curiosity got the better of her, leaned over and looked at my hand.

She said nothing and merely handed me a fist full of 100-dollar bills with a wink. Others chuckled.

"You can't do that!" The Sixth did not seem happy with this turn of events.

"It's a private loan," retorted the royal exchequer.

"But he can never repay you, and besides, its against the rules to sponsor another player." A tic had developed in his cheek, wobbling his chewed cigarette.

"Then it's a gift. Here, Davy, another 500 for you to play with," she announced, passing me another wad and rubbing the point home.

"But!" Alexis's unlit cigarette positively jiggled. He hadn't foreseen that an unknown heiress would come to my rescue.

"But what, Alexi?" she challenged. "Nothing in the rules says I can't give my money away."

The exchange had gotten everyone's attention. A gent who did not like to loose face, the Sixth muttered something conciliatory.

"I'll see you," I said, pushing forward my few chips and the required balance in 100-dollar bills. A sharp kick on my ankle urged me to add boldly, "And I'll raise you another hundred."

The game had now escalated to the realm of a real currency, with big bills at that. We had started the evening with 500-drachma denominations (a little over $2), and now I was betting for more than I earned all summer—in one deal.

The Sixth sat back silently for a minute, eating a fresh, unlit cigarette. He looked at his cards again and smiled, noting I only had a bill or two left.

A twitchy fox with a larger wallet, he had gambled in some of the biggest casinos around the world and been known to loose and win trunkfuls of cash in a single evening. He was a fellow accustomed to playing for high stakes.

"Your hundred, and I raise you four." He took five crisp bills from his purse.

A bag to my right was rummaged, and an emphatic hand foisted another deck of large bills at me—ignoring my protests.

"Another present for my favorite Irishman. A thousand," she announced.

Alexi leaned on one elbow, his jaw working furiously. His bluff was being called in a most unexpected way. Luckily he had picked up an ace to match the pair he had drawn, which was cause for further prolonged contemplation. He still held a decent hand, despite being countersteamrolled.

"Don't expect me to be giving you any money," the ship owner teased, eliciting a titter or three. The twist of events had added some spice to the game, and I got the feeling that my participation had become incidental.

This mob wouldn't have batted an eye if the stakes had three more zeros tacked onto the end, so this was about something other than money. It had become a jovial rivalry between serious brokers, and I was just a pawn who happened to be holding kings and queens.

The princess leaned over my shoulder for a closer look at what I held.

"Err, Devid, do not show your hand." Alexi didn't approve of the informality and was drawing attention to the conspiracy.

"What? I can't look at Davy's hand?" she admonished. "I'm out. What do you care?"

Alexi decided to follow through with his bravado, hoisted his chin, and upped the pot a full grand, taking me to my limit.

"See you," I said quickly, hoping to stop the escalating atmosphere and ignoring the hand nudging me in the ribs with a fan of more bills.

The Sixth noticed the proffered wad and quickly laid down his triple aces, not wishing to risk more against a seemingly bottomless bag of cash.

"Three kings," I said laying down the trio to a sympathetic murmur, which broke into applause when I added, "And two ladies. Actually three," with a wink back at the princess.

I insisted on giving the "present" back immediately, whereupon the princess insisted that she didn't want any of the drachmas, but if I insisted on returning the winnings, she would keep the dollars. Even the "loose-change" drachmas came to about two months' salary—a good night at the table for an amateur.

"We'll find some other way of using this," she joked while stuffing the greenbacks into her bag. "Cards should be fun, and wasn't that fun, Alexi?"

The Sixth called it a night, and I don't think he ever played cards with me again.

I did, however, have a lot of fun as a guest of their royal highnesses in London and the Caribbean—where we played cards for toothpicks. Winning isn't always about raking in the biggest pile of chips.

Alexi remains a dear friend and one of the most colorful characters a bloke could hope to meet.

23

MICES AND MEN

The island has a knack for doing the unexpected, sometimes sabotaging the best laid plans of mice and men.

Having turned my hand to a number of tasks, I had thought that accepting the offer of longer-term employment in a secure environment was a step forward. I have mentioned a couple of the memorable events from my involvement with the White Mansion, but the first rhubarb happened only an hour after I arrived for my first day of work on a Tuesday.

The intercom buzzed. I assumed it was the Sixth, requesting morning coffee and a welcome chat.

"Devid, I have just been awoken by the chief of police, who wants to see you in his office now—with your passport," said my new boss, sounding understandably irked.

"Why, Alexi?" I asked, perplexed. This was the first such summons I'd ever had, and the word "passport" had a bad ring.

"He didn't say. He was pretty upset. You had better go down now."

Impressive start, I thought. I couldn't figure out what had induced the chief to trace me to the mansion only minutes after I had turned up for the job.

I racked my brains walking down the hill. The only possible rhubarb that might involve the law had to do with a small rental disagreement. A few weeks earlier, I'd passed on a phone number to a blonde looking for accommodation—just a favor for an acquaintance. The securing of discount digs for three months, during the height of the season, is no mean feat. A studio with a view, kitchenette, private bathroom, and private terrace for sunbathing—I had figured Blondie would love it. She didn't and moved out after a couple of days. An encounter between a small field mouse and said tenant had precipitated her flight, and there was an ongoing rhubarb over the deposit, but I didn't imagine for one minute that this merited police chiefs calling tycoons before breakfast.

The rhubarb had started when I was sitting at the Three Brothers, another of the island's lunchtime social hubs, and Blondie had come thundering up to my table the second day after she'd moved into the apartment.

"Mices in the room," she panted. "I didn't sleep, and I had to go to the doctor. I have blood pressure and had heart palpitations."

Little field mice were fairly common on that side of the hill, so I wasn't all that surprised. I actually thought she might be kidding. Anyone half as familiar with Hydra as she knew that we share the Rock with rats and roaches—not to mention *serrandapothia* (poisonous centipedes) and tarantulas.

"Mouse, singular; mice, many. How many?" I tried to lighten the crisis.

"At least one."

I laughed. "Don't you get mice in Tel Aviv?" I received a scowl in response, my humor failing dismally.

I made amends and marched up the hill with her to purchase poison pellets from Four Corners. I sprinkled a few under the sink and explained that the mice would eat them and then return to their nest, somewhere outside the house, where they would fall into a permanent sleep.

I left, feeling sure that Blondie had been appeased.

A couple of days later—déjà vu.

"All okay?" I smiled at the incoming frown.

"I moved out. I found ze dead mices, so I go, juz like that," she moaned.

The mouse had chosen not to die under a bush but elected to perish instead in the center of a china salad bowl. Blondie had opened the sink cupboard the following morning and found the ex-mouse.

"I couldn't touch it, so I throw ze bowl out ze window,"

Three stories up—lucky, I thought, that no pedestrians had been passing below.

The fact that large, intermittently occupied stone houses on Greek islands sometimes attract little mice was no excuse.

"I come for 'oliday not to 'ave zees stresses. I want my deposit back."

Blondie did have a point: there was no small print in the rental contract covering wildlife invasions. Nor did any clause in the agreement mention full reimbursement in the event that mouse and mice-phobic tenant meeting under the sink.

Blondie had been most insistent that she couldn't wait for Jeannette, who managed the house, to return and demanded instant reimbursement. So I had approached her Barefootness with the problem as she was a co-agent and a friend of the LA-based house owner, Charles. Plus Jeannette and the Countess were close buddies.

The Countess had agreed to repay Blondie, and Jeannette or Charles could repay her later.

"Tell her Monday morning outside the bank," her Barefootness had said. I did and imagined matters were settled.

On Sunday evening after a boat picnic, her Barefootness wanted to know the inside story. I explained that a mouse had caused all the *fassaria.*

"A mouse? The cheek! She's a big girl. What about the lost bookings from people we turned away? Well, I'm not paying her."

On Monday morning I called her Barefootness, hoping for a change of heart.

"I haven't changed my mind. She can go and jump. Jeannette will back me up too."

Blondie waited a futile hour outside the bank apparently and then headed straight to the precinct. The chief uniform on duty had been obliged to phone the countess then and there.

"Absolutely not, Gregori. She cannot demand like this. She must wait and talk to Jeannette. Or she can phone the owner in Los Angeles, if she wants." Click.

The cop told Blondie as much, so she had stormed out in search of me.

Later that day, Felix—a Norwegian novelist not to be confused with my tortoise—bellowed to me from his usual elevated table at the Three Brothers. He had semi-retired to the cafes of Hydra and taken over the plaintiff's vacated studio. A jovial fellow with wispy hair and no aversion to mice, Felix was a rare commodity, whose presence added a lot of flavor to the island.

Felix possessed a unique intellect, humor, and a distinctive style. He attracted an audience wherever he sat. Impeccably spoken, in a gold waistcoat waving a long cigarette holder, he would blurt out whatever came to mind, sometimes preceded by a distinctive windup chuckle.

"Halloo, David, yuk—yuk—yuk. The blonde battleship is looking for you," he called, referring no doubt to the plaintiff's considerable bulk.

I thanked him for the warning and fled uphill.

I had already told Blondie a dozen times that Jeannette would deal with the deposit when she returned from Othonis. The funds were banked, and as I had no access to the account, I couldn't do any more.

This favor was rapidly going wrong. It's unpleasant having to avoid one's usual haunts because of a rhubarb on the loose.

* * *

"Battleship?" It hadn't taken long for Blondie to get wind of Felix's quip. "What is zees?"

"Large," chimed a spoon at breakfast the next morning.

"*Megalo*," confirmed a second, stirring.

Digestion took a couple of seconds.

"I know anuzzer battleshitz. I'll give zem a battleshitz alright," she'd fumed and steamed off to the coppers.

With mutters of embassy involvement, she'd staged a sit-down protest in the chief's office, threatening not to budge until she had her money.

"Wezzer from Zanette, David, the Countess, or Felix," she didn't care. She had a flask and lunch on hand.

Such determined, bulky anchorage discouraged any thoughts of physical eviction by even the bravest constable—hence the early-morning phone call to the White Mansion.

So my guess had been right—the mices had conspired, culminating with waking the Sixth. When I finally arrived at the station, passport in hand, I found her Barefootness, Felix, and the Battleship all talking at once and the chief staring at the ceiling.

Actually, Felix was chortling loudly, slapping his thigh and saying things like, “Isn’t this wonderful.” Felix loved theater, and he had the best seat in the house.

The bespectacled, stand-in police chief held our passports up. Clearly frustrated with his inability to take control of the proceedings unfolding in his office, he raised his voice above the din.

“Okay, no passports back! Nobody!”

This got instant silence.

“Until everybody shake hands and be friends.”

More silence.

“In front of me.” After a pause, he emphasized, “Here! Now! Or I keep the passports.”

The paperwork would be enormous if nobody shook.

On the one hand there was the Barefoot Countess, whose connections ranked at the top of any ladder, and on the other, the Blonde plaintiff, her embassy, and the formidable Tina of Venice, a second battleship in the wings, as an ally if need be.

“Jeannette is in charge of the house. She is in Othonis and is returning next week,” said her Barefootness, presenting unity with Jeannette and her considerable local influence. Island solidarity and the longevity of Hydra landownership versus part-time tourist point being made.

"No! I stay here until I get my money. You can keep my passport," declared the Battleship, determined to remain at anchor.

Her Barefootness started to name powerful lawyers.

"Yuk, yuk," the chortle chipped. "All this for less than $200 rent. Isn't it marvelous? One couldn't write such a script. Yuk, yuk."

Gregori and a couple of his uniforms looked on, helpless in the face of this standoff. The interim chief doffed his cap and looked imploringly at her Barefootness.

"*Parakalo*, Madam. Pay her. For me. I would myself, but it is not allowed—"

Eventually hands were shaken and passports returned. I headed straight back to the White Mansion. The Sixth was sitting by the pool.

"Hi, Alexi, you'll never believe what that was all about," I said.

"I know, Devid," he said sagely over his shades. "This blonde is tough. She beat you all using one little mouse."

24

MONASTERY MONSTER

"Hey man, check this stone carving out. It must be centuries old!"

Our excavations had already unearthed two layers of floor. Under wooden planking, we had discovered ceramic tiling, and now it seemed there was a third, possibly original floor made of sandstone slabs. Lourens had exposed a cross carved with old Cyrillic script, presumably by ancient monks.

Lourens and I were working at the top of the mountain on the restoration of an old monastery above the harbor. Even at that elevation, recognizable noises echoed up from the port. The amphitheater's effectiveness does wonders with the acoustics; one can hear phones ringing in the evening quiet.

Lourens, a gifted artist from South Africa, looked and behaved like a combat veteran of that country's old bush wars. He was the kind of fellow you wanted on your side if you were going to be mugged—or doing heavy manual.

One aspect about living full time on the Rock is that the cast changes continually. As a result long-term inmates tend to withhold themselves from the holidaymaking throngs and befriend those who stay more selectively.

The syndrome is well-known: close friendships struck up on vacation and promises to write dwindle into ever more infrequent postcards—a bit pointless if one is living in the postcard.

A colonial voice on the port once said, "I won't speak to anyone who hasn't been here for at least two years." At the time I thought the dictum snobbish, but over the years I've come to understand what the speaker meant.

If a new character was still around after the awnings and chairs were gone in the fall, then the chances of making his or her better acquaintance rose considerably. One got to know people over a winter, and bonds developed. Sadly, most mates don't do more than a couple of years on the island before the lure of the first world entices them away again. So one becomes hesitant about building bridges.

"A South African painter is thinking of staying for the winter. Perhaps you should meet him," said Canadian Colin's pipe from an adjacent table. He knew I had some history in that part of the world.

"Well, let's see if he does first, shall we?" I was even more disinclined than usual. The last thing I wanted was to find myself discussing the artist's country's political dilemma. In frustration I had given up on its policies, along with the rat race, years before.

"That African bloke is still here. He seems quite nice and has heard about you," said the pipe some time after the first rains.

"What sort of South African? They come in many shapes, dialects, and sizes?"

"White. Looks like a mercenary," Colin had puffed.

This sounded ominous. "Language?"

"Strong accent. Afrikaans, I think." The pipe obviously didn't know what a Boer mercenary type potentially represented. Mr. Mandela was still in jail. The proposition sounded something akin to being asked to pal up with a Nazi in 1946.

The following day muscular, unkempt stubble at the taverna table next to me started sketching on the paper tablecloth. A few pints later we discovered we were in the same political camp, and so I became mates with a South African bulldozer.

Lourens became my working partner. No handyman job was to large, including the dismantling of old monasteries. He would add pencil sketches to our documentation of the dig if we unearthed anything of interest during the day. The carved flagstone merited a drawing, so we downed tools as it was late afternoon anyway.

Just as we were sitting down to enjoy an after-work cigarette before clambering down the mountain, we heard voices filtering up from the valley below us. They carried clearly in an unfamiliar, singsong language. It was rare for anyone to come up the deserted hill at dusk, even locals.

A large arched doorway dominated the entrance of the ageing structure. A pair of heavy wooden doors held together by a thick rusted padlock and chain gave it a desolate look.

Lourens and I peered through the crack between the lopsided doors and were amazed to see three Japanese tourists out exploring. Overnighters from the Orient were rare, as their groups seldom stayed longer than the allotted hour off the cruise boat.

A guy with a camera bag and two elegantly dressed ladies were ambling gently up a disused donkey path toward us.

Lourens put a finger to his lips as we watched their progress.

When they were about thirty meters from the entrance, I heard a guttural roar over my shoulder. At the same moment Lourens grabbed the doors and began shaking them violently. The chain rattled dramatically. Puffs of masonry fell.

I nearly had a heart attack and looked down at the hikers. They'd stopped dead in their tracks. The women had their hands to their mouths, apparently stifling screams of horror; the fellow had dropped into a crouch and was staring at the monastery, jaw on the path.

Lourens let rip with a second, louder rattle and a roar more fearsome than the first. The visitors took flight, and I feared for their ankles as they bounded back down the precarious slope.

"That was really mean," I told him.

"No man, just think of the story they can tell their mates back home. They'll always remember this walk," he said, grinning. "Now they've had a real adventure."

"You do realize that not all tourists feel that encountering a Yeti in a haunted house is an essential ingredient to their holiday, mate."

"Ja, but now they have something to tell their kids. I bet you they'll always recall Hydra before the Acropolis even." Lourens had a habit of looking at things from a different perspective.

Lourens's daughter started attending the local kindergarten, and during one lunch we were sitting at the Three Brothers watching her and a gang of kids squabbling over some pencils on the steps outside the taverna.

"Listen to my little girl, man. She has picked up the language in a few short weeks," he said, beaming with pride.

"Do you know what she's saying, Old Bean?"

I explained that her language translated would have made him blush. He shouted at her in Afrikaans to stop.

"*Lollie, moonie, moonie, kom heer.*"

There was a stunned silence among the Greek diners. Lourens sensed disapproval from the adjacent tables.

"What's the matter with them, hey?" he asked.

"You have just called to your daughter using the crudest Greek word for female genitalia. They probably reckon you are trying to top your daughter in linguism as she merely referred to her mates in the colloquial for 'wanker,'" I laughed.

Lourens begged me explain the faux pas to the frowning moustaches.

"Strange language, Afrikaans," said one.

"No wonder they say it's all Greek to me," answered Lourens.

25

SEWAGE AND CEMENT

Georgo needed a hand to clean up the street outside his house.

"There are some cement splashes that need chipping off, and my back cannot cope," he explained. "Just a little job."

Georgo owned one of the island's grand mansions situated high above the port in the labyrinth of the upper town's cobblestone streets. According to Georgo, he had taken matters into his own hands to solve an ongoing problem with a leaky *vothros* (septic tank) in the neighborhood. For some time there had been a rhubarb about a foul odor wafting through the area. A various selection of plaintiffs had made numerous complaints to the municipality and police on the issue. Georgo had returned from the Big Olive that spring and decided to fix the problem for once and for all by blocking the hole permanently.

"How much cement did you use?" I inquired.

"Fifteen bags," he said with the certainty of a man who knows that fifteen bags of cement would staunch a flood never mind plug a leak.

I swept the street before attacking the few cement spots with a hammer.

"*Tee kanees etho?*"

I was used to black-shawled *yayas* (grandmothers) coming to investigate any proceedings and asking what one was doing. But the *yaya* didn't seem pleased with my answer that I was helping *Keerios* Georgo tidy the road, as she started to babble and gesticulate with gusto.

"*Oxi, oxi.*" A waging finger indicated that I should cease work. I was accustomed to free advice, and experience had taught me not to pay too much heed. I suggested to the old dear that she take the matter up with the house owner and continued chipping away.

She banged on the massive front door. When she got no reply, I assumed that Georgo was deep within the rambling house and hadn't heard the knock. She waddled off, muttering.

A couple of minutes later she returned with reinforcements—three *yayas* all shouting at once. My efforts to improve the street were not getting the appreciation I had hoped. I reiterated that Georgo was the man they should be talking to and continued filling a rubbish bag.

Yayas may appear like helpless little old ladies dressed in black and just being nosey, but they are in fact the real authority in island society. *Yayas* know who, where, why, and what about anything that moves in any neighborhood. They have an information network bar none, as well as troops of family to enlist if required. One does not argue with *yayas*.

The noise attracted more people, none of whom seemed pleased with what I was doing. I started to wonder if perhaps I was encroaching on municipal territory and therefore not entitled to work on public property. I told the growing mob that I was merely the assistant; they should direct complaints to my employer.

More rapping on the door failed to produce Georgo.

I caught the word *astinomia* (police) during the debate. Someone else mentioned the *dimarxhos* (mayor). Still, I wasn't concerned, as the mayor knew me. He spoke English and, most importantly, knew the influential estate owner for whom I was working.

I had almost finished when two uniforms arrived and declared my labors illegal. I was officially requested to relinquish the hammer.

The whole neighborhood had assembled by this stage, and I suppose I shouldn't have been surprised when the balding dome of his mayorship puffed into view. Good, I thought. He would translate and explain to the irate locals and police that I was merely an innocent laborer before stoning started.

"*Tee kanees etho?*" asked the glistening dome, pointing to my bag of rubble, his air of authority silencing the rhubarb.

"Ah, Mr. Mayor. Glad you're here. Just helping Georgo tidy the street," I said, hoping that he would view my task in a favorable light. Instead, he burst into emphatic Greek from which I gleaned that he had sided with the mob and suddenly lost his linguistic skills.

By now I was perplexed. Where was Georgo, and why was a lynch mob gathering over a bit of sweeping?

My Greek wasn't that good, but I did pick up that the abundant rhetoric included a demand for me to report to the police station with my passport.

"Mr. Mayor, I know you speak English. What's all the fuss? Am I not helping the municipality do its job?" I retaliated.

The statement failed to provoke a conversation in my mother tongue and instead produced a stream of invective about what sounded very much like "tampering with evidence."

A couple of black shawls were trying to lead the mayor further up hill. The fifteen bags of cement had created a dyke, it seemed, backing the sewage up. Apparently houses behind Georgo's mansion were awash, someone had fallen ill, and plague was deemed immanent.

Unblocking the drainage would take dynamite, one villager added. Others suggested using the explosives in a less productive manner. The mayor gave me another verbal reprimand in Greek for the benefit of the crowd.

I'd had enough. I downed tools and hammered on the door. Surely Georgo must have heard the noise in the street by then.

He eventually appeared and cast assurances to the throng that the problem would be taken care of officially. My endeavors were merely temporary cosmetics to win favor with the local populous while the real matter was investigated.

Some further dialog ensued, the upshot being that his mayorship did not grant me further right of labor, and at what I took to be grunt of dismissal, I dispersed with the rest.

Later that afternoon I bumped into the mayor on the port.

"Hello, David, how are you? Nice day we're having," he chirped, his English remembered and the morning's event apparently forgiven and forgotten.

INTERMISSION

A VARIOUS SELECTION OF PHOTOS

Pan's postcard from his bar, ca. 1983.

David's mum, Clare, with Anthony Kingsmill and her now husband, Colin, outside the Liako, 1986.

Michalis Metaxa, our picnic captain and fossil expert.

Bluebell with friends in Molos.

The usual suspects at Chris's Dirty Corner, ca. 1990.

Mavro Manolis, ca. 1985.

Dirty Corner, our hole-in-the-wall hangout during the 1980s and 1990s.

Antony, with a familiar glass of porridge.

Little Willie, newly minted chef, at the Moita, ca. 1993.

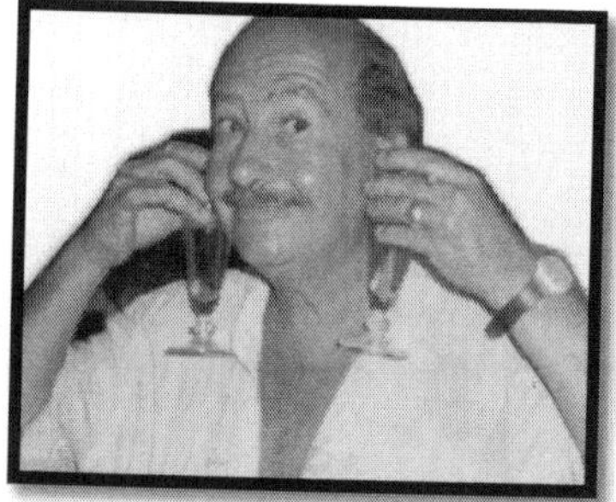

Leonard Bernstein (affectionately nicknamed "Beerstain") horsing around with his kokinelli.

German Willy and Clive at the Liako.

Don Lowe and David with Maggie at the Pirofani's opening, 1992.

Her Barefootness, Christina, with Sasha and Doris.

Christina and Jeannette in Clive's garden in 2006.

Ouzo Jimmy and Jeffrey at the Breakfast Club, ca. 1987.

Jesse and David at the Up 'n' High.

Douglas, surveying "breakfast," ca. 1988.

Brummy Mark in his black hat, late 1980s.

The Banker either before or after his spectacles fell down the well.

Canadian Colin with pipe.

HydraNet partner Michael Giese, ca. 1996.

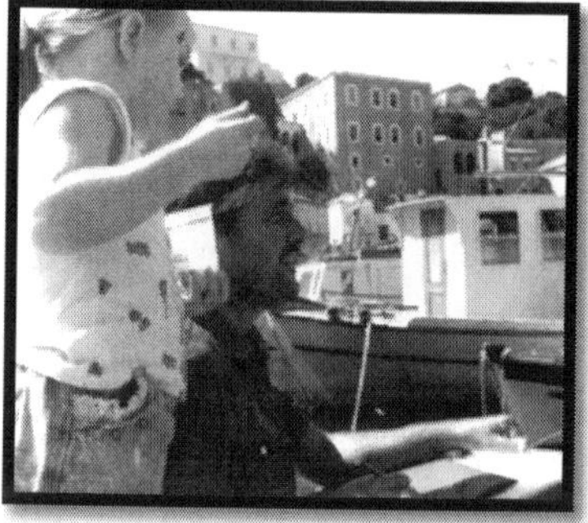

Lourens sketching with daughter Lollie on the port.

Elizabeth, the Noodle, with her goat's head trophy, aboard the Zoë Zoë.

Maggie and David at the Breakfast Club, ca. 1989.

The Banker teeing off at the Hermes outside the Breakfast Club, late 1980s.

Bill conducting business on the island's first "mobile" phone at Gunter and Lilly's Moita Restaurant.

Douglas with Michael Giese riding back to Kamini from Vlichos.

Longtime Hydra inmate Aussie Skipper Brian.

Madam Paouri's image on the 1,000-drachma note.

The old guard at Tassos: David Gore-Booth (the ambassador), Nick Craze, Michael Kelland (the Banker), and Mr. Bill.

David digging for the beard's bullion in the Brownings' courtyard.

Gunter and Lilly.

Swedish Anita and David at the Bahia's bar, ca. 1985.

Tablecloth drawing of Felix and Ouzo Jimmy at the Three Brothers Taverna, sketched by Lourens Purén in 1988.

David and Clive in the back of a flying dolphin (hydrofoil).

The HydraNet Internet office.

Pavlos shooting Judas, Pascha, ca. 2007.

Stathis, on his 70th birthday, 2006.

Ingeborg, late 1980s.

Charlotte and Bill, early 1990s.

Bill and Gunter in Vlichos, ca. 2009.

Irish Tony, Canadian Colin, and North Carolinian English teacher Chris.

Jeannette, Sasha, and Doris.

Irish Tony in a port café.

Theo and Roger ("The Bard") Green at the opening of the Pirofani Restaurant, 2013.

Maggie and Stathis dancing on the eve of his 70th birthday.

David with Roger Green and William Pownall after a reading of the "Thirty-Ninth Pslam of David."

James, David, and Ferri in SoHo, London.

David with BBC's Mike Bushell filming a documentary about Hydra for the 2004 Athens Olympics.

Felix the Tortoise and Lizzy the Cat at play.

The mustachio (left) and mates at Dimitra's market, Kamini Valley.

Michael Lawrence, ca. 2008.

Mr. Bill, much missed.

Alexis Mardas, aka "Magic Alex" or "the Sixth Beatle."

William Pownall, whose painting graces the cover of this book, at his studio high above Hydra Town, ca. 2004.

David and his father, Neil, on "Pavlos's Lazy Terrace" at David and Jennifer's spitaki.

Many thanks to Sasha Jaeger, Kelly Shea, Susan Purén, Anita Geise, Lisa Kelland, Charlotte Hilding, and any others we've missed for helping us collect these photos.

26

THE BREAKFAST CLUB

"You no more order *omeletta* here!"

My friend Eva, owner of one of my favorite tavernas, was apparently banishing me from the Breakfast Club. I had been an executive member, status achieved for excellence in paid-up attendance—about six breakfasts a week for half a decade, winter and summer.

"Your *omeletta* just cost me several thousand drachmas," Eva laughed.

As far as I knew I'd never run a tab with her for more than twenty-four hours, but clearly there was a matter of lost profit to discuss. Later, the ever-cheerful Eva added in her amused manner, "We must talk." Beneath the banter there was an obvious need to renegotiate my membership rules.

The Liako was my combined breakfast venue and office. Banishment would be akin to exile from the dinning room at one's clubhouse.

Eva knew how hard it was at times to eke out work and that half my average daily budget, about 500 drachmas, would be allocated to occupying a seat at one of her tables. Sometimes—most times—for hours a day. At forty drachmas per pint and the same for eggs, one could park for a considerable period on a fiver.

I went principally for the port-front theater; eggs and beer were the entrance fee. The Breakfast Club—hub for part-time and year-round expats, tourists, and locals alike, a polygamy of nationalities and backgrounds—was open morning until late at night, 355 days a year.

Eva would serve anything under or over the grill at all times in the days when nobody raised an eyebrow if beer was the beverage of preference before noon. The Liako had become my lounge, and it had a phone. A lot of us waited years for a private line.

Private phones were uncommon in the later 1980s, so you can imagine the commotion at the Breakfast Club one day when Bill turned up with a cordless phone that could receive and make calls like a "normal" telephone, the dinosaur equivalent of today's cell phones. We were astonished by the leap in technology and superbly impressed when Bill phoned the bar inside the Liako to order his cocktail.

It worked like this: Bill's wife ran a language school on Donkeyshit Lane, and he had rigged an antenna on the roof that sent radio signals to his phone. Bill and his contraption, with its six-inch rubberized aerial, gained notoriety in no time and became that summer's star attraction.

The Banker got wind of Bill's communications leap and, not to be outdone, decided to bring his own portable port phone from the States when he came out for Easter. The trouble was that, in those days, Greece had strict importation laws and taxes, especially on electronic goods, so he devised an ingenious way to smuggle his phone through customs on his way back to the Rock from New York.

The antenna came in lengths of metal that would have set off the airport detectors, so he placed the parts in a golf bag along with a number of clubs. After installing the transmitter on the terrace of his house, which overlooked the harbor, he too proudly wandered down to the Liako sporting his newer model, which had a telescopic retractable aerial and therefore claimed the communications spotlight.

Bill and the Bank became dueling dial-up rivals to the amusement of all, including the staff summoned at various waterholes. The phones only worked in the port, however; Kamini and Vlichos were out of range.

The bank was quite pleased with how he had circumnavigated the airport customs police and one morning brought his four-iron down to show off.

When the *Hermes* cruise boat came into port, he decided to give the Breakfast Clubbers a giggle and pretended to whack a golf ball at the mooring ship. Fits of laughter ensued when it became apparent that the teed-up golf ball was an egg. All manner of theater took place at the Liako.

During the previous tough winter, Eva had been an immeasurable ally in my rivalry with the port-front cats.

When a gent is earning 500 "drachulas" an hour for sporadic menial labor, then watches the port cats snag a week's wages' worth of lunch off adjacent tables as soon as the Japanese tourists rush back to their boat each day, he gets to thinking.

Who is supposed to be top of this food chain?

Perfectly good, tasty, untouched *kalamari* (squid) and prawns, at a value well above the daily winter budget, were being devoured by the same toms who regularly sprayed one's shopping or coat tails. This was territorial stuff.

"*Kah neechie wah*," gold shop owners would say in greeting the island's winter tourists, 95 percent of whom hailed from Japan. The *Hermes* "three-islands-in-one-day" cruise boat, affectionately nicknamed the *Herpes* as it would blight our view of the opposite side of the harbor, would disgorge a couple of hundred visitors for an hour each afternoon.

The Liako was the first taverna tourists passed as they got off the boat and obviously the last before they reembarked. Many were attracted by the lifeless *octopothia* (octopuses) Eva strung up alongside the tables, and they would sit down to order her finest seafood.

At least one table would hustle off leaving substantial parts of their lunch untouched. No sooner had they stood than fur and claws would swoop and skedaddle with freshly grilled tentacles. One needed tactics.

A quickly chucked glass of water usually kept the competition at bay until it was socially acceptable—that is, the gangplank had been traversed—to lean across to the next table for first dibs on the morsels.

Eva had apparently watched my maneuvers with some amusement.

"*Oxi*, wait," she tutted one afternoon as I sidled over to the barely touched platters. "I take."

Five minutes later she came out with a seafood platter—my "leftovers" on a fresh plate and reheated. The day's rescuings included prawns on rice with fresh octopus on the side—a feast fit for an executive of the club.

I had dined well that winter. But now it was going summer, and it seemed rules had changed.

I decided to square matters away with Eva. One shouldn't cost the innkeeper money to frequent her establishment, especially when she had been so generous during the lean months.

"*Ella*, Eva, what?"

Apparently the boys had been splashing out on breakfast just before my arrival. The club's "A-team" breakfasters that day had initially had a hankering for lobster, prawns, some salads, and some mezes. All was written down.

A few minutes after they ordered, I took a seat and chirped, "I'll just have my usual, please, Eva."

"What's your usual?" Wall Street inquired, peering over his rescued spectacles.

"An omelet."

"Actually that sounds much better than a heavy lunch in the sun. I'll just have what David's having as well, Eva, *parakalo*."

"Me toos" echoed around the table.

A several-thousand-drachma food tab diminished instantly to about 200.

From then on, I simply got a "cat-plate," as in tasty, free leftovers if I was in the company of well-heeled appetites, and I never again ordered eggs when others were dining on shellfish, winter or summer.

The Breakfast Club stayed open for over a decade. Eventually crowds of human traffic offloading from tour boats pressurized the ambiance. And the advent of phones in every home and especially the introduction of a few dozen television stations changed the way we lived and dined on the Rock forever.

27

EGGANOMICS

We have all heard the old saw about studying at the "University of Life." Well, I can testify to the truth of that cliché, having attended a five-year course in "egganomics."

The Breakfast Club at the Liako was the venue for the morning meal for most all inmates. More than live theater for those with in interest in human behavior, it was an open-air classroom with a spectacular harbor view.

One can often tell a person's character by the way he eats his breakfast. The standard—and just about the only—traditional breakfast available was bacon and eggs. The accompanying beverage, however, did vary from customer to customer, irrespective of time of day: Jimmy naturally had ouzo, others vodka; many favored the local cognac, Metaxa, in colder months. For the most part, Amstel lager was the most popular choice. A few actually had coffee or tea.

Tough-as-old-boots German Willy ordered his eggs on the rubbery side.

"I must be able to bounce mien fork on ze yokes, ja. Zees runny eggs alvays get on mein chin."

Ouzo Jimmy's laid-backness, on the other hand, infiltrated his chewing. He perhaps holds the world record for slow eating: we once clocked three and a half hours for his plate to be cleaned—a two-eggs-and-a-couple-slivers-of-bacon marathon. Douglas attacked his eggs with the ferocity and intensity that was his being, slashing the yolks at once, left and right.

Mr. Bill always carried a small bottle of Tabasco in his pocket and drowned his breakfast with spicy red sauce. Canadian Colin ate the white of his egg first, trimming it down as though to see if he could leave the yokes whiteless. Jeff liked variety in life and so peppered one egg and salted the other.

The rest of us simply dipped bread into the yokes and consumed our morning meal normally.

One day an English tourist threw a spanner into our simple breakfast routine. After squinting at the menu, he enquired whether Eva did scrambled eggs.

"What is these?"

We helped the fellow in describing this mysterious dish. Eva merely shrugged in disbelief. Smashing eggs before cooking them seemed silly.

Jeff and I decided to demonstrate and went backstage to prepare the visitor's breakfast. Eva and her chef watched in fascination at the ease of scrambling eggs. I suggested that this egg preparation, popular with foreigners, should be added to the menu.

The visitor loved his eggs, and sure enough, the very next day the chalk blackboard menu outside proudly advertised the new offering, the first of its kind on the island: "scrabbled eggs."

* * *

Greek cuisine is highly regarded for taste and health reasons the world over, but all cultures are known for certain dishes that do not appeal to those of weaker gastronomic disposition. Take the Scots and their beloved haggis—basically porridge cooked for hours in a sheep's' stomach along with bits of interior organs from all regions of the abdomen.

The Greeks at Pascha have their version of haggis, called *kokkoretsi*. Granted, these traditional meals originated back in the days when no part of an animal went to waste. And as there was no refrigeration, and as entrails were the first to go rancid, they were the first consumed—branded a delicacy no doubt to persuade people to partake of the ghoulish plates, much as Popeye's spinach eating was designed to encourage youth to eat their greens in Western society.

Kokkoretsi is, to some of us, up there with haggis when it comes to edible treats with a difference. Essentially it is a dish consumed after midnight on the Saturday before Easter Sunday (Pascha). A goat's innards are wrapped in its intestines and rotated on a spit over coals for a while. (In this area I remain in complete ignorance and beg forgiveness to those who know the subtle nuances of this recipe.)

I am gent blessed with a stomach for almost every kind of food, except when it comes to the midnight meal at Pascha—and I have tried on a few occasions, even with a pre-bellyful of beer.

Once we were invited to Stathis's for traditional lamb on the spit on Easter Sunday. In all seriousness, our host offered my newly-arrived-from-England, ten-year-old stepdaughter, Harriet, the ultimate delicacy. Stathis poked a fork into lunch's eyeball, popped it out with a soft sucking noise, and proffered it to the wide-eyed, ashen-faced little girl, who shook her head vigorously in the negative.

I will never forget her look of fascinated horror as Stathis relished that "best part," wiped his lips with a napkin, and then proceeded to crack the skull open by wedging a carving knife into the cranium, relishing what he found inside with the same gusto with which he relished life.

28

A PERFECT MURDER

The setting was perfect—a rambling, empty pension, isolated under the lip of the hill, overlooking Kamini's little harbor. It was a resort of some elevation, known for great sunsets and fluctuating management, but the tourists had gone and only the hardcore inmates remained—plotting.

Bill, Robbie, and myself sat hunched at the bar, which quartered a large living/dining area, wondering what to do about Michael, who was feeding the fire, excessively, at the other end of the room. He was a fairly new addition to the expat community, a Californian artist, who had departed the West Coast but remained in the sixties, especially when filled to the gills.

"We're going to run out of furniture bits to burn," grumbled Robbie, the pension's warden, a burly Australian bloke who had served with the British Special Forces in Burma.

"Aye, *Malaka*, I've told ya to go easy with the wood," he drawled at Mike's frizzy mop, silhouetted by the flames. "If ya wanna burn things, I told ya to bring yer own."

It was still common practice to scrump for wood en route to visiting friends with fireplaces in the early nineties. Mike had wobbled in empty handed and uninvited.

"Relax, man." Mike was well into sixties mode. His thick glasses glimmered back, "Have a pop."

"I'll pop him alright," Robbie muttered to us. And that's how it started.

How far did one go in removing an unwanted guest? Mike had a rhinoceros hide, and there reached a point when he failed to notice that discussion of the wrong company in the wrong place referred to him, no matter how many well-aimed comments were fired in his direction.

Mike had turned up, sheets into the wind, flying a spinnaker in fact, just as it was getting dark, attracted by chimney smoke and a light.

He was a flamboyant character, still finding his feet in the community, but back then too much character sometimes infiltrated his personality to the point of stage domination. He was a big lad with a balance problem when too immersed in the sixties, at which point he also constantly went outside to pee—a constant disturbance to three mates playing cards.

Was one eventually driven to murder?

"Point him in the direction of the pool," said Bill. "That ought to do it."

The pool in question was in fact a four-meter-square concrete hole, an open cisterna. A terrace and benched wall surrounded it, making it a quaint spot to dip after the hot climb up in summer. When it had water.

Now, blue paint peeled off the sides, and the pump house equipment was gathering rust. Its function as a bath two seasons deceased, Robbie had decided to turn the thing into a rock garden. He had placed cactus and spiked aloes among the boulders at the bottom, explaining the need for arid, non-mosquito-larva-generating conditions, when questioned about the "garden" part.

"Three meters down onto that lot—not a chance mate." Bill was keen on the bunji-trap plot. "He'd fall in even if it wasn't dark."

But there was an equal chance sixties mode would bounce and merely cause itself grievous bodily harm. We would then be in a bit of a pickle.

Not perfect. An "accident"—undetectable and terminal—was needed.

Sparks flew across the room when a piece of dry bed board exploded; an ember got trapped in Mike's wire.

"Mike, your head's on fire!" White smoke was beginning to curl, carrying a whiff of burning mattress.

"Yeah, right man, like I'm gonna believe that." Mike had been unaware of the pyrotechnics going on next to him.

"That's it—murder by way of not extinguishing flaming gate-crashers. Let him burn," piped Robbie.

Debate at the bar contemplated stench and police reports. There would definitely be a rhubarb about the incineration of said artist.

Not perfect.

"Hey, man, it's getting warm over here—"

Sixties was leaning toward the fire, hands out stretched, oblivious of the looming bush fire on his head; the fizzling was audible.

Robbie grabbed a glass of beer, the closest fluid on hand, as he headed toward Mike in haste.

"Hey, man!" Mike raised his forearms to fend off the Burl, unaware that he needed dousing. Hair hissed.

"What did you do that for, man? Hey, I'll bring my own wood next time!"

Guffaws from the bar only confused him more. Although only a handful of hair (hardly noticeable in Mike's case) got flamed, the stench was more than adequate olfactory evidence that a "happening" concerning his wool had occurred, thus confirming our explanation for the douche.

"Man, that was close," said a dripping Mike, sitting down. "Think I'll have one to steady my nerves."

We went back to plotting, leaving the pyromaniac to ponder his near-death experience. It didn't take Mike long to forget about the wood rationing, and he turfed another precious piece of bed onto the blaze.

"Think. For real," growled Robbie, who had resorted to burning old furniture as all loose wood in the immediate neighborhood had already been scavenged. Times were tough, and ordering in legitimate quantities was out of budget.

One night coming up Donkeyshit, Robbie asked me to give him a hand with an old electricity pole. The island had new ones installed the previous year, and apparently the old poles were up for grabs.

"Think of the benefit of a great log fire, aye?" Robbie encouraged as we struggled up semi-lit cobbled alleys. The task left me winded for days and earned me weeks of free fire.

The flaw in our dubious efforts became apparent when we finally managed to get the first chainsawed piece to burn. Tar, chemicals, and a various selection of industrial preservers had been lacquered on over the years.

"Toxic," was Bill's description.

Bill was playing "musical residences" and was staying that winter with Robbie in the deserted pension. I would sometimes give Robbie a hand, and the day's chores would often drift into dinner, wine, and the fire.

Watching Mike drinking his beer in the corner, Bill suggested, "Give him the whole case. Maybe he'll drown," the elements of earth, that is, Robbie's "garden," and fire having failed.

"Hey, man, can I just sleep here next to the fire." Sixties was already horizontal on the couch, snuggling in for the night.

"I'm not waking up to that first thing in the morning. That's it, he's going." Robbie roused Mike and guided him out the door.

Robbie ran a loose barracks in the off-season; suspects used to straggle in and were welcome to take potluck, generally from a big bowl of communal pasta. The sergeant's mess was a hospitable, easygoing place.

But there were rules, apart from bringing wood and/or a beverage of choice. Guests were encouraged to remain perpendicular for the duration of the visit and to use combustibles sparingly. That was all.

It could not be said that Robbie ran a tight ship. Eviction suggested gross misconduct.

We were still chuckling over Mike's antics when he returned, fiddling with a jammed fly.

"Hey, man, its cold out there." Having watered the plants, he had returned for a just-one-for-the-roader.

"Why don't you use a toilet like civilized people, *Malaka*," Bill joked.

"I like nature, man," slurred Mike, draping an arm around Bill's shoulders before heading back to the diminishing woodpile.

"There's the plan—the perfect murder." Mike's wrestle with the zipper had given me an idea. "Tell Michael he must use the outside loo."

"But we don't have an outside toilet," said Robbie.

"Exactly—but you do have an old pump house that looks like one from the exterior." I could see Robbie wasn't with me yet. "What did we find living in there the other day?"

The burly sergeant started to grin.

"Yeah, but how do we keep him in there? He'll make an awful racket for a while."

"There's a two way latch on the door—we close it during the event and leave it in the unlocked position after the deed is done."

"We're alone on the hill; the wind is howling. Even if someone did venture up, it would be too late," added Robbie enthusiastically.

"Perfect," he rumbled. "Not a trace—scot-free."

"What, what?" Bill was keen to catch up.

They're nicknamed B-52s around here—huge, ferocious-looking brown hornets with yellow markings. Although not normally aggressive, they are known to carry a whacking sting if antagonized. We had found a colony of them billeting in the old pump room. They'd built a multistory nest of red-brown mud, some feet in height and one in diameter, a magnificent structure like a pile of enormous, stacked pancakes. Hundreds of wasps guarded and fanned the entrances; at night the winged sentries would be home and silent. A trap.

More sparks flew as Michael heaped another plank, adding fuel to our plan.

"Point Michael into the outhouse, latch the door, and spray a squirt of insecticide through the keyhole," mulled Robbie. "That should get them going."

"In any event," quipped Bill, "an autopsy would show the victim to have been in no state to find the door handle even without a swarm of angry wasps."

We searched for the flaw and found none.

It was a prank of top-job proportions. Wintertime seemed to encourage pranks on the island. Perhaps in the absence of other distractions, and to escape cabin fever, inmates created harmless amusement on themselves.

"Once in the middle of the night, we were surrounded by policemen who burst in from every angle with a warrant," Bill recalled, "just Robbie, myself and JJ (the miniature Yorkshire terrier Bill looked after), sitting here at the bar with a couple of candles. Someone had said we were running a cathouse, a house full of *poutanas* (prostitutes) mate. Can you imagine, up here in the middle of winter?" Bill pulled the end of his nose. "Nothing happened. They just laughed and joined us at the bar."

The prospect of our "murder" was made so probable that Robbie promptly locked the pump house door, permanently, in case a real accident happened.

Years later, when Michael had become a prominent artist on the island, I was helping him place a brass plaque on the pedestal of a bronze he was having publicly erected, and I told him about his near murder.

He grinned at me incomprehensibly for a second, unsure whether I was telling him the truth or winding his clock.

"Hey, man, it was the sixties. What can I say, I'm sorry—shit happened to a lot of us back then," he joked. "Many didn't make it, you know."

Suspecting he was going to launch into the tale of the untimely death of his mate Jim Morrison of The Doors due to excess sixties stuff, I chipped, "And some made it until the mid-nineties without even knowing they had."

29

SUBS AND SLUGS

"It's like James Bond," said Günter, peering at footage that the miniature submarine was beaming back to our quarter-deck. After that "James" became our nickname for the submerged robot.

Hi-tech equipment littered the boat; diving gear dripped. Our luxury yacht indeed looked like something from a spy movie, and I was the owner through peculiar circumstances.

We were searching for the wreckage of a sunken luxury cruise boat valued, according to the Lloyd's representative on board with us, at over $750,000. It was said to have been pirated, then torched, somewhere along the Corfus coast-line. I had found myself promoted from first mate to owner of the vessel for the duration of this operation.

This safari was looking up. What had started out as a quick crewing job was turning into a dinkum deep-sea treasure hunt. We had been testing the yacht in Corfus Bay before potential buyers showed up to make an offer, when we got wind of the maritime rhubarb.

The previous evening, a Cambridge accent at the other end of the taverna was trying to get a point across to Hellenic port police and was being drowned out by a local fisherman and a couple of file-wielding officials.

From what I could gather the fisherman, who claimed to have the largest vessel in Corfus Bay, was adamant that his canted-deck boat could accommodate the wetsuits and their electronic paraphernalia.

Lloyd's was concerned about the weather—February in the Med is unpredictable and, he also pointed out, the equipment was worth more than the boat. Below deck facilities were a requirement.

The Coast Guard only had a Zodiac in the vicinity, and anyway, Lloyd's would have had to foot the bill, a uniform explained.

"*Freedom C* would be perfect for them," I said to Günter, whose boat we had come to flog. It was spacious and opulently equipped. Corfus, a rather remote little village on the Peloponnesian coast, had little to offer in the way of ocean-going vessels.

Günter told me that if I brokered the deal, he would cut me in for a third of the charter. He suggested I appear to be the owner of the yacht, and he my captain. This would explain who controlled the helm during salvage operations.

"Vot vil I say to Lilly?" asked Günter. Lilly, his wife, had made me promise that we would "behave," concerned perhaps that the lure of distant ports would take us into troubled waters.

"Tell her the truth. She'll understand the delay," I suggested.

Günter decided to wait and see.

Mr. Lloyd's loved the proposal, and we agreed upon a decent daily rate, plus a handsome bonus if it was proved that arson had caused the sinkage.

"If this can find keys still stuck in the ignition on the fly bridge, for instance," he pointed to the mini-sub's aluminum trunk, "then we would have a case, and you would be entitled to a percentage of the insurance value."

"Done," said I. "This is Captain Günter—"

They had seven days to find the wreck or call the search off.

A deep and jagged coastline surrounds Corfus Bay; hence, it's a favorite with local scuttlers, it being only a three hours' sail from Piraeus. Law dictates that the Greek port police authorize and accompany any such underwater investigation to prevent submerged historical relics being nabbed, so a half dozen badges clambered on board when we left shortly after first light.

The little remote-controlled yellow submarine was amazing—providing camera angling, zoom, and adjustable lights at depths well below normal scuba. A couple of false alarms had the English and Greek divers bailing overboard to investigate rusting keels. Fish and plummeting seascapes were scanned all day.

"Ve have *James Bond* the mini-submarine, some divers and police, and a man from Lloyd's," Günter explained that night into the taverna's phone.

"I don't know how long. Maybe ve find it tomorrow—but no longer than a veek."

"She vants to speak to you," he said, thrusting the hand piece at me.

I confirmed that yes, we did have a submarine called James on board, and we were working for Lloyd's of London on a piracy case.

Lilly wanted to know if we had been drinking.

"I told you she vouldn't believe us," said my captain.

The novelty had worn thin by the third day, and the crew dwindled to a skeleton. *James* suddenly found some solid evidence of a recently sunken luxury boat that afternoon—debris of satellite coms, railings, and batteries—but it was getting late, so we simply marked the spot.

Lilly was on the dockside when we returned, having taken a various selection of transport modes terminating in a long taxi ride to get there. She had decided to see for herself and was most impressed—and I dare say relieved—to find that *James* really existed.

It took another day to ascertain that most of the wreckage had slid down to uneconomical depths. Only a very expensive salvage operation could recover further evidence, but the footage they had taped might be sufficient for a conviction once they reviewed it under closer inspection back at the lab.

"We will let you know if we have been successful," said Lloyd's as he piled *James* into a truck and waved good-bye.

"Where are our wages?"

Günter grinned, knowing full well that I had nothing in writing.

"Depends on the result. They know where we live and will post us something according to the review, whether just our fee or with a bonus remains to be seen."

"Uh-huh. I suppose it was worth it just for the adventure and experience." He sounded skeptical. "It was vinter, after all, and ve ver here anyway."

Freedom C was sold the following day.

The next season Günter and Lilly opened a restaurant on Hydra, called the Moita after another vessel Günter had once owned, and it became a regular hang out with island hobnobbers.

One lunch I asked for the *log* (short for *logariasmos*, or bill), and when he came out with my change, Günter shoved a huge wad of drachmas into my hand.

"Your change, Sir," he said, trying to keep a poker face, knowing it would cause a stir among the clientele.

It took a second—months had passed since *James* had departed.

"You mean wages, Captain? The Double-O department coughed up, right?"

"Ja, a surprise for all of us at the post office this morning. I had nearly forgotten."

Sometimes I would give Lilly and Günter a hand in the restaurant.

"There are sixteen Norwegian guys here off a yacht. Their boss turns fifty tomorrow, and they want a party here," Günter explained one day. "These guys drink a lot, so I need help on the bar and with orders."

A jovial band of "Scandahooligan's" had "hej-hoed" their way through a few toasts by the time the Caesar salad was served.

"Excuse me, sir," an arm beckoned. "There is something in my salad."

The table pretended not to notice as I went over. The largest, blackest, slimiest slug imaginable writhed on the lettuce. Had I not spent over a decade examining local fauna and flora, I might have been caught, but I knew no such beast could be native to Greece. I decided not to give their prank away and called Lilly over. "Petite" accurately describes her.

She squealed in surprise. The Norwegians continued to look appropriately shocked at the slithering garnish, hej-grumbling, one pointing to the bougainvillea above the table.

Günter sauntered over.

"Fokkin'-shit, I'm sorry, gentlemen. Did you vant that grilled?" he asked, turning to go. "I vill get the chef."

Little Willy was then hauled from the galley to inspect the dish and looked down in disbelief. He had worked his way up through the kitchens of Amsterdam and returned to Greece experienced enough to handle a commercial galley. His reappearance had coincided with Günter's opening the new restaurant.

"But I washed the lettuce," he squawked. The yachtsmen guffawed, no longer able to contain their mirth.

Günter wanted to keep the giant slug, his motives mysterious. Turned out this seafaring, jet-set slug was not for sale.

"No, no, we take him to Spetses tomorrow. This slug has traveled half way around the world with us, and only once did we get offered a meal—but, of course, we paid!"

"But you guys handled it the best so far," chuckled their blond-bearded leader. "We insist on buying you a drink."

I asked Günter what he had intended doing with the giant, black slug.

"Pickling it, of course," he said, his eyes glinting over gold-rimmed glasses. "And putting it in someone's cocktail."

Günter spent a season or two behind the bar thumbing fancy yacht magazines, reminiscing and window-shopping well beyond the restaurant's income capability. He eventually returned to his first-world career, the shipping business, where he gets to visit boat shows.

30

THE BEARD'S BULLION

Once upon a time the island was rich—very rich.

Its citizens had struck a deal with the ruling Ottomans whereby, in return for donating their first-born sons to the sultan's fleet, they would be granted license to trade freely. As a result the Hydriots plied the Mediterranean unhindered by the occupying Turkish Empire, accumulating wealth and power. To this day, as evidence of their success, the captains' spectacular stone mansions adorn the amphitheater that forms the little harbor.

According to island legend, in the absence of a national banking system, inhabitants of the time were prone to hiding their wealth in the cisternas (rainwater tanks) of their houses. The Orthodox Church in Greece enjoyed vast prosperity, and one local Hydriot priest, Baba Jannis, was said to have hoarded several hundred Louis XVI gold sovereigns. In current value the stash would exceed a million pounds sterling.

Even today the church carries considerable clout in the community. Citizens can be seen genuflecting and kissing the hands of long-bearded men in black robes on the streets. Distinctive, authoritative clerical figures wearing stovepipe hats, concealing manes of unshorn hair, waft to the front of queues in banks and post offices.

When the old beard passed on, his fortune never surfaced. The treasure, however, was rumored still to be buried somewhere on the grounds of his vestry. Today a grand manor occupies this site, and for many years it was owned by a retired English diplomat and his wife. The original church still stands adjacent.

"I'm going to Switzerland next week, and I'll pick up an auger as we seem to have exhausted all the island's alternative mining tools," said Rob. An auger was a ferocious-looking rock-munching device that tunnels.

I looked at the paraphernalia we had accumulated in our excavation—everything from the house vacuum cleaner to sharpened fence posts. Even a pneumatic *kanga* (jackhammer) was proving too puny. The island isn't nicknamed the Rock for nothing. I had to agree—we definitely needed a more robust tool if our dig was to proceed. We went inside to discuss our options.

It is the nature of any small society to gossip, and we were only too aware of the ridicule we would face if word got out that the distinguished gent and myself were looking for buried bullion.

Rob had initially hired an Albanian fellow to assist with the manual labor under the guise of dealing with an encroaching root system that had tunneled into the foundations of the house.

"There doesn't appear to be anything of an intrusive nature here, *Keerios*," said the help. Rob felt it prudent to let the fellow go rather than let him in on the wild scheme. Plus, by paying the lad, he would quite possibly be throwing hard-earned pension money into a bottomless pit—literally.

Rob and Audrey Browning were of New Age ilk, convinced not only that their house was planted on top of hidden gold but also that it was constructed on ancient lay lines, invisible energy lines that had healing powers and good karma. They had completely renovated the mansion upon purchase and at the time had not come across the original priest's cisterna. Nor were they aware of the mythical coins until years later.

They had reached a point in life when they were contemplating selling their home and moving back to England. The house was situated near the top of the town's steep hill, and the climb had become less charming as time passed. Convinced that the tales of lost gold should be investigated before they sold off, they had consulted the Ouija board.

There was, according to the departed priest's spirit, a fortune lying buried underneath the back courtyard. A definite downward thrust of a divining rod backed the beard up. There appeared to be a lot of supernatural evidence supporting the theory of hidden treasure.

The fact that the courtyard was enclosed and out of sight meant that the dig could take place in secret. I had known the Browning's for over a decade, and they knew me to be a man who could keep his own council.

Rob had meticulously recorded Audrey's cryptic Ouija board conversations with the departed beard. He'd drawn up plans, made measurements, and come up with an assessment worth investigating. If I threw in my lot and some muscle, they would cut me in for a third of the treasure. I was fully aware that despite the huge house, they lived on a retired diplomat's pension and were not able to justify the going rate for manual labor on a long shot.

I had nothing to loose, apart from a little sweat, by participating in this venture. In fact, I found the prospect of our treasure hunt exciting. I knew the island and its history well enough to know that the Hydriots of old had squirreled their savings in obscure places. The bottom of a water-filled cisterna was a known favorite.

Upon my arrival we would sit down each morning to discuss what the Ouija board had told Audry the night before. Rob had leaflets from Geneva coin collectors giving the value of sovereigns. He had drawn up progress graphs and the angles of our dig. We would ponder the next few feet.

Audrey would periodically appear with chilled *musta*, a local nonalcoholic grape juice, to quench our thirst and replenish our body fluids. We would hack and chop at the tunnel face. With each change in shale texture, we inspected the *bazi*, or rubble, for signs of hope. Three meters down and under, we came across what appeared to be lime, which, according to historical documents, was an important ingredient in the construction of old water wells.

This gave us encouragement and impetus to dig on. We would occasionally flood the pit with water in an attempt to soften the ground, which then created mud. We would generally knock off before lunch, and I would make my way down to the port only partially cleaned of the grime.

"A spot of gardening at the Browning's," I would say to the quizzical expressions on the harbor front. After some weeks it was noted that every time I had finished a spot of gardening, I resembled a tin miner more than a horticulturalist. Comments like "What are they planting, a forest?" were frequent.

I looked forward to my mornings on the Brownings' front terrace, discussing and dreaming, sipping tea and musta in our shorts. I was happy measuring, plotting, and passing the morning in good company. Better than fishing (anyone could do that), we were digging for hidden treasure. It was a grand hobby.

We had a strong rumor, time, a historical location in an enclosed area, imagination, and a sense of dare. Why not? We had nothing to loose.

Eventually the excavated pile filled the back courtyard, and anyone looking out the kitchen window was bound, at the very least, to comment on the mine dump. By this time electric lighting had to be used at the face. So we made the painful decision to fill the hole in and replaced the *plakakia* (stone tiles), vowing to reopen the tunnel the following season.

We never did. Audrey needed a hip operation, Rob's joints wouldn't tolerate the strain, I opened an Internet shop in the port—life had moved on. The Browning's sold their mansion and moved back to Blighty, where the hills aren't quite so steep and cabs have wheels.

I wonder if the new owner would like to know the location of this dig. We could possibly find an adventurous young Irishman to man the auger. A fitting end would be to mail a slice of the treasure check to the poltergeists who initiated the find, Mr. and Mrs. Ouija, c/o London, with thanks and vindication!

31

SPIDERS AND SLEEP

I returned to my bunker from dinner at the Brownings one night, and taking off my jacket in the gloom before turning on the bedside lamp, I noticed a black sock on my bed, caught in the corner six inches above the pillow.

The sock stood up when I switched on the main light. It had eight legs as long as my little finger.

Africa offers a larger variety of arachnids and other microterrors, so I had some experience in dealing with this type of invasion. I also know that rare species should be protected; nature conservation becomes second nature with some upbringings.

The spider didn't take much coaxing onto the end of a broom. I awkwardly carried it outside and placed it under the lemon tree of the *yaya* from whom I rented a couple of rooms and a tiny outside ablution.

We had a most amicable accommodation arrangement. She would surprise me with the odd kitchen treat; I would lend a periodic hand with the hammer or shopping. She nurtured the little garden; I enjoyed fresh basil and lemons. We respected personal space—the perfect *yaya* for a bloke on his own.

It was spring on the island. Flowers and buzzing insects were everywhere. Also, I discovered, the tarantula's had come out of hibernation and were beginning to stake out their summer hunting grounds.

Sharing a small room with a spider that large would have had a detrimental affect on sleep, African past or no. My eight-legged friend could have the garden; indoors was for humans. Me.

The next morning, my *yaya* assured me that I had been very unlucky as she had only seen two in all her years of living there. She occupied the other blocked-off half of a small L-shaped cottage and had her own separate outside loo.

A crack in the wall above my bed had widened a centimeter during a recent seismological event, and even though the spider was probably too big to have emerged through it, other crawlies could, so I moved the bed into an opposite corner of the room.

Almost to the day a year later, I returned one evening to again find my hairy friend above the bed, just a few inches from my pillow. I got the broom, thinking that if this was the same spider, then he'd lost a lost of weight—and was a lot more agile!

It scuttled up the broom handle, which I dropped like a hot coal. Luckily, the little blighter ran up the wall, not under furniture, and I was able to encourage it slowly onto the brush.

The *yaya* told me it was probably the same one; it just hadn't had a substantial meal yet.

A couple nights later, a juvenile, about two and a half inches in diameter, occupied the corner behind the television, diagonally opposite the bed. I used scrunched paper to apprehend this arachnid, and both were placed into the kitchen garbage bag.

I lay in bed feeling guilty that I had been a bit harsh on the spider when it dawned on me that it could, with its fangs, chew its way through a layer of plastic—and escape into the kitchenette.

I got up and tied a second bag over the rubbish. No sooner was I horizontal than I figured if it could escape through one bag, then why not two?

Slumber would be easier knowing the spider was outside, so I got up again, put on a robe, and took the bag out to the shower, where an escape wouldn't be drastic and the *skoopethia* (rubbish) would still be safe from marauding cats. I figured I would carry it down the hill in the morning.

One less *tarantoola* in the neighborhood would surely reduce the odds of another of these "unusual" encounters. I dismissed the subject from mind.

After the late movie the following night, I had just switched off the light when I heard, and felt, a plop on the bed next to me.

Had a small pebble fallen from the ceiling? A pebble would have fallen against the wall side, not on the pillow next to my head.

I flipped on the bedside lamp just in time to see four hairy legs disappear between the mattress and the wall. Further attempts to capture the little swine failed when it eight-legged it underneath the bed frame.

I gingerly inspected each sheet, blanket, and pillow for the invader as I stripped the bunk. Sympathy and a conservationist mind-set waned rapidly when the search progressed to shaking out every dusty old boot and shoe piled under the double bed.

Hunting spiders and moving furniture in the middle of the night tends to discourage kip and encourage irritation. The heavy mattress overturned, dustier suitcases dragged out—eventually the little bastard broke cover, scuttled for the door, and was unceremoniously assisted outside by a swift sweep.

Worried that I might have damaged a leg, I went outside to inspect.

"*Tee echies?*" asked the *yaya* in her gown, wanting to know what I was doing with a torch under the lemon tree in the early hours.

"*Po-po-po!* Another one?" she responded. "Most unusual."

She was equally perplexed as to why I hadn't stomped on it in the first place. "Next year we only have more."

The following day, I popped over to my neighbor's house, where a couple of Syrian mates were renovating. There was a yelp from the garden as one of them had uncovered a juvenile nestling under some leaves.

"Where we come from, these things can kill you." Stomp.

I belatedly argued that the Hydra breed was comparatively docile and not known to be deadly. Also, for some reason, they only seemed to inhabit one side of the hill, a limited colony. I still wasn't convinced genocide was the way to go with an endangered species.

This conviction changed the next day.

After I had seated myself in the tiny outhouse (I had to bend slightly in the shower to avoid hitting roof beams and watch out for elbows when drying), I went to grab a roll.

Directly in front of my hand was the mother of all tarantulas—fat and hairy as a mouse, about to spawn several hundred offspring by the look of it.

The loo brush broke. I took solace in the fact that this hunt had been motivated by self-defense. I already had the jitters after only half a dozen territorial disputes; a new generation of them was too appalling to contemplate. Tarantulas are nocturnal hunters, so upon entering the bunker at night, I had already taken to scouring the corners and ceilings and shaking sheets. Divisions of her brood would have had me on the street, and such secure, comfortable, long-term bachelor digs were hard to come by.

It got worse.

A couple of days later, I was drying my back off after a cooling, midnight shower, when I felt what I thought was an olive twig or locust leg snagged in the towel. My little bathroom stood under an olive tree, and bits blew in periodically between the tiles.

I felt a quick, sharp pain in my left index finger.

As I pulled my hand from behind my back I saw, with horror, the daddy of all tarantulas hanging from my fingertip—hairy inches, multiple legs, splayed in the air.

I instinctively flicked and simultaneously banged my head on the beam, yelping.

The only decent armament, the loo brush, hadn't yet been replaced after my disagreement with mummy spider. The perpetrator had vanished, so dazed and starkers I dashed into the garden in search of a club, light flooding out the open door.

"*Tee echies?*" Yaya had come to investigate the commotion and hadn't quite comprehended the sight before her. I was sucking one index, and covering with the other hand.

"*Pali tarantoola.*" Another, I explained, backing naked and still unarmed into the loo.

The only weapon on hand inside was the toilet-paper bin itself or a toothbrush. When I lifted the metal disposer, my adversary made a break for the back of the porcelain.

I missed with a noisy swipe, and it dashed toward my dripping self. I was then motivated to get really active with the dustbin.

The *yaya* could only hear an unholy racket going on in the tiny bathroom, and her voice sounded concerned.

"*Eesai endaxi?*" Was I okay?

Had her tenant finally gone around the twist? Cavorting naked in the garden at midnight and now making enough noise to wake the dead. Other lights in the neighborhood went on.

I eventually emerged, wrapped, holding one of the eight limp legs.

"*Bravo sou!*" said the *yaya*, applauding the dangle.

A week later, the inverted and curled corpse was still lying beneath the olive tree, so big that the ants hadn't managed to move the exoskeleton. My mate, an Australian skipper, had come to visit and was impressed when I showed him the evidence to go with two small puncture marks on my finger.

"*Bravo sou!*" said the *yaya* for the umpteenth time as she passed, still happy that I had finally learned the law of the jungle.

"It's your *spiti* (house), and you are the man."

It took this man some weeks before he stopped shaking out shoes and towels. I still suspect that the *yaya*'s magnified spectacles were always underprescribed: two in twenty years indeed!

32

TWO TONYS AND THE TRAUMATIC TRINKET

Bill and I would usually spend St. Patrick's Day preparing stew and practicing the art of making, and sampling, Irish coffee. Tony, the only other Paddy on the island was a builder and part-time fisherman who lived in Vlichos, a little village down the coast. He had promised to bring some Guinness and was due to arrive before the rest of the gang turned up that evening.

He hadn't showed by the time the party was in full swing, so I gave him a call, thinking it was unusual for my fellow countryman to be missing out on our national day. He sounded exhausted.

"I can't tell you why now, and you probably won't believe me when I do, but a funny thing happened," he said. "And it's certainly not something that I would try to describe over the phone. But when I do tell you, you have got to promise me you won't tell a soul."

As excuses for missing a party go, this one tops the list.

Tony had apparently been suffering from a dreadful cold that particular blustery day and decided to spend it in bed, gathering his resources for our St Patrick's bash.

"The wind was howling, and the sea had gotten really rough, when I got a phone call from my neighbor, Jorgo, to say my boat was in danger of being smashed against the rocks. He advised me to drag my caïque up the beach."

Tony went onto to describe how he had forced himself out from under the covers, dragged on his "wellie boots," and gone down to pull his boat out of harm's way.

"It weighed a ton, and in my weakened condition, I only managed to shift it a couple of meters."

He'd returned home, got undressed, and climbed back into bed. No sooner had he settled when the phone rang again.

"Leatherboy this time, wanting to know if I had a hack-saw."

Leatherboy Tony was the only other expat resident of Vlichos, so nicknamed not just to alleviate confusion between the two Tonys but because of his affection for leather gear. In summer his black leather shorts promenaded along the harbor front. In winter he would exchange his hosen for tight biker pants. He was a noticeable fellow in the small village. Leatherboy Tony and Irish Tony—it stopped us muddling the two.

"Hi, Tone, can I come around and borrow a little saw?" Irish Tony had one of the best-equipped private workshops on the island. Leatherboy was a musician and cook, not usually prone to handyman stuff.

"Sure," Irish Tony had said. "But I am in bed with the flu, so just let yourself in downstairs and help yourself."

No sooner had Irish Tony nodded off when the phone went again. Jorgo informed him that the waves had increased and that Tony's boat still wasn't safe.

"So I got all dressed up again, this time with a coat because it had started raining too, and managed to drag the boat up another couple of feet."

On cue, when the Irishman was just dozing off between the sheets, the phone rang again. This time Leatherboy's voice had a hint of distress in it, but Irish Tony was feeling too off-color himself to take much notice.

"Err—I think I need a pair of pliers as well."

"Just come and take whatever you want," said Irish Tony, beginning to loose patience with matters.

"I swear, I had just nodded of when the bleedin' phone went again," he explained. "It was Jorgo to tell me that the sea had gotten even rougher and that the waves were now crashing right up the beach."

Tony had dutifully donned his foul-weather gear and gone out for a third time to secure his craft. By now it was the middle of the afternoon and the chances of a siesta before the party were looking slim, but he decided to try to catch a nap anyway.

"The frigging phone went again, I tell you." This time Leatherboy's voice emitted distinctly strained sounds.

"I can't do this by myself. I need help."

"What?"

"Well, err, it's a bit difficult to describe," squeaked Leatherboy. "It's awkward to explain, but I think I need to use your vice."

"What's the problem?"

"I'll have to show you," whined Leatherboy. "But you have to promise that you will never tell anyone."

"Just tell me what the problem is."

"Well, I would go to a hospital, but what with this weather, there are no ferries off the island," Leatherboy added to emphasize the level of crisis.

Intrigued, Irish Tony got dressed for the fourth time and went outside and down to the workshop.

"I saw Leatherboy hobbling painfully along the path to my house, like a fella who had been the victim of a serious assault."

I believe the device is called a cock ring, something a man inserts over his penis to maintain an erection and prolong orgasm. Leatherboy had apparently been experimenting with this gadget at home alone and found he couldn't get it off. The more he fiddled, the more the swelling increased and the more difficult it became to dislodge.

It certainly wasn't the sort of predicament he wished to share. So he had limped over to Irish Tony's workshop and picked up a small hacksaw with the intent of cutting said metal tourniquet off.

The trouble was, by the time he got home, the swelling had all but covered the gadget. Bent double and with shaking hands, he found the task impossible.

Still loath to share his plight, he figured that if he could grab the ring with a pair of pliers and saw carefully he might solve the problem.

He had limped the half kilometer to the workshop and back, only to find the affliction had increased yet more in size and darkened in color. Attempting to grasp the trinket by now proved beyond the limit of tolerance.

After some hours of ever-increasing pain, he had feared he was at serious risk of permanently loosing valuable anatomical bits. The prospect of a whole night in this condition was too awful to contemplate.

"I'm not going to even tell you the condition he was in, poor bloke," said Irish Tony, shuddering at the memory. "You shoulda' seen his eyes when he saw I had the fever shakes, making the hacksaw vibrate. So while you lot were having a grand ol' time, I was performing a delicate surgery on some bloke's winkle in my workshop vice. I missed the party but I tell you something, it won't be a St. Paddy's I'll forget in a hurry."

Nor apparently will Leatherboy, who can still sport his shorts with pride on whatever island he's ultimately migrated to.

33

PEDRO THE PAINTER

"You gotta help me man," said Pedro over the phone sounding more distraught than usual.

"Boogie is dead!"

Pedro the Painter, an American artist, spent most of his time trying to simplify life. The trouble was, the more he simplified it, the more complicated it became. He was not a man accustomed to timepieces; indeed, he didn't consult calendars either. It was well known that Pedro and punctuality were not words to utter in the same breath. He took island living to slower level.

On my way over the hill, I pondered my friend's latest predicament. His charge had suddenly kicked the bucket under mysterious circumstances. He certainly seemed to be having a run of bad luck.

Only the day before he had called me from Athens wanting to know the DEH (electricity office) phone number.

"Do you think the National Electric Company of Greece can switch individual apartments off?"

I told him I doubted it and wanted to know why.

He explained that he had decided to escape the island and took a mutual acquaintance up on an offer to stay in her swish Kolonaki apartment while she was away. Just as the early-morning hydrofoil was pulling out of the harbor, he remembered that in his haste to make the first dolphin, he had forgotten to turn the electric stove off and was concerned about combustibility.

I inquired as to alternative means of gaining access to his flat.

"Only the landlord has a spare set of keys, and the house is a mess," he said. "Plus, I don't want him to think I'm a fire hazard."

He decided the best thing to do was to cut short his stay in the Big Olive and return to the island on the next dolphin, the first of which was early the next day. Stressed about his abode, but figuring that there was little he could do about the situation, he picked up a few vital art supplies and took himself to dinner.

Pedro was a good-looking bloke not known for discarding flirtational opportunities—especially when on parole in the big city. This meant a late night had followed.

Having nodded off shortly before dawn, having brought a friend back to the flat for a nightcap, he had overslept and not heard the alarm go off.

"First thing I knew was when the phone rang to say there was a taxi waiting outside the apartment, and I only had half-an-hour to make the hydrofoil."

It being out of season, there were only two dolphins a day to and from the Rock, one in the early morning and one in the late afternoon. He dared not miss the early boat; smoldering ruins were beginning to haunt his imagination.

He had just made the hydrofoil and was settling back in his seat, mulling over the chaos that had been the trip, when an awful thought dawned on him.

In his haste to flee he had scrunched up the sheets, emptied the ashtrays and generally squared the flat away as best he could in forty-five seconds before legging it for the waiting cab.

"I was feeling a little slothful for not properly tidying up my hostess's apartment when it suddenly struck me," Pedro said. "The condom—the used condom—was still lying on the floor beside the bed on the side opposite the door!"

He had followed instructions and left the keys inside the apartment on the kitchen table before pulling the Yale-locked front door behind him. Without access back in, there was no way the evidence could be cleared up before the owner got back, even if he made a turn-around trip back to Athens.

He would have to explain the item in question with much embarrassment, perhaps over a nice dinner?

He was still stewing over this pickle when he got off the boat and was immediately accosted by a lady in need of help. Damsels in distress were Pedro's specialty, and with his guard already lowered, he accepted the mission.

"Ahh, Pedro, just the man I wanted to see."

Lena, his pretty neighbor, was about to board the same boat on its way back to Athens and had asked Pedro if he wouldn't mind dog sitting for a couple of days.

All he had to do was pop over in the morning, throw some food in a bowl, and let the doggie have a run around the terrace before locking it inside for the night. The mutt, Boogie, was a highly pedigreed miniature Yorkshire terrier, no bigger than some sewer rats, and would be no problem he was assured. It sounded simple enough.

"Thank you, Pedro, you saved my life," expressed Lena. "Here are the keys to the flat, and there's dog food in the fridge."

I arrived to find Pedro pacing the terrace in a state of distress. He point to an ominous six-inch stain on the tiles outside his front door.

"A Boogie stain man. I've scrubbed with detergent, chlorine, hot water, and it still won't disappear."

"What happened," I asked. "How did a perfectly healthy young dog die within twenty-four hours under your care?"

"I don't know," he moaned. "I got up, fed the dog, let it out on the terrace while I popped down to Four Corners supermarket to get some coffee, and when I came back, there was Boogie. I couldn't have been gone ten minutes, and I returned to see this ball of fluff just lying there in a dark puddle—pink tongue hanging out."

Lena's terrace was situated above Pedro's house, so the little dog must have fallen the height of a full story and died instantly.

"There's been a large grey cat loitering about the neighborhood. Maybe it chased Boogie. Some leap for the mutt to have cleared the wall. I didn't know they could jump that high."

"What did you do with the corpse?" I inquired.

"Well, I didn't know whether Lena would like to bury the pet herself, and I didn't want it attracting flies, so I put it in her freezer."

The look on my face prompted him to add quickly, "I did wrap it in a plastic bag so it wouldn't contaminate the food."

"What am I going to say to Lena? She loved that mutt."

He had no contact number for Lena and decided the only thing to do was inform her friend Iris, in the hope that the news could be broken gently to her before she got up the hill. Visions of her opening the fridge and finding a frozen dog were appalling.

"She'll freak out," said Pedro. "I toyed with the idea of leaving a warning note on the freezer door but that seemed even more bizarre. I just hope we can catch her before she heads up home."

We were still pondering the burial of a frozen dog on our way down to the port, when Iris spotted us.

"Ahh, Pedro, just the man I wanted to see," said Iris, with her geriatric blind mongrel in tow. "I have to go to Athens, and I was wondering if you wouldn't mind looking after Fluffy for a few days?"

Seeing the look of incredulity on my friend's face, I couldn't help but guffaw and quickly apologized to Iris, who must have thought my response rude.

"Trust me, Iris. Pedro is out of the dog-sitting, keyholding business for a while."

Pedro has returned to the first world, but nobody predicts he won't be back.

34

DONKEY WALKABOUT

Putting along the coast, peering with binoculars, I was at my wit's end. How could such a large animal have vanished? Particularly a high-profile donkey like Dardo. Three days, with everyone on the island looking out for him, and still no sign of the blighter.

I had discovered a broken tether rope when I went to feed him in the morning and scouted the immediate area as he rarely wandered far. Normally he responded heartily to the call for breakfast.

My second port of call was down to Four Corners supermarket where he had been known to *klepsie* (steal) the vegetables on display—a favorite habit of runaway donkeys as I had already discovered with Bluebell.

"*Oxi*," Dimitri tutted. "I would have noticed the thief."

Dimitri's shop stood on an important junction in the Kamini-port road, and little traffic, mule or man, passed unremarked. A large, unattended appetite would certainly have been noted.

I extended my search, spreading the word further a field. The port shopkeepers, other vegetable grocers, Kamini-ites, and the muleteer union—nothing. Nobody had seen Dardo.

Considering this community knew exactly which cat belonged to whom, and where that person lived, the loss of a very distinctive donkey was extraordinary. A Cypriot donkey is a breed as large as a mule. Dardo was retired and had a conspicuous grey coat and big head. He would infiltrate port-front tavernas to nuzzle for bread. Everyone knew Dardo.

Concluding that someone had borrowed him or was playing a prank, I gave up looking at sunset.

By the second morning he still hadn't turned up. The police put out an APB and further spots were investigated—Mandraki Bay to Palameetha. It was established that Dardo hadn't been seen boarding a fishing boat, hydrofoil, ferry or water taxi, which meant he was definitely still on the Rock.

By day three I took up the offer to motor around the island on a mate's caïque, as by then the vanishing of Dardo had become an island mystery that demanded solving.

It was getting late, and we were headed back to the harbor when I spotted a long shadow behind a shrub. An open patch of land, adjacent to an old mansion, smack between Kamini and the port—I noted the spot.

The loudest hee-haw you can imagine greeted me, big ears up. Dardo had been grazing randomly and managed to wrap the dragging rope around the base of a bush a few times. Eventually the rope became so short he was harnessed right up against a well-nibbled shrub, a mere couple hundred meters from home.

"Ahh, you found him," chortled Felix from his usual chair as Dardo and I passed by the Three Brothers next day.

"Gone walk about, had he?"

"No, actually, Felix, I went walkabout; he went standabout!"

35

AU PAIRS AND ELECTRICIANS

"I propose a new pomp," said Top-Job, surveying the shiny red bomb that was the water pump.

"Another one! *Ella*, Yannis," I exclaimed pointing to a line of eight laid out, corpse-like, in varying stages of rust. "This one didn't even last six months!"

"But you have swimming pool. This is the problem." His was tone emphatic. "I will go to my laboratory to get a new pomp."

Yannis's vocabulary was extraordinary. He would come out with surprising words made even more so by the look of him. A hard-working fellow, covered in grime, sporting flip-flops for nine months of the year, with thin, wispy hair wafting, he was a jovial soul with an unusual lexicon.

"A man must have water; otherwise he will dehydrate," he stated as he trundled off with his little donkey carrying the toolbox—a bad sign.

"You coming straight back, Yanni?" I called hopefully after the departing wisp.

"*Amessos*," immediately, he waved, not looking back. "I need the Lion to carry the new pomp." Top-Job had named his donkey Leo because it "was strong like a lion."

Feisty is a polite word for the little donkey's behavior. Parked outside Top-Job's lab halfway up Donkeyshit Lane, he did not attract petting like most of the patient mules on the port, as he was prone instead to foot stomping and, on occasion, nipping.

Leo was also an incessant chewer. He had a close call one afternoon when a low-slung, high-voltage cable swung into chomping range.

Imagined consequences, both comic and tragic, were amplified when Yannis, yanking Leo's chin rope away from the partially gnawed cable, bellowed, "Again you biting things! I should let you eat this, but where I get a new donkey this time?"

Some days later Top-Job and Leo turned up at the house, replacement red pomp in the saddle. A family illness had caused the delay this time.

"I hope this one lasts, Yanni," I said dryly, watching him lay number nine to rest, the brightest in a row of fading-red ex-pumps.

"But we need the three phase," which essentially meant upgrading a building's entire electrical wiring system. This was his standard reply to most electrical enigmas, a procedure that I knew to interpret as involving major cost and complication.

"He knows about this," was all Yannis said, referring no doubt to the house owner.

The house was in my neighborhood, and I kept an eye on it. The owner was in shipping, a Turkish Jew who threw generous *Pascha* (Easter) parties involving—unusually—suckling pigs rather than traditional Greek lamb.

A fellow of individual style and hospitality, Morey had bought a pair of adjacent houses on the hill's apex and built a pool where a dividing back wall used to be. Numerous young olive trees surrounded by slate terracing filled the estate. Space to entertain, and he did, with flair.

He called a few days later to ask me if I would give a helping hand when the family, which included two young sprogs, came out for a festive fortnight.

"With pleasure," I replied. "Doing what?"

A pause while he found the name of my intended profession.

"Our au pair, shall we say." The fellow had wicked humor. "Has Yannis come?"

I explained about the usual procedure with the pump a week prior.

"Well, he has a couple of little jobs to do for me also, but he's probably waiting until after Christmas," he mused with the surety of a fellow who understood island time.

He was right—work is generally postponed once schools let out until after New Year's. Barring an emergency, the chance of obtaining industry is beyond optimism.

I checked the house before going down to meet the mid-morning boat on a cold grey day. The family, some frozen geese, smoked salmon, a bag of truffles, and bundles of other unobtainable delicacies disembarked. They were looking forward to their cozy home after a fraught trip.

I assured Morey as we followed the mules up Donkey-shit that the house was immaculate. The maid had done a sparkling job; there were new candles, clean carpets, fresh duvets and towels, neatly placed wood in the fireplace, and basic victuals from Four Corners in the fridge. The even had hot running water.

I had covered all eventualities and knew they would be impressed.

"No worries! You guys settle in and give me a call once you have rested," I said, leaving them to continue the final leg up to the house.

The phone was ringing as I approached my apartment.

"You were up here this morning right—and everything was normal—yes?" Morey's voice had a strange pitch, like he was suppressing something.

"Two hours before your boat came in, why?" I couldn't think of anything abnormal with the home.

"Well, Yannis is here with his drill, and he says he thought we were coming tomorrow," he paused and added, "but even next week would have been premature by the looks—"

I went directly up.

Yannis's drill had, in a couple of hours, gouged trenches of proportion, horizontally and perpendicularly, along almost every interior wall, smothering freshly washed crockery with dust and sprinkling sheets and furniture with rubble. Pebbles were strewn across the floor. Industrious stuff! Top Job's three-phase project had gotten off to a flying start.

"The time is run away." Yannis was dismantling the drill in the background. "I want to do top job for Mister Morey, and I wait for special parts from Switzerland. I know Mister Morey is from the Swiss, very good quality, only the best, but there was delay with the transportation." Morey was headquartered in Geneva.

Yannis was short on time but never short on answers. Morey grinned good-naturedly as he took me outside.

"And look," he chuckled, "he's even going to install the new garden lights!"

The manicured multiterraced garden with its swimming pool looked like a mini–war zone. The drill had made fast work, decimating the exterior walls too. I was amazed at how understanding Morey was being under the circumstances.

"I could laugh, or I could cry," was his philosophic response. "This is Hydra, I'm lucky an electrician turned up at all, and I am on holiday."

"And the air is moving very fast, ees difficult," said the wisp as he and his apprentice scurried past, bristling with tools. "But I will fix everything." Indeed a brisk breeze was scattering dust into everything.

Moray opted for peace and quiet—the drilling stopped. It was decided that if basic amenities worked, then perhaps the excavating and cementing could be postponed until the holiday was over.

By nightfall the house was swept, the lights and appliances worked (gaping trenches not withstanding), and the family had running water. The goose was delicious, and I recommend that any bachelor alone take up au pairing over the festive season. It's like being a member of a family and lending a little extra help, like putting the kids to bed after cocktail hour.

A few months later, Top-Job and I were inspecting the remains of a washing machine at a different site, Clive's house.

"But they have the laundry machine, this is the problem," tutted Yannis with the same conviction as he had about the red pump. "It must have the three phase."

"Perfect," I said to Yannis, "they're coming tomorrow, so we can start immediately."

He looked at me sideways and chuckled as he ran a hand through the wisp in contemplation.

"Better I take it to my laboratory for fix," he said, loading Leo with the faulty appliance.

Working with Yannis was a treat, an endless source of entertainment and jargon. It must be said, in real electrical or plumbing emergencies, Leo was roused, and Top-Job saved the day many a time. His skills were in such demand that he spared little time for lab work.

The washing machine sat in the laboratory for four years—awaiting a "special part" from some distant oriental factory.

"It is old, so it is complex to find this part. They don't manufacture this kind anymore, and they have to investigate," became his standard reply as I walked down Donkey-shit past his lab, giving berth to Leo.

"But I have very good new German washing machine," would drift down after me, "and I will install it for you free."

Eventually three phase got installed, and a new automatic machine was delivered before the part ever materialized. The client noted this point after the new machine was connected.

"I am still waiting for the supplies, then maybe you will have a spare machine too," were Top-Job's parting words as he dragged Leo off.

Perhaps one day he will delve into the pile of pending electronics in his laboratory and restructure his business as Top-Job's Antiques and Uninvestigated Spare Parts.

36

ANOTHER TOP-JOB

New house owners on the island have to contend with the fact that their home may be called by another name, sometimes for years after they have lived in it.

Newly renovated villas of opulence, lovingly called "Bougainvillea Sunset," may still get "Oh, you mean the Blogg House" two decades later. It depends on what era the building is associated with and who haunted the place at the time.

Top-Job had recently installed three-phase electricity in Solveigh's house, known as the Fisher House to others who remembered when Sam F was the owner. Another bunch knew it as Mardas's little house, referring its subsequent owner, and once it was even rumored to be Joan Collins's house on account of the fact that we had taken her round to show her the Sixth's chef's cottage, and Sasha, Joan's son, had said he liked it.

Anyway, now it was Solveigh's house, and she was putting her very distinctive stamp on the place. A German lass of stock, with energy and organizational genes that surpassed those of most mortals, she was married to a gentle surgeon, Georgo, a smoker with a smile.

Georgo retained his practice in Athens and commuted weekends, leaving Solveigh to organize the house. What started out as a lick 'o paint job grew into a project that included creation of a studio, darkroom, laundry … all requiring a various selection of appliances, which required updated electrics.

Top-Job had installed the new power system throughout the house and garden as promised well before Christmas, and she looked forward to a relaxing break in the fully functional comfort of her new home.

She decided to celebrate that year with a pre-Christmas party and invited a mixed bag of guests and nationalities—Dutch poets, Canadian writers, English artists, doctors, lawyers, and locals. Affectionate grizzly bear hugs welcomed them all as they trickled in. A huge, undecorated pine tree adorned the high-ceilinged living room, as was the German tradition. Guests were encouraged to each add their touch by choosing baubles and trinkets from a box at the tree's base … a nice touch.

Visitors cooed and complimented Solveigh on the new design, particularly the kitchen. She had proudly laid the banquet out on the sideboard and centerpiece of an open-plan kitchen. Dark wood, white marble, copper utensils, thickly carpeted throughout, it was something out of a Christmas "country kitchen" catalog.

The house and the party were a huge success and started the festive season on a high note.

Solveigh decided to pop into Athens for the day to do some last minute errands before the city closed for the holidays. Before leaving on the early hydrofoil, timers and central heating devices were set—lighting Teutonically automated.

Expecting to see her newly wired cozy house aglow when she unlocked the front door that evening, she was greeted instead by an eerie darkness. Laden with shopping she stepped inside and into a foot of cold water.

"It was like a swimming pool in the kitchen. Things floated." Solveigh had gotten quite excited about the matter and immediately shared her hysteria with Top-Job, the prime suspect behind the sabotage.

Yannis was good in emergencies and came straight round with his little donkey Leo. If she was expecting him to show some remorse over the atrocity, then she was mistaken. Surveying the carnage before him, he said proudly, "You see, Madam, top job—only the best. If you hadn't had my engineering and three phase, maybe you have no house. It could have burned down, or an electrocution could have occurred. The safety system is working very well. The problem is the water heater, is very old, and is better to have new with the three phase."

Yannis was adept at taking the wind out of sails and reaping full benefit of the change in power supply. "I fix everything now. You are lucky it didn't occur when you had your guests."

Sure enough, the old *thermofisino* had sprung a leak, which directed itself, gully-like, straight to a hole in the top of the wall, right above where Top-Job had buried new electrical wiring—a 240-volt faucet!

"You see," he boasted after wading across the kitchen to the fuse board, torch in hand. "The safety fuse is fully functional. Nothing really bad can happen."

37

THE MEDIATOR

From what I could gather, George and his comrade Tomas had decided on their first night to go out for dinner before their first day on the job. Rubin had been dead against the idea of his workforce leaving the premises, claiming that he wanted them all up bright and early at 7:30, ready to commence graft.

There had been some sort of disagreement, the upshot of which was that when the Albanians went out for dinner, Rubin had set a home time. George had steamed off, and as the evening progressed, his indignation grew. Being told when to be home smacked of curfew, and George had a fundamental and intense dislike for those sorts of rules—an attitude for which he had served a dozen years behind bars.

Convinced he held the moral high ground, he opted to ignore the home time and stayed for a nightcap or two after the meal. George and Tomas returned to find the high electric gate to the house locked. The buzzer failed to get any response. George began to make a racket. A deceptively frail looking fellow, he yanked one of the bars loose on the gate and managed to squeeze through the gap.

An agitated Rubin tapped his watch as he greeted George. What happened next is subject to different points of view, but the upshot of the discussion progressed to the point of George grabbing a carving knife and waving it menacingly under Rubin's nose.

"I tell you, be back by ten o'clock. It is now midnight. How you get up in the morning?" Rubin had whined at George before the weapon had been drawn.

"I haven't officially started work yet, and in any case, so long as I turn up for work and do a good job for the hours I am employed, what I do with my spare time is non of your f***ing business." George launched his case in voluminous tones.

"I'm the boss, and I say you cannot work so good if you have been out all night partying. If you do this again, I tell Solveigh." Rubin was an enthusiastic foreman and probably would have made a great corporal.

"And how dare you lock us out! Who do you think you are? You know what we do in Albania to people who lock other people in or out?" George was smarting and had no intention of taking orders.

"You no in Albania now. Here I am in charge. I call Solveigh. You see"—Rubin went to get the phone on the floor of the empty lounge—"you no more go out in the evening."

Tomas apparently begged George to cool down, telling him to think about the income and ignore the Argentinean fool. But out came the knife.

I got on well with the Albanians; they were generally a reserved lot who kept to themselves, unlike most of the other polygamy of nationalities that had infiltrated the Rock's society.

There was one personal drawback with this influx of folk: it didn't take long for my piecemeal work to evaporate. Prior to their arrival, I had been just about the only full-time handyman, and there was always demand for a cheerful pair of hands and legs. A lick 'o paint here, a garden to prune there kept the wolf from the door.

Soon, however, fairly needy unskilled labor on the island was abundant—probably a good thing for me in the long run as it forced me to look for alternatives. Otherwise, I may well have just remained "Er … David,"* Jack-of-dwindling-all forever.

My skills and background allowed me to move up the ladder and accept some responsibility. I began managing houses (holding keys and handling accounts was a step above the odd jobs I had been doing).

Solveigh met me off the boat when it landed at Zea Marina port in Piraeus and filled me in on what she knew as she drove us out to her house in Kiffisia, a well-to-do suburb on the outskirts of Athens. She had left the renovating team there the previous evening.

Within hours of her departure a rhubarb of mega proportions had erupted between Argentina and Albania, culminating in the former refusing to come out of a locked room for fear of being knifed.

We arrived at the mansion to find Tomas painting and George sitting with a newspaper and coffee.

"He won't tell me what to do. Says I threatened him," George said calmly. "I just told him that having spent half my life in jail, I was not about to be locked up by anyone."

Rubin and sidekick remained barricaded in the basement, where they had taken refuge the previous evening for fear of having their throats slit in the night.

---

* See appendix A for an explanation of this honorific.

"I no work with these man. He no listen, and he want to keel me. I go back Hydra," announced the animated South American.

I had George promise through the door that hostilities were at an end and a state of cease-fire existed. It was agreed that instructions would pass through me and that operations would commence on different floors. Rubin and his mate would paint upstairs, and George and Thomas would commence work in the basement. Rubin was thence coaxed out of his bunker.

Sensing that George was still smoldering, I took him off for a cooling beer and souvlaki at the taverna. He would rather leave and go back to the island than take orders from that man. I let him get it off his chest.

"No f***ing body is ever going to lock me up again. If I want to stay out all night, I can, just so long as the job is done, right?" George dared me with dark eyes.

I mollified the fellow over another pint and highlighted the advantages of securing independence by acquiring an upholstered wallet. I said that I would be there, and he wouldn't even have to talk to Rubin—and yes, we were free men out to enjoy ourselves after a hard day's graft.

He and I would have a grand time; plus the wages were good and the environment comfortable. We had a good giggle at the how those given the title "boss" turn into mini-Hitlers.

"I'll deal with Rubin. Don't let one stupid chap ruin this opportunity for you. Think of the savings; plus if you leave, then he wins. You need this job. And Solveigh is a really nice lady and always very fair. She will see you right at the end."

My Albanian mate's confidence secured, we ambled back to the house. The gate was locked.

"The bastard has locked us out again. You see what I mean? The guy is a *malaka*." George pressed violently on the buzzer a few times. The gate was eight or nine feet high, not an easy hurdle.

Solveigh had called me in for my supposed diplomatic skills to settle the matter before some grievous bodily harm befell the Argentinean "foreman." I had taken the chore on because gainful employment and a break from the Rock for a few days sounded like a decent opportunity. The last thing I had expected was to find myself banished to a night on the pavement with an enraged Albanian for company.

I thought about the situation I had gotten myself into. Rubin was a gentle fellow with a pedantic nature. A sandy-haired stickler who had suffered severe acne as a kid, he was the nephew of an artistic Argentinian chap who owned a shop and house on the Rock. His nature suited Solveigh's meticulousness, and he had been made foreman of the project. I didn't know Rubin's sidekick; he was a backpacker from Buenos Ares who had stayed with Rubin and elected to stay at the offer of a part-time job.

George had been one of the first Albanians to hit the Rock. Before Albania's communist regime collapsed following the fall of the Berlin Wall, George had supposedly spent the previous twelve years in solitary for political dissent. Once freed, he headed, like thousands of others, for Greece in search of work.

A small man with an understandably big chip, George was fluent in English, a poet with a sensitive side, and yet here I was with the "mild" fellow threatening to garrote the boss once we got inside.

Thomas let us in and explained that Rubin and mate had yet again barricaded themselves in the basement, perhaps fearing that the alleged new Albanian-Irish alliance would lead to actual throat slitting in retaliation for being locked on the street.

I called Solveigh to admit that I had failed in my mission, that half her labor force had again imprisoned themselves in the basement, and it was all I could do to stop the other half from spilling blood. She agreed to come around first thing the following morning, and the upshot of the affair was that Rubin would not emerge from his den until Irish and Albanians had left the building—for good.

A compromise of sorts was reached as it was agreed that timid Thomas could remain, take orders, and stay in at night. Solveigh's husband, Georgo the surgeon, ferried George and me down to the hydrofoil to Hydra, giggling with me at the absurdity that it took years for the rest of the parties to the rhubarb to see.

38

NOT A TOP-JOB

Anyone who has had dealings on the island involving electrics or plumbing knows that these matters can get convoluted. Simple leaks can turn into floods; a dickey appliance can cause suburban blackouts.

Project management sounded like a decent occupation, an elevation in industry that hinted at less menial labor—a bloke in charge.

I took the job of overseeing some renovations on a neighbor's estate hoping this would be an easier way to earn an income. I quickly learned that the phrase "taking charge" applied to anything in this environment is a delusion and that "project manager" translates into "mug who sits and waits forever."

One comes to expect the unexpected as part of doing any house maintenance and can be forgiven for suspecting the electricians and plumbers are in conspiracy. When they do eventually report for duty, it does not necessarily mean anything so optimistic as the start of work.

"But I cannot put the wiring until after the plumber has been." Top-Job's wispy dome jerked in the negative. "The water must come before the electricity. Otherwise we can have fatal accident."

Top-Job referred no doubt to an incident in which a heater had been installed above the shower in a Swedish-owned cottage, resulting in the near electrocution of Mummy Viking. Luckily she had not been standing under the nozzle and merely tested the water temperature with her hand while still standing outside the curtain in rubber-soled sandals. As it was, she looked like Tina Turner on a bad hair day that evening.

"I will arrange with the plumber and come back." The fact that Top-Job hadn't turned up with Leo the donkey and his tool chest was perhaps a clue that he hadn't actually scheduled the commencement of electrical operations anyway.

"But Yanni, where is Leo?"

He knew what I was angling at.

"He is at the laboratory waiting. I have to check the system first to see what I need. Then I bring Leo and the right equipment"—Top-Job was never without plausible counterargument—"so as not to make the poor donkey carry the unnecessary."

"When, Yanni?" Chances of a straight answer were slim, but it did no harm to ask.

"*Methavrio* the plumber will come, and I will come after." The wisp trotted off with his customary over-the-shoulder wave.

The day after tomorrow gave one hope that plumbing would commence within the week—maybe.

The word *avrio* is used with such frequency that it has lost its credibility—like *manyana* in Latin American countries. So *methavrio* sounds almost like a fixed appointment, as it indicates that tomorrow is booked and such things as schedules are being kept.

A fortnight later the plumber turned up. My suspicions were already aroused when he too arrived solo. On the job, he usually brought a sidekick, who also lugged the tools.

"But the electrician has not been!" The chap looked appropriately disappointed. "First must come the electricity—with no *revma*, I have no tools, and I must cut tiles and pipes. I will speak to Yannis."

"When?"

"*Methavrio* he will be here, and I will come after." Familiar circles.

"Next time bring Benny." We both knew that dragging an employee and tools along showed more commitment to activity.

Top-Job and Leo arrived the following week with a *kanga* drill. A half-hour's trench carving in the walls created a mini bombsite.

Yannis started packing up. "I'm afraid we need the plumber. I must know where he is putting the pipes, because I cannot put the electrical cable close," he explained, a dusty frown molded onto his forehead. "It is illegal to have the water and electricity together—and very dangerous."

"The safety is the first," he said over his shoulder as he headed down the lane. "I will send the plumber."

"But he won't do anything without *revma*." The situation had the makings of a perpetual tail chase.

The project progressed slowly but surely. Lines were drawn to indicate future piping, a temporary electrical outlet installed so plumbing could proceed with power tools. More electrical stuff and more pipes ensued, followed by a couple of repeat performances of the above when it came to the installation of a hot water heater, which required electrical and plumbing coordination on the same item.

Two blokes could juggle several dozen projects at once, working on several houses, swapping days and hours according to need and what they knew they could get away with—and drive the project manager to drink and insanity.

One of the most bizarre experiences in the field of water and electricity had to be when Kiwi Clive and I were helping Caprice Willy open his restaurant.

Clive was tough, an All Black with a white beard. He built houses for a living and could wield both a screwdriver and soldering iron to skilled effect. In fact, his name should have been Jack.

"You are not going to believe this. Come see—I need a witness."

Clive was in the men's outside loo. We had been installing a new hand basin and generally helping Willy get it together. I assumed the summons involved wildlife: a sewer rat or *serrandapothi*.

A cloud of steam billowed from the porcelain.

"No wonder Willy was grumbling about the electricity bill. Some bright spark has plumbed the hot water into the lavatory tank." Clive shook his white curls in dismay. "A dozen liters of near-boiling water, flushed literally clean down the drain every time someone has a piss."

The last-known plumber to fiddle in the place turned out, naturally, not to be a local tradesman but some Italian kid who had long since left the island.

"Not a top job, but an Italian job, one could say. Don't worry. I'll fix it." Clive got out his soldering stick. "This has to top the lot. Never in all my years—"

"Thanks, guys, that's great, and it should cut my electric bill a lot," said Willy, admiring new hot and cold running down the right pipes. "Before you go, would you mind having a quick look at the ice machine? It's making a funny noise."

Clive was handy with appliances too, and we went to have a look inside.

An industrial monster filling the back corner of the kitchen churned away like a tractor in duress. It took the three of us to shift it away from the wall, and Clive crawled behind the mechanism.

Suddenly language appropriate to a rugby locker room erupted from behind the icer. Clive reversed out on all fours.

"Bloody pipe burned me." Clive's elbow had nudged a scalding conduit. "Some lunatic has plumbed the hot water into the ice machine. No wonder it doesn't stop for a breather."

Presumably the Italian job again. The device had spent the month before opening converting boiling water into cocktail cubes.

"Just when you think you have seen it all, this place hits you with another one." Clive got out the soldering stick again.

"Boring its not," I agreed. "Have you checked the phone isn't wired directly into the electrical system, Willy?"

He paused for a minute.

"I used the phone, and it seems alright." He appeared to think the question quite normal. The island does that to one.

39

DEAD-ICATION TO ART

"Yuk, what's that stink?" Elizabeth, an aspiring New York artist, stopped in her tracks. I recognized the whiff of something deceased and was keen to head in the opposite direction.

"Nothing you want to know about. Let's check out the other side of the beach."

The two of us had been exploring an uninhabited little island off the coast of the Peloponnese. We had anchored in the crystal waters of a secluded bay and rowed a dingy to shore.

Zoë Zoë was a magnificent twin-masted wooden sloop captained by an Australian friend, Brian, a longtime inmate. He had sailed the Aegean extensively for three decades and knew exactly where to find "undiscovered" coves, private anchorages being our preference.

Elizabeth and I had rowed the inflatable tender ashore and spent the morning clambering around the island. One old stone hut ruin provided the only indication of previous human habitation; a few wild rabbit and goat droppings appeared to be the only evidence of current life.

Elizabeth had opted to spend her sabbatical year working on Hydra, an island known to attract artists, on the recommendation of Pedro the Painter. She was focused on her art and had a tendency to be bit scattered about other matters in life. Thus she had acquired an affectionate nickname: the Noodle.

I had invited her to join us on an end-of-season cruise, a last run before permanent winter mooring, and we had spent a enjoyable couple of days sailing the Greek waters in perfect autumn weather.

Undeterred, the Noodle insisted on investigating the smell and walked over to the precipice. At the bottom of a small cliff lay a partially decomposed ram. It must have lost its footing and plunged into the ravine. The once handsome beast had sported splendid corkscrew horns; now, its brown-and-white skin was drawn taught, revealing white ribs.

"Oooh," crowed Elizabeth, surveying the ex-goat. "That's just what I've been looking for."

This from a smidge of a lass who collected sick kitties and refused to kill invading ants.

"You're kidding, right?" Most young ladies would have gagged at the sight. "What on earth do you want with a decaying corpse?"

"To sculpt! Come on, let's find a way down. I need that skull." The fact that it was still attached to the decomposing body didn't seem to have crossed her mind.

The previous evening we had pulled into a little fishing village, and the Noodle had spotted some exotic, brightly colored fish in the market.

"I need a selection of those to paint when we get back," she announced. "I want that blue one, a couple of those reds, and that—"

Our captain pointed out that we still had a couple of days at sea. The stench of aging fish, in the confined quarters of the sloop, might not be such a good idea.

"What if I wrap them in double plastic and put them in the fridge." Freezing was not an option in our galley.

A reluctant compromise was struck.

Smell has a way of permeating everything, and every time we went to the galley icebox, a waft of fish market infiltrated the cabin, plastic bags not withstanding. It had already attracted commentary from the crew.

Asking the skipper if my guest could bring a rotting skull on board as well seemed like pushing it.

"I'm going to need a sharp knife to cut its head off and slice some of the dead skin away. Will you go back to the boat and get one—and maybe some pliers," she bubbled happily. "I've always wanted to do a ram's head sculpture. What a find!"

The yacht's klaxon sounded lunch while I swam back to the sloop, having left the tender for her and the trophy.

"You'll never guess what the Noodle wants to do now," I said. The first mate was putting the final touches on lunch. Fried sausages and eggs disguised the smell of fish.

"I'll need to borrow that knife when you're finished."

"Absolutely not." The captain and mate didn't have the stomach for semi-decaying skulls either, not to mention the use of a galley knife in the operation. I swam back to shore and delivered the captain's ruling.

"But I'll pick it clean," said the Noodle, who by this time had completed the decapitation with manual wrenching and was down at the water's edge. "I'll wash it off in sea water. They won't smell a thing."

"Well, you go back and negotiate with the skipper," I said jokingly, not wishing to jeopardize my berth on the vessel.

She did and won—on the proviso that the skull would be odorless. But even with scrubbing and picking, skeletons manage to retain some pong.

"Only when you put your nose up close," the Noodle implored when she returned with her prize. Trouble was we didn't have plastic bags big enough to cover the head, but once on board she wasn't going surrender her trophy.

There was no denying her dead-ication to art, and such enthusiasm had to be commended and accommodated. I came up with a plan that seemed to satisfy the crew.

"Let's attach it to a rope and dangle it in the water off the stern."

That evening we moored in another small bay with a couple of other yachts. The sailing community is a friendly bunch, and we invited a family over for cocktails just as it was getting dark.

A piercing shriek sounded suddenly from the deck above, followed by a large splash. Our guest's ten-year-old daughter had decided to investigate the rope hanging off the back of the sloop. An ashen-faced kid appeared in the hatchway.

"What were you using for bait?" she squeaked.

40

MISPLACED RUMORS AND STATELY RHUBARBS

An argument had broken out between two of the island's most informed gossips as to whether George Bush Senior or Michael Jackson was staying on the Rock.

"It can't be the former US president. He always stays as a guest on a huge yacht and only ever gets off for a brief walk—if he gets off at all," a fellow aptly nicknamed Radio Kamini insisted. "And besides, according to the news he is vacationing off Santorini at the moment. It's definitely Michael Jackson."

"If Alexi Mardas still owned the villa in Molos, then maybe you would have a point, but he sold it months ago to a wealthy Greek with high political connections," answered the Hydra Herald, a chap who kept his ear to the cobblestones and his oar in everything. "What possible connection would the King of Pop have with a Greek politician?"

Molos, an isolated bay halfway down the west side of Hydra and accessible by boat, had a long, white-walled villa along the back of the beach, flanked only by a couple of usually unoccupied houses. Not a shop, tavern, or beach umbrella in sight.

Both claims were feasible, and opinion bounced back and forth between taverna tables that evening. Not in dispute was that first a fisherman and then a boat of picnickers had been hounded off the beach by toughs wielding submachine guns earlier in the day.

"According to witnesses, these guys were not American CIA but foreigners," Radio Kamini countered. "The president would never be surrounded by private body guards, where as Michael Jackson would, and indeed does, employ a private army. Anyway, Alexi is close friends with the person who bought Molos and could well have influenced the invitation."

It was a plausible explanation as the Sixth was well known to have hosted many rich and famous acquaintances on the island. I knew firsthand that even though Joan Collins stayed in the White Mansion above the port, she was most fond of the luxurious complex at Molos. Indeed, it was rumored for a while that she was the new buyer.

Also Alexis's friendship with the late John Lennon lent credibility to inclusion of a musical celebrity in the gossip and was a strong card in Radio Kamini's favor. "Its just the sort of retreat that MJ would love, and Bush's security would never allow him to stay in some semi-deserted bay, particularly with what has been going on in the Balkans."

The mid-1990s were a turbulent time for our neighbors to the north, and Greece, despite its NATO membership, was naturally inclined to support its Serbian Orthodox brothers. US politicians visiting Athens were greeted with mass protests and civil disturbances necessitating the use of tear gas—hardly the climate for an ex-prez to be sunning on a public beach.

"But that's just it, the beach is no longer public. Bodyguards are chasing everyone off. Even boats aren't allowed to tie up at the little pier," harked the Herald. "It's typical of the American's. They think they can go anywhere and that they own everything."

By midnight more information had trickled in about the fisherman's version of events. The mercenaries spoke Russian, it seemed.

"Yeltsin!" said the Herald.

"Gorbachev!" Radio Kamini chimed.

Yeltsin was here to dry out on doctor's orders. Gorby was on another autobiographical retreat.

Debate about who was billeting in Molos then shifted focus. It didn't matter who was staying out there—they had no right to kick us off "our" beach. Late-night cocktails and camaraderie fueled indignation.

Another inmate pointed out that it was against the law to commandeer any beach, as they are public domain in Greece, and it was decided that a large picnic party to Molos should be arranged for the following day. Additional stakes on our claim to public access were suggested—a barbeque on the shore and perhaps a bit of beach volleyball in front of the opulent entrance.

Unbeknownst to this group, another bunch had gotten wind of a celebrity visitation and also decided to take a caïque load down to Molos the following day, presumably in hopes of bumping into Michael on his midday swim or something. The fisherman had told his mates about the eviction, and they too had decided to clean their nets in the same quiet bay on the morrow.

Whatever the reason for this famous individual's staying out at Molos, it was not for the purpose of attracting attention, so when a flotilla of local craft hove into view the next morning, the Slavic swat team went into headless-chicken mode. Dealing with incoming armadas was not in the Kremlin bodyguard manual, it seemed. A lot of strutting and ineffectual waving was accompanied by chattering walkie-talkies.

Anchor was dropped not far from a fancy, sleek motorboat, presumably associated with the VIP, tied up at the pier. A sandy-haired coxswain with a Kalashnikov loitered on the upper deck looking conspicuous.

"Nazdarovia!" A couple of picnickers raised their glasses to the deadpan sentry, offering him a beer. The quiet, secluded retreat had just turned into a circus.

Then the port police turned up and putted slowly around the bay in their inflatable Zodiac, at which point the guys with guns retreated into the complex. Large, arched, wooden double doors closed behind them and locked. The celeb's private retreat had just become beach party headquarters.

That evening, armed with more information, Radio Kamini and Hydra Herald were again in dispute.

"Now the poor bloke is a prisoner. He's probably paid a lot of money for his privacy. It's not how we treat celebrities on this island," Radio Kamini said, suggesting that locals had overreacted.

"Ah! But only if they come in peace will we leave them in peace," retorted the Herald. "If they come waving guns around and dictating where we may swim, then it's an invasion, and we are quite entitled to retaliate."

The Herald camp, keen on holding daily beach parties in retaliation until the invader had left, rhubarbed their approval. Had camping been allowed on the island, I suspect a few would have overnighted on the beach.

"But guys, it depends on who the visitor is, doesn't it? Hitler and Mother Teresa must surely merit different approaches right?" Radio Kamini was equally quick with counterargument. "If it were Bush, I would say protest by all means, and if it were Michael Jackson, I would say give the man his space."

More rhubarbs in favor of the Radio's point of view rippled.

This reignited speculation as to who the Molos guest actually was and whether further protest barbeques would be needed.

"I'm telling you, it's Yeltsin. Gorby doesn't have the means; nor does he merit a full swat team for protection these days. Yeltsin on the other hand always travels with a platoon of ex-KGB," the Herald said logically. "Besides, everyone knows that his doctors have been suggesting he go on a dry-out retreat for health reasons. Molos would be ideal."

"I'll bet you anything it's Gorby, and of course he has body guards," Radio Kamini countered. "After all, he's been here before and liked the island. Hell, he supposedly even bought a painting from Michael Lawrence. And I don't think Yeltsin has even been to Greece—so why would he come here as first choice?"

Others claimed to have spoken to eyewitnesses. One couple was said to have seen Mr. Gorbachev on the poop deck of the launch; another had spotted Mr. Yeltsin strolling the grounds.

"Perhaps they are both here?" I quipped. "Maybe for a clandestine game of poker with Monsieurs Bush and Jackson?"

No guns were reported outside the complex after that, and the rebellion dwindled. One morning soon after the launch was gone. The Russians had left, and by that time the matter had already been relegated to the gossip archives.

A few weeks later my phone rang. Ingeborg sounded most business-like.

"Why didn't you tell me he was on the island? You know this is exactly the kind of story I like." She was a Dutch television journalist with a reputation for taking on hard news. "But noooo, I have to read all about it in the *Sunday Times.*"

"What are you talking about?" I was clueless.

"Come on, you are supposed to know what goes on in Hydra. Don't tell me you didn't know he was staying in Molos, considering your history with the place." Ingeborg was referring to the days when I was associated with the Sixth and once put a donkey out to pasture there. "There is a whole double-spread story about it, photos of Molos and all."

"So Mr. Yeltsin and/or Mr. Gorbachov stayed in Molos for a few days. What's the big deal? Loads of heads of state visit the Rock, you know that." A victim of Paparazzi telescopic invasion hardly seemed worth the interest of a journalist of Ingeborg's caliber. She tackled real news that got to the core of social issues, not celebrity gossip.

"You really don't know, do you?" she said, "Marco Milosevic was using the place as a hide out."

Marco was the son of the infamous Serb leader, at the time perhaps the world's most notorious bad guy. He was a fellow reputed to have a lavish taste for things like fast, expensive motorboats that can disappear in the middle of the night.

41

ROUTERS AND E-RHUBARBS

Living on a small island, particularly in a fourth-world foreign country where communications systems are sparse, one often gets left behind by mainstream society.

In 1996, while visiting some friends in Sweden, my first time abroad in years, I "discovered" the Internet. The fourteen-year-old son of my host had a full-color monitor—a novelty—and a computer that could perform magic. Always a gadget fan, I was drawn into the kid's bedroom, attracted by the amazing audiovisual graphics of a game he was playing.

He gave me a demonstration of what his machine could do, showing me digital photos and sophisticated word-processing programs. Up until then, the most advanced machine I had worked on was an "antique" Apricot. For those who don't remember, it was an early competitor to the first Apple computers, back at the beginning of the eighties. It weighed two tons, was mouse-less, and had a smallish curved green screen.

Plus, Windows 95 appeared to be much more user-friendly. It played music, and one could create just about anything on paper.

"You can download stuff off the Internet," the lad added. My expression went blank.

"You know, e-mail?"

I hadn't a clue.

I did have a business card with a mate's details. He had been waffling that summer on his annual holiday from Canada about computerized coms, but it hadn't meant a thing to me. The card apparently included a e-address, as I learned when the kid identified a string of letters surrounding an "@" symbol.

"Let's send him a message. For the price of a local phone call, you can send dozens," he explained.

I couldn't imagine communicating with Ottawa for less than the cost of a stamp.

We got a reply within minutes. I was hooked.

My enthusiasm was probably doubly accentuated by the fact that this technology had come to me out of the blue. When I had moved to the island, vinyl and cassette were the only forms of household music on tap. One day in 1988, a bloke from LA showed up with a CD. I remember being amazed at the technological leap: a small round mirror and lasers yielded great sound, and I hadn't even heard of it.

The World Wide Web made an even greater impression. We had nothing like it on Hydra. To me this inexpensive means of communicating and accessing the world's biggest library, especially on an island that didn't cater to avid English readers, was as powerful as any invention I could think of. Up there with wheels and fire!

I sensed this was my answer to changing my way of life. After a dozen years as jack-of-all, the time had come to get behind a desk again. Apparently, all I needed was a computer, electricity, and a phone line. I reviewed these simple facts: the island had electricity, I had a phone (to give an example of island speed, I had waited nearly five years for the line), and I could devise a way of obtaining a computer (as my wallet didn't instantly extend that far).

On my return to Greece I already had it in mind to create a "digital telex office" and build an information "magazine" about the island on the World Wide Web. I'd open a room on the port for e-mailing, a place for notices, advertisements, real estate inquiries, news, and printable discount coupons for participants whereby an advertising page printed out special deals at various establishments—an amalgamation of all my pre-island skills from my abandoned career in advertising.

A friend, Michael, was coming to live full-time on Hydra, having had enough of Scandinavian winters. He needed something to do in his semi-retirement on the Rock and loved the idea of partnering with me in the digital telex office.

As he was himself just exiting first-world commerce, I assumed he was clued up in the techno basics of the mid-nineties. Because I was burbling about what could be done on the Internet, he assumed I was fairly proficient.

So we went into Athens to see about an Internet service provider and to price equipment.

The start-up connection alone, we were told, would cost $12,000 to $15,000. Back then, Greeks often quoted prices in dollars when talking about large amounts. It sounded like less than asking for tens of millions of drachmas.

But I'd been assured that with three basic ingredients, I could have coms in the Himalayan hinterland. Routers and cable cost per meter were not necessary, according to the advice I got from my teenage Swedish expert.

No way was my partner going to cough up that amount of capital to bring the Internet to the island.

I assured him it could be done. If the Mongolians could get connected, then so could we. Eventually, we invested in a couple of PCs, a scanner, and a printer when we found a less expensive way to hook up to Athens.

As I didn't want to show my partner how much of an amateur I was in technologistics, I didn't leap into the boxes as soon as we hauled them back to the island and into our little office. He too agreed we should paint the place and build some basic furniture before unpacking. Little did I know he was just as nervous as I was about unpacking as he had even less online experience than I did.

We eventually plugged and played, learning by trial and error, and opened Hydra's first Internet cyberpromotions office a couple of years before its time by island pace.

The compromise was that we had to make a long-distance call to Athens for Web access, which cost a lot more than the projected local call. We got around that by only dialing in briefly to check mail, and if anyone wanted to surf, they could cover the long-distance phone charge.

Initially, not everyone received this wondrous new communications system with open arms. Mates, some of them travelled expats, not just locals, considered e-mail a gimmick. The fax was all the world needed. The Internet was just a con to get people to buy computers, a passing fad. For kids.

Change always meets with some opposition; indeed, I had balked at "progress" on the island myself. But this seemed inevitable, and pioneering it felt like a logical step for me to take.

Islanders really do have a speed of their own. It's one of the nice things about living here, if a little frustrating at times. But enough expat and passing tourist business justified keeping the HydraNet shop alive, and coms technology changed so fast that we were soon vindicated. I slowly got the hang of driving Windows and Netscaping, attaching images and documents, and Photoshopping, and people came around to seeing that this gimmick was here to stay.

I got a real kick shortly after opening at being able to send photographs of a wedding to Sydney and New York simultaneously within minutes of the event.

I guess the novelty started to wear thin for us when it became apparent that e-mail was also a vehicle for idle natter and "ers."

The technology began to spread rapidly, and within the year a new service provider had opened a small branch on a neighboring island with the same area code, so the cost of surfing dropped dramatically. Dialing Athens had made connecting more expensive than most places.

Even with this improvement, there was no automatic-hunting line for the five numbers we were provided. No two numbers were in sequence, and more often than not the lines were engaged. And because the island was still on antiquated analog phone lines, we were lucky to get connected at 10,000 bps, super slow in current technoterms. Lines barely held the signal some days, and disconnection was frequent. Downloading simple e-mail, never mind attachments, was always a gamble.

I was assured of an immanent switch to digital phone lines and that they would make all the difference to e-coms. Every few weeks I inquired of progress in this direction at the OTE, the country's national (and only) telephone company.

"Before the millennium for sure," was the eternal response.

Three years later, a few hours shy of countdown to the year 2000, it eventually happened, but by then the Net had become a digital quagmire. Even on the island the novelty had worn thin. Everybody had his own techno specialist and website, all claiming better service.

I closed the HydraNet Internet office and shifted my cyberoperation home.

42

DIGITAL DAVE

I knew the island was starting to understand what my little shop actually did about two years into the operation when some local sought me out on the port, at night, the day after Princess Di's death.

"*Keerie* David, we want to send a photograph to England—*tora!*" a moustache announced. "Your machine can do this, we hear?"

My posted office hours were 10:00 to 14:30, six days a week, and rarely were those hours fully occupied, so a special request at night, particularly from a local, was a novel first.

For a couple of seasons I had tried to introduce the concept of the Internet to this small island community, which was still, for the most part, struggling with the introduction of electronic cash registers. Indeed computers were much regarded with suspicion and associated either with some form of tax-tracking device or kiddie's video games.

Princess Di had spent some time on the Rock the week before her death, and the island prided itself on the fact that she wasn't hounded by the Paparazzi during her visit. Dignitaries and the famous are not unknown sights to island inhabitants, and the community respects privacy etiquette.

But upon Diana's demise, wind of quick dollars for last-known photos of her had filtered onto the port, and a second-rate candid taken from a semi-secluded vantage surfaced.

The submission of this picture for cash generated much moral debate at the time. But it was my opportunity to show what Internet connections could do. I could showcase my technology *yia to mellon* (for the future) at last, and my kudus as a service soared.

The fact that the photo did eventually appear in the press was irrelevant; the moustaches had seen proof that the Internet worked. But it wasn't until some months later, when I sold a house via the Web—a house that had seemed fairly priced at 45 million drachmas but hadn't had a nibble in four years—that local punters really came over the fence.

* * *

I learned a very valuable lesson during the sale of this house: never consider a deal done, even if all parties shake hands in front of a lawyer, until the paperwork is signed. Especially on a Friday afternoon!

"See you all back here in my office, first thing, Monday morning," I said after everyone shook hands. Jenny, the lawyer, would complete the legal paperwork over the weekend; keys and autographs would be traded on Monday too. My client went off to pop the champagne.

According to the rules of cricket, we had sealed the deal. The fact that cricket isn't a known sport on the Rock hadn't dawned on me.

"She wants more money," said my guy in a tizz at 7:30 a.m. on Saturday. "She says she got an offer from a German for half a million more." A bidding war ensued.

This was back in the days before mobile phones. Negotiating between parties, whose daytime destinations stretched from Vlichos to Mandraki, represented miles of legwork.

My guy, being of royal Dutch ancestry but born and reared in the Far East, was accustomed to a culture that places a lot of value on saving face. The German, it transpired, was an editor and close buddy of a wealthy contingent of arty publishing types, countrymen who had already accumulated much property on that side of the hill.

As the weekend progressed, the French expatriocracy allied itself with incoming Flemish/Thai blue blood, as did the Russians. In short everyone got involved.

The outgoing resident, Alexandra, an artist, had two small kids to support and naturally rooted for both sides. She was the chief spokesperson for the family. A brother in New York and a sister holidaying on the island were equal inheritors and only added to the negotiating equation.

The trouble was that all through the bidding, the bloke from Bali, the united German home-owners' group, Alexandra, and the consenting siblings all had to be included, step-by-step, in the unexpectedly ongoing negotiations. The furthest sunbathing beaches from town seemed to be the venues of choice for bartering.

Having gathered both sisters, I would use the office phone to persuade the New York brother to accept the latest offer from my client. More deutsche marks would then enter the fray, and the process would be repeated.

There comes a point when long-term real estate futures outweigh the current value of the amount being asked and common financial sense takes over, making complete piracy out of the question. Another property would have been located before that happened. Live punters get snapped up or chased away.

There was a serious risk of pissing both sides off with the escalating price and widespread community involvement, sending the deal south, perhaps to Crete. Getting the sellers to agree among themselves was a feat in itself. Multilateral rhubarbs had developed.

Half an hour before my bloke left on the Monday mid-morning dolphin, a parting, "take-it-or-leave-it-shot" had been accepted. Hydrofoil tickets were altered, and my man bought a quaint little house that he subsequently upgraded into a villa of some opulence.

Fishermen and muleteers all suddenly had *spitia*, or houses, for sale—often at hugely inflated prices—and came to me to advertise them on the Internet. After all, my "gimmick" had landed a sale right near the heart of town, and my client had been prepared to go to financial war and pay even more than the asking price—unheard of in local land trading; usually one haggled down. So my first sale via the Internet had made island taverna headline news.

My taste for the real estate business, on the other hand, had been quenched; it wasn't a game for cricketers (blokes who played by tacit rules)—or so I hoped.

The transaction did, however, prove to the island that serious trading could be achieved with *komputers*. I just hadn't anticipated how far one would have to walk with this new information technology.

Digital Dave stuck as a nickname for a couple of seasons, but the future caught up, and I moved on.

43

CO-COORDINATING KONDOURIOTIS

Since 1821 the Hydriots have celebrated their most famous naval victory at the end of every June with a festival called Miaoulia.

During the War of Independence, the Hydriots decided the time had come to throw their maritime weight behind the revolution, which aimed to end 400 years of Turkish rule. Until this point the islanders had cut a deal with the ruling Ottomans whereby, if they sent their eldest sons into the service of the sultans' fleet, they would be allowed to trade freely. In this manner they accumulated wealth and power—and a fleet of armed merchantmen.

In 1821, one of the most successful fleet owners, later known as Grand Admiral Miaoulis, successfully deployed a surprise attack on the Turks' warships. He sent fireboats out, much as Lord Nelson had done on occasion, and toasted the Ottoman navy.

Ever since the locals have shown their appreciation for Admiral Miaoulis's bravery with a pyrotechnical nautical event called "The Happening." Islander's dress up as Revolutionaries and assault an old caïques, which is ultimately blown up.

This little island pageant was taken to a new level when Hydra mayor Konstantinos Anastopoulos introduced a spectacular sound and light show and marching bands, which attracted an island full of Athenians. The event now makes the national television news every year.

After Miaoulia in 2005, the year after the 2004 Athens Olympics, I went down to the port on a Friday afternoon. A frigate was moored off the harbor entrance. A marching band milled about with sailors in full dress. A couple of beards, suits, and fellows with lots of braids and glitter on their uniforms stood about looking important. The port was setup exactly as it would be for Miaoulia. A stage had been constructed in the middle of the port. Top-Job types fiddled with microphones and large speakers for music.

Normally the municipal office kept me informed of island events so that I could post them on my Hydra information website, and I was curious as to what this pomp and circumstance was all about.

The mayor's secretary, Martina, informed me that the following day was to commence a new annual weekend celebrating another famous, though lesser-known, Hydriot hero of the same war, Admiral Kondouriotis.

The country was enjoying a post-Olympic economic boom, and it stood to reason that if the island could sport two such celebratory weekends, tourist revenues would double. Thus the Hydriots' second most famous pirate was unearthed and dusted off.

The tone of these celebrations of the Greeks vanquishing the Turks had changed after 1999, when both countries suffered sever earthquakes. Subsequent mutual relief efforts had evaporated centuries of animosity overnight. The Greeks had sent rescue squads to help in the Turkish calamity, and Turkey was in turn the first to reciprocate when Athens suffered a similar natural disaster a few months later. The rapprochement had been dubbed "seismic diplomacy" at the time.

So this new ritual would be about appreciating the lessons gleaned from past troubles and forging new friendships, as opposed to the old "lest we never forget we 'toasted' our enemies" type of attitude. I got the theme.

"I could have had an announcement up weeks ago," I told the mayor's secretary.

Martina was most apologetic and explained that, what with all the logistics of organizing the event—the navy, the march band, the invitations to dignitaries, and other logical operations—they just had not thought about publicizing it on the Internet as well.

"Fair enough, I suppose. Silly but understandable." They promised to keep me informed in future.

On the way up Donkeyshit I bumped into Anna-Marie, a neighbor who was also the curator of Hydra's Kondouriotis Museum, housed in the admiral's family mansion. I gave her some gentle ribbing for not letting me know about the upcoming festival.

"How am I supposed to promote this place if nobody tells me anything? This is a big event. You of all people should have informed me."

Anna Marie exploded, "Let you know?" She dragged me just down the street past Four Corners and pointed to a newly tacked poster on a wooden telephone pole where most public announcements were usually advertised.

"I found out half an hour ago when I saw this. Grand opening of my museum, tomorrow, admiral and dignitaries and everyone else to be afforded free entrance until five o'clock."

She flicked the pole with her fingers. "This was the first I heard, or should I say saw, about it."

Clearly she wasn't making this up.

"Imagine if the entourage had turned up and I tried charge them an entrance fee, or I had to take my kid to the doctor. The museum could have been closed. Apparently informing the curator wasn't on the list of priorities either, so don't you complain!"

The event went off without a hitch but with less fanfare than the Miaoulia festival. Kondouriotis continues to be remembered annually but does not hold the same attraction or merit the same marching bands and battleships as his former naval compatriot.

44

UN-REAL ESTATE

"You are absolutely sure the paperwork is in order? Not even a small percentage of an ecclesiastical nature?"

The policeman bobbed enthusiastically in response to my question.

"*Kathera! Olla endaxi!*" The paperwork was clean and ready, he reiterated for the fifth time.

The policeman had recently inherited the house, and it is not uncommon for the last will and testament of the deceased to contain partial "bequeathment" of the property to the church. A gesture to the beards and the Almighty at a time when these things are a sound investment, purchasing a ticket through the pearly gates, can throw a spanner into the deed of sale.

I wanted to be certain as I knew the pitfalls, having been down the same road before. I knew to make sure that ownership of any property for sale was not in dispute from any quarter.

He had asked me to sell his house four days earlier, and I had clients flying in specially to purchase. Via the magic of the Internet, digital photos, and an honest appraisal, a couple in France on the lookout for just such an old house were on their way. They had been on the hunt for a couple of years, and I was pretty sure they would love it.

I had clearly explained to the cop that these people had changed their travel plans and were only coming for two days, specifically to buy his land. They would be at the house Friday at noon with money to put down. The prospect of an immanent well-padded wallet usually did the trick.

They came, they saw, they wanted to sign.

"*Theeskolo*, difficult," tutted the cop. His eyebrows jerked in negative unison.

The inheritance paperwork for his wife's house had acquired four siblings. All had agreed to the sale in principle, but no actual signatures had been obtained. It was simply a matter of acquiring their John Hancocks. Lawyers were instructed to get to work.

"*Avrio*," by tomorrow, the policeman said—plenty of time before the punters had to leave.

I was highly skeptical that four signatures could be acquired in twenty-four hours, but maybe with a live punter on the island with cash in hand, they would materialize.

"*Mikro probleema*," said the policeman's wife, herself a senior white apron at the local hospital, the next morning, an hour before the departing boat.

The small problem was that one of relatives had died and left his portion of the house to his four kids. They were scattered across the country, and getting their agreement would take a couple more days. Now we had eight additional owners, some not on the island.

Our customers went home unable to place a deposit, and the purchase was left hanging.

"*Theeskolo*," lamented the lawyer a couple of days later when I called to see if any progress had been made.

Three of the grand siblings had been located and were willing to sign, but the fourth had also subsequently perished. A prolific fellow apparently, he mentioned eight offspring in his will. Two had emigrated, and another was at sea.

To say that logistics were becoming convoluted would be an understatement. It was early November, and the clients wished to complete the purchase before Christmas. Sixteen signatures could be gathered before then, the lawyers assured.

To cut a long story short, eventually thirty-eight sellers agreed on paper. But the paper did not confirm the meterage stated on the original plan. The surveyor had guessed the size, being unable to come out to the island.

The deal was saved when he promised to come on the next boat—with a tape measure. All in all, the deal took seven months and enough paperwork to topple a donkey.

* * *

Sometimes a deal is struck whereby the grandparents get to stay in their part of the building for the rest of their days.

A Dutchman purchased a decent sized home in Kamini some years ago. The upstairs comprised a self-contained two-bedroom apartment, a *yaya* and *pappou* flat.

Tragically, but luckily for the new owners, the old guy kicked the bucket three weeks after they took possession, and the *yaya*, unable to face living in the same space packed with memories, elected to vacate the premises.

Things don't always work out as planned, however.

"That Belgian girl has done the same thing and bought a big house on the hill," Ouzo Jimmy told me. He picked up a lot of trivia on his rounds. "Says there is a very old, sickly *yaya* called Maria who lives in a granny flat on the top floor."

Keeria Maria was a well-known character. She was a large, ancient woman with badly swollen ankles, barely ambulant with a sturdy walking stick. The kids of the neighborhood steered well clear of her and regarded her as a bit of a loon.

For over twenty more years *Keeria* Maria hung in there, waddling along to the Four Corners grocery and feeding a dozen stray cats on her doorstep.

45

LAW AND DISORDER

Nobody else appeared to notice the chaos. To them this was normal—these throngs of cell phones and clutched legal files, interspersed with gesticulating, often unwashed clients of dubious income, all believing in the freedom to exercise vocal rights. Among these, the animated and the chain-smoking inhabitants of Greece's largest criminal court, I felt like the alien that I was by status. (It tickled a few expats to be documented as aliens on their visas.)

It takes permanent island dwellers a bit of time to adjust to traffic and city bustle when visiting the "Big Olive" after an extended period on the Rock. Being in a crowded Supreme Court for the first time was doubly intimidating.

Thirty-eight hours earlier I had been fairly relaxed, assured by my "suit" that this was a cut-and-dried case. The plaintiff, an heiress, was supposedly out of the country and wouldn't be in court. A "no-show" on her part should lead to a ruling in my favor.

She had met a cowboy and had taken to raising steers in Arizona. Also, my alleged crimes were trivial in comparison to her usual shenanigans in front of the wigs, he had assured me, because she had filed frivolous lawsuits on several previous occasions. Showing up certainly didn't merit the travel time and expense from her angle.

"Shut and open case, no problem," repeated my lawyer.

Then he had called the night before the trial to inform me that I would have to take the stand. He wanted to know if my Greek was good enough to plead innocence of the complaint.

What then was this new rhubarb, I had inquired.

With the cowgirl absent, apparently the judicial system was still quite keen on being reimbursed for the four years of work it had taken to set a court date. The matter of outstanding expenses for justice hadn't occurred to me. Any contestant turning up could well end up footing bill for the whole caboodle, it seemed.

It was a disturbing phone call that kept me awake with worry. Doubts began to creep. I barely scraped by in island pidgin. Judicial Greek was way above my understanding—and in Greece, one is guilty until proved innocent!

I tried to think of the positives. Surely I was in the clear, having just the previous day managed to assemble a legally binding document from an elusive witness and friend of the complainant assuring my innocence: an affidavit proving that somebody else had occupied the scene of the crime after my departure.

More distressing was the fact that my lawyer suddenly couldn't act as my translator. And he wanted to know if I could muster any other dignitaries to testify on my behalf if things got rough. At this late stage!

I spent a couple of hours pretending sleep but didn't get a wink. I may have donned a jacket and tie, but I was far from sharp that morning.

Fahgan Ntevint ("nt" in Greek spells an English "d") was the seventh criminal on the agenda posted in the hall.

According to local sources in the know smoking nearby, it could be hours before I was called.

A bellow from the corner of the courtroom seemed to demand silence, and the volume sank to a murmur-rhubarb. The clock behind the pulpit said nine fifteen. Proceedings were getting underway only a quarter of an hour late. Punctual in fact by most Hellenic watches!

My mate and moral support, Stathis, and I had left for the Supreme Court in Piraeus with ample time—time that had evaporated quickly with regular stops to ask barely ambulant geriatric gentlemen, the only folks slow enough to catch at rush hour, for directions.

We were late but still on time, if you know what I mean. Shy on sleep but not on caffeine, I twitched around the foyer as *numero ena* (number one) took the dock. The appearance of another staunch ally, Karin, did much to bolster flagging reserves. Although not officially in a position to do so, she agreed to take the stand to vouch for my integrity if necessary.

"Don't worry," she assured. "This is Greece. People go to court over the price of a loaf of bread."

The court was in the middle of the second case, about forty minutes into the proceedings, when Stathis announced that he was just popping out to feed the parking meter.

Case number three was a nonevent; four, five, and six were quickly executed or postponed.

"*Fahgan Ntevint numero epta*" was called—and my exalted witness was still out feeding the parking meter! Panic and abdominal butterflies suddenly hampered regular breathing.

The lawyer gestured for me to come to the front of the courtroom. Three Beaks glowered down at me while my legal representative apologetically explained that my only witness was temporarily detained.

I flashed the lady judges, tough-looking birds, what I hoped was my best "ignore-the-unkempt-hair-I'm-an-honest-Joe" smile.

The middle Judge sternly interrupted my attorney's bid for time and blurted something directly at me.

"*Signomee?*" I begged ignorance.

My lawyer quickly explained that I was an *xeni* with limited Hellenic conversational skills. The word *xeni*, for some horrifying reason, caused a stir in the spectator arena, and silence descended for the first time.

An alien was to be convicted—always a novelty.

I had waited four years to get to this point only to have my one and only defense witness vanish. I imagined the court noting the delay as a sign of disrespect as we were told to remove ourselves.

We were banished back to the smoky lobby until we had got our act together—more time to jitter. By the time Stathis returned, victim number eight was half convicted.

The timepiece on the wall read 10:20 a.m. when my lawyer managed to jump back into the queue. In the process he ousted a particularly vocal balding fellow wielding a huge file, which could have taken hours.

Again there was that annoying silence as the judge read the charges out loud. Interest and silence seemed to intensify when it became apparent that the complainant was also extraterrestrial—if absent.

My council quietly told me he wasn't going to produce my precious jail-saving affidavit unless it was really necessary. He explained that it only proved that the *klepsied* goods (three sketches and half a dozen videos) could have vanished after I handed the keys over. My coveted written statement failed to mention whether the missing items were still in the house after I left.

Stathis took the stand, but because he had translated the original police summons years before, he was deemed an unacceptable witness and dismissed. My mouth felt as though I'd been sucking dry chalk. Spiffing!

The chief wig beckoned me to the prisoner's box, and much as when composure overcomes stage fright or the whistle blows at the beginning of a rugby match, I stepped confidently forward, calm as a clam.

I knew that my rudimentary preschool Greek would never stand up to the legal jargon of the High Court and begged forgiveness for my inadequate linguistic ability. Mercifully, Stathis was then sworn in as my translator.

Twitters from the audience at my lingual faux pas and confusion among translators, the bench, and myself in a mixture of two languages gave the proceedings a surreal air.

My imagination leads me to believe that until the middle beak inquired as to what my current occupation was, the verdict had hung in the balance. The deficit in bureaucratic coffers held large appeal, in that the judiciary should be reimbursed for the time and paperwork, and I was the only potential participant in the room.

I addressed the bench, explaining that the mayor of Hydra and I were working in close contact to promote tourism for the island over the Internet, hopefully implying that I was of more value to the country as a free man. I added that I was not a fellow of wealth and that while I sympathized with the bureaucratic deficit for these proceedings, I would be unable to cover the judicial costs.

The three then conferred briefly behind raised folders.

"Innocent, acquitted, not guilty," my lawyer simultaneously confirmed. Absent party to cover all costs to the state. With a bow and an *efharisto poli*, I walked.

And then I went for the haircut I had hoped to get before showing up in court. Delays had prevented my obtaining a final grooming to enhance the clean image I'd hoped to project. Like I said, just about everything in this country is prone to its own sense of timing!

But better late than—

46

PROPERTY PIRATES

Patience and timing are essential ingredients when dealing in all matters of home ownership on the island. Laws that can be threaded back to the days of the philosophers still influence the right to land in Greece. Two plus millennia of red tape!

A couple of meaningless splashes of white paint on a rock may not mean much to the average hiker, but to the local inhabitants they represent a geological chess game. The ownership of land is disputed down to the pebble.

A classic case of brinkmanship was demonstrated over a few square meters of vacant land a few of years back. A fellow who had recently completed building three villas on a plot of land overlooking the harbor was keen to expand his enterprise. One he day paced out a couple of meters from his boundary wall and dropped a splash of *asvesti* (whitewash) on a pair of rocks; then he left it for a year. No one arrived; no one complained; no one claimed the land.

The following year he freshened the fading *asvesti* with larger dollops of white and painted a couple rocks more to add definition to the perimeter. Again, no arrivals, no complaints, no claims.

Another year he dug a slit trench; the following, actual foundations were excavated. Next season the concrete foundation was laid, a year later a meter of stonework was masoned—you get the picture.

As the final roof tile went into place eleven years later, there was a knock on the new front door.

"*Kalimera*, thank you for building me a beautiful little house on my land. Here are my papers," said the unexpected visitor. Keys were handed over!

If the pirate had only waited twelve years to install that final roof tile, the occupational and squatting rules would have changed in his favor, and he would have been able to keep his claim. But the owner of the land had bided just the right amount of time and got a new house, free of charge, for his patience.

* * *

One would think that biding one's time to the right house for the right price would lead to an easy transaction.

Pedro the Painter had spent nearly a decade looking for the perfect little *spitaki* to buy. Knowing the island, he understood that decisions over property purchases were not to be rushed. Patience must be maintained until the right item comes along—and finally it did.

A "renovators dream" on Hydra realistically translated means "start-from-scratch ruin." The intended property was within the artist's budget, and if he put his creative juices to work, along with some hard labor, he could put together a comfortable little cottage.

Pedro was well known and liked on the island and rarely associated with detrimental gossip—until, that is, he shook hands on the purchase of his long-sought *spitaki*.

"I've never had so many people shout at me," said Pedro the next morning, looking distressed. "Wherever I went, people I've known and liked for years were coming up and giving me shit. All of them claimed a sixteenth share in the ownership of my intended purchase."

The lesson of course is to check the paperwork before palm spitting.

Then there are balls that curve just when you think they're over the plate.

"I sold it yesterday. I didn't think you were serious, and anyway your customers might not like it." The jet-lagged prospective buyers looked on in disbelief. Newlyweds who had honeymooned on the island the previous summer, they had come a long way to do the deal.

"But Christo," I said, "I told you these people were flying all they way in from Singapore and that they had seen the place and were coming to sign."

I had given them an honest description. They knew the location and had seen photographs on the website. We had even arranged the final price with the owner. I therefore had mistakenly assumed we were well beyond first-option status.

A hefty last-minute cash wallet had hijacked the deal the day before. A shrug and an apology—*Tee nah kanomay* (what can we do)—was all we got.

Not surprisingly, the young couple took this as a bad omen and gave up on the idea of a Greek island holiday home altogether.

* * *

An elderly Dutchman who was helping clear out his daughter's garden and the neighborhood *platia* (empty square) outside her front door decided he would burn the excess rubbish. The fact that he was wearing a woolen jumper and jeans did nothing to deter a local moustache with a hose.

"I don't know what I've done, but they're very excited," said Hans, dripping in the doorway.

The hosing incident was investigated.

Turns out the *platia* was in much dispute with several parties; even the *demos* (municipality) was in contention for its rightful ownership. The pending result had been lingering for years on a judicial desk somewhere.

Labor of any kind upon this type of land can be misconstrued as staking a claim. This apparently included the raking and burning of leaves. Hence the hose. Then a couple of the adjacent black shawls had emerged to verify land "jumpmanship."

"Not even the *demos* may clean this *platia*," wagged a finger, which would account for the lack of land care and Hans's attempt to clean things up.

Experience teaches one to ask the right questions and ignore the "right" answers. There are a lot of right answers, depending on whom you ask and what century of law is being employed. The trick is to collect as many answers as possible and go with the majority.

47

VAGRANT FIRST CLASS

I had never seen such a tough-looking cop on the island before, and he was scrutinizing my passport with incredulity.

"*Sim-pa-paway*, *Afriki*, *eenai?*" Telly Savalas with dark stubble looked at me in disbelief. My birthplace, Bulawayo, in what had been known as Southern Rhodesia, had caught his attention. I suspect that if he had come across any Zimbabweans before, they probably weren't blue-eyed white men who spoke bad Greek.

I explained that I had been sort of accidentally born there by coincidental circumstances to do with parental migration but that I had moved back to Ireland when I was still in nappies.

"*Eirlandos?*" A thick, hairy forefinger tapped the booklet. I nodded, he nodded, and he reached into a drawer.

Out came a serious-looking official folder, and I began to reflect on how my naivety had gotten me into this predicament. Twenty years before I had hung up my first-world gloves for a simpler, uncomplicated island life, and here I was back in the ring, sparring with red tape—and all because I had thought it a grand idea to get a little boat license.

Only lure of fun could have enticed me to register for anything at all for no reason other than the fact that I hate standing around bureaucratic institutions. An invitation to go sailing had tempted me to do something out of character: visit the civil service.

I had also talked myself into it for a second reason. I figured that by 2005 perhaps the time had come to acquire some sort of identification other than my passport—something in the language of my adopted country being preferable. What better than a small boat license?

The seed had been planted a fortnight earlier when then stepdaughter Harriet's boyfriend had come around waving a smart looking "driver's license" complete with his photo and stamps. The kids had been loaned a small putt-putt boat to fool around in for the summer.

"Did you have to take any tests?"

I was accustomed to the idea of qualifying for such licensing, as mopeds and small motorbikes differed legally from larger machines in terms of operating requirements.

"No, its only for a little boat up to thirty horsepower, for fishing," Stam shrugged. "You just pay a little money to the port police, and they will get it for you. Easy."

But there was a catch: one required a citizen's registration number in order to obtain said identification—something called an "afeeme" number—which I didn't possess.

I was about to give up on the idea, figuring it was not going to be worth the hassle, when I bumped into James of the Brownings, a fellow inmate who had recently purchased a house in our neighborhood. He was coincidentally spouting on about how simple it had been to obtain his afeeme number, which happens to be required for ownership of any sort of property in Greece these days.

"I just popped up to the mayor's accounting office, passport in hand, paid them ten euros, and it was there the next day. Simple really," he urged.

I am a firm believer in timing, so I took this as an auspicious signal and trundled off to the office with my passport and a tenner.

A new lass, whom I didn't recognize, occupied the secretarial seat. She started copying info from my passport onto an official-looking form.

"You must have somebody Greek who knows you. Can you find someone?" she inquired.

"Of course! Loads of locals know me. You can ask him, if you like," I said pointing toward the next office.

"*O Keerios Demarxos?*" She looked both surprised and impressed with my suggestion that the mayor could verify who I was.

"He has known me for years. He is an old friend, and we have had lots of dealings," I said matter-of-factly.

She duly wrote this onto the form.

I didn't realize at the time that when she said someone who "knows" me, she meant someone who would stand guarantor to my integrity, a person prepared, theoretically, to vouch for me in court. One would normally at least have the courtesy to ask the intended "legal" sponsor if he or she was prepared accept the honor, especially the lord mayor.

I told her about James Browning's experience to confirm it was really that easy.

"No problem," she assured me, poking at the form. "For you, even easier. You are from here a long time." I thought that was a nice way of putting it.

I was told I could collect my document the following day, *avrio.*

The next day I was informed that Mayor Kosta had kindly endorsed my application without hesitation, but the head office in Poros apparently needed to check out a few more things. Could I come back again *avrio*?

Six days later I stuck my head around the door and popped the question first. "*Avrio?*"

She grinned and nodded. HQ was still busy on my file.

I began to wonder why my afeeme was taking so long to process, although if it hadn't been for the fact that James had actually received his the next day, I wouldn't have.

I could only guess, but I figured that the system had unearthed my name in a twenty-year-old file or something—from a time when the EU was still referred to here as the EEC and when aliens had to register everything in order to do business in the country, from blood type to stool and urine results. I once had a large temporary folder, presumably untouched since the bar folded and I joined the ranks of the officially unemployed two decades previously.

When news did arrive back on about day sixteen, the secretary clicked sympathetically.

"You must go straight to the police with your passport." She handed me some forms. "It's not because of us. It's the head office which wants this."

Standing in front of Telly at the local precinct, cursing my naivety, I finally gave the matter some thought. Of course it was never going to be that simple. The world had changed since 9/11, never mind 1985. Big Brother had matured. I wasn't worried, just disinclined to grapple with long-winded bureaucrats over a silly boat license.

I'm sure it's the Irish blood, but when in doubt I tend to engage the opposition—verbally. I was about to embark on my history with the island in credential-sharing chit-chat, when Georgo emerged from an adjacent office—in uniform what's more. He was senior in the precinct and had done my original paperwork back in the EEC days.

"*Yassou, Davie, tee khanees*," he said, immediately greeting me in his usual jovial fashion.

We exchange friendly banter about seasons and family.

"*Ah, to xerees?*" Telly looked up with a smile, relieved to see that the police chief knew me. With my credentials thus established, the rubber stamp appeared. Stamp, stamp, and one euro for the paperwork later, I had a new official document containing more numbers and rhubarbs on me.

"They have to check these days to make sure you aren't a terrorist, that's all," the mayor's secretary explained to me back at her desk. "But we have another problem. Now you must go to the TAP office."

I had no idea where or what a "tap" office was, and the thought of whipping James at cards or backgammon (unlikely) began to seem appealing. The expression on my face must have prompted her.

"It's just so they can check you do not have any financial liabilities against you and that you have no debts," she soothed.

I had no worries in that department either. Being a man of no means, thus no debt, I was sure my name wouldn't set of any bells or raise any flags. I had always considered myself ahead of the game by staying out of the mortgage department and living in hand-to-mouth street.

Being out of the system meant that I had acquired nothing that required my having to register for anything, if you get my meaning. I prided myself on the fact that I stood on my own two feet without expecting a hand out from state or others. With not even a donkey to my name, I knew I didn't qualify as an income to be chased, so I was confident.

The new generation also occupied the front desk at the TAP office under the Port Police. A young, gum-chewing lass with vacant civil servant genes waved the piece of paper I had given her over her shoulder.

"*Tee naf toe?*" She chirped to nobody in sight, asking who I was.

"*Aftos eena o David,*" said a woman's voice from behind the filling cabinets at the back of the office. The voice went on to say briefly that I was known and was neither a vagrant nor a fellow with taxable assets or debts.

"*Endaxi,*" said the rotating gum with a wide smile. Stamp, stamp, no charge. Yet more paperwork, all for the sake of being legal to drive a motorized bathtub—and fish for one's dinner.

"Okay now?" I asked back at the mayor's office.

"*Endaxi*, I hope," she smiled. "*Avrio.*"

"All OK," she beamed the next morning, handing over a stamped and approved document. "But the extra work means fifteen euro."

Literally cheap at half the price, and I was even happier when a friendly young bloke in a white naval suit copied my passport and afeeme, kept a pair of photos, and said I could collect my license the following morning—and I did.

Trouble was, I noticed it expired in less than two years. Perhaps it would be wise to start renewing soon?

* * *

I have since been granted full residence, complete with card, official stamps, and photo—a citizen of the island with voting rights and everything!

48

A PERMANENT SMILE

A simple trip to the dentist on the island can offer extremely daunting medical complications if things, while you're in the chair, do not go according to plan.

"Oops!" uttered not once but twice—perhaps the scariest word in the dictionary when one is semi-horizontal with a cheekful of cotton wool.

I had thought this, my final visit, after weeks of substantial bridge and root-canal work would be a piece of cake—the final fixing to a new smile.

My dentist shook his head and reached for a device that I had never seen before—a tool four times the size of his biggest drill! He had initially tried removing the new bridge manually, but the dental work was jammed tight.

Not only did the new machine resemble a mini jackhammer, but it felt like one. We were attempting to dislodge the bridge with brute force.

"*Oxi*," he frowned, picking up the syringe. His usual humming had stopped—ominous.

The skull jarring jackhammer got more enthusiastic as the bridge remained cemented. The cranium-rattling whacks sounded awfully loud.

He sighed and stopped, removing the instrument. Perhaps it was getting heavy?

"Can't we just leave it? It looks good and seems to work well?" I inquired jokingly.

"We must remove it. I try one more time," he flexed his hand and got the hammer.

I expected to feel splinters and prayed the fixture came loose. I couldn't imagine what horrors lay beyond if the bridge failed to dislodge. Perhaps minor explosives? Even worse, a trip into Athens and the unknown dental labyrinth of a big city for further mouth surgery.

I think he too was much relieved when the bridge finally budged. After all that, the root canal bit seemed like a day in the park.

"We fix it permanently now?" he asked. "It's comfortable, yes?"

After the "temporary" fixing, permanent had an until-death ring about it. I nodded keenly.

Seems I now sport a better smile for life—especially as the new chompers have proved too that they can take a hammering.

49

FIFTY MILES IS WORLDS APART

Almost all of the muleteers sport mobile phones these days, a misleading gadget that could cause one to think that the island is indeed connected to the first world and therefore the scheduling associated with it.

If you like laid-back, then this is the place—and not just because nothing moves faster than a donkey plod. The co-ordination of six signatures can take eight months, planning permission a generation. So just turning up gives one an edge—being punctual earns huge kudos.

It can be frustrating to those who wish to achieve something, anything, the same day they plan it to happen. In fact there must be world records in matters concerning completion of task going into extra time.

When one's technician is known as Spiros the Specter (*Phantasmos* in Greek), and to others with less humor and more impatient moons under their belt, as Spiros the *Pseftis* (Liar), be prepared to be very laid-back about waiting for the bloke to show. Take up a hobby while you wait—like growing a beard.

Getting excited with the bloke after two years of waiting for the air conditioner to be serviced is an exercise in futility. Nothing can be achieved by staking out his brother's cafe with handcuff's, threatening boycotts, or even kidnapping his dog—the chap always has a get-out clause. While Top-Job employs an encyclopedia of plausible excuses, the Phantasm, a friendly Ghost with expertise and no clock, or calendar for that matter, merely uses one line that absolves him of any guilt.

"I was working for the government television on a technical matter."

It is known that Spiros had a hand in the erection of a television mast above the town some years ago. Such inferred excellence and demand for his profession is beyond question for most mortals, and further explanation and argument are a waste of time. Whatever your rhubarb, you still come second in matters of national satellite communication.

Some have tried circumnavigating the monopolies and made the mistake of importing their own professionals from the Big Olive. This alternative is not only uneconomical because of transportation costs but could invite future rebellion in a time of emergency.

"Call your man in Athena," a restaurateur got told when her kitchen developed a flood one evening—candlelight dinners in a pond. So such outsourcing can come with an eventual price tag.

But the contrast between life on the Rock and the world beyond goes further than our differences in time-keeping and transportation modes.

When I give folk from the first world my postal address—Fagan, Hydra, Greece—they immediately feel compelled to complicate it by asking for codes, streets, numbers, credentials, stuff for the machine that seems to be running the rest of the planet these days. Skeptics accustomed to a society ruled by numbers may need convincing, but keeping it simple works best.

Not so long ago an expatriate received a dog-eared, moth-eaten parcel that had somehow managed to travel half way around the world, twice, before landing on the Rock. No one knows for sure how this happened, but it evoked some speculation because the aforementioned mail had been franked in places as far away as Moscow and Montreal.

There was nothing obviously untoward about the address upon initial inspection; nor were the contents of the parcel extraordinary, just a couple of paperbacks, but it had also visited the United States a couple of times, as well as France and Italy.

It was addressed to

> Mademoiselle "Jane Doe"
> Poste Restante
> Hydra 18040 Ελλαδα

So how did the package go on such an extended walkabout? Someone suggested that it went to both France and Quebec because the sender had quirkily titled the recipient "mademoiselle." Another pointed out that the package may have been returned to the States, where it appeared to have come from originally, because the zip code for Hydra, 18040, is also the zip code for Easton, Pennsylvania.

It was then astutely decided that it had gone to a Russian post office because some bright spark had noticed that "Greece" had been written in an alphabet resembling Russian. Nobody could quite figure out why it had vacationed in Italy, except that Poste Restante sounded like an Italian pasta or something.

According to the stamp marks, in most cases the parcel had sat in an unknown/pending pile for a few weeks before some clerk had decided to pass the buck onto the next "logical" country.

Keeping it simple works best. A sorting clerk in any post office anywhere initially looks at the address's bottom line and puts the piece of mail in the relevant bin or pigeonhole. So, if it says Greece, it will go into an overseas box, then a European box, where it is then stuck in a mailbag destined for Athens. Once in Athens, it is then subsorted into suburbs, regions, or islands; so, something marked Hydra comes here. Once here, well, they know who we are and deposit any items of post into the box labeled "D–F." My wife and I once received an envelop from Johannesburg addressed only:

While we do not advocate everyone keeping it quite that simple, Christmas greetings were received well in advance of the holiday—in itself a miracle at that time of year when high seas can interfere with mail delivery for weeks on end.

A mere fifty or so miles from one of Europe's' major capitals, the island might as well be 50,000, and fifty years behind. Take the contrast to an everyday chore like shopping.

A typical exchange of useful information on the island would include "Four Corners has some avocados in, but if you want a couple, you'd better go now. The box won't last." One also appreciates normally mundane salad more when it becomes an exotic imported delicacy. Seasons too play a big part in availability; stocks of simple things like fresh lettuce can disappear for months.

Five customers is a crowd in Four Corners, and there is no room for shopping baskets. A trip to the neighborhood supermarket is a social event. As there is rarely an unfamiliar face in the crammed little shop, one chats with others while waiting to have one's future guacamole weighed.

The limited selection of veg and fruit is piled and tilted on plastic crates outside and needs protection from passing donkeys on the browse. Wasps and other unwelcome airborne scavengers can get very enthusiastic about a new batch of fruit, and one must be careful not to get stung when selecting.

"They should cover the fruit and veggie boxes. This can't be too hygienic." One part-timer, always on the lookout for something to improve, took her idea to the shop owner. Insects with landing rights on the grapes could spread disease, she pointed out.

"They come fresh from the tree. You think the wasps only come to my shop?" The merchant mustache gave her a look that implied her idea was ludicrous. "You must always wash the fruits before eating, even if they are from the refrigerator. You don't know this?"

Sometimes the first world is left stuck for an answer.

Until recently, Kamini was probably one of the last places where one's supermarket shopping receipt came hand-scripted on a page torn from an outdated diary. For instance, this receipt, issued December 6, 2010, is dated January 17, 2008:

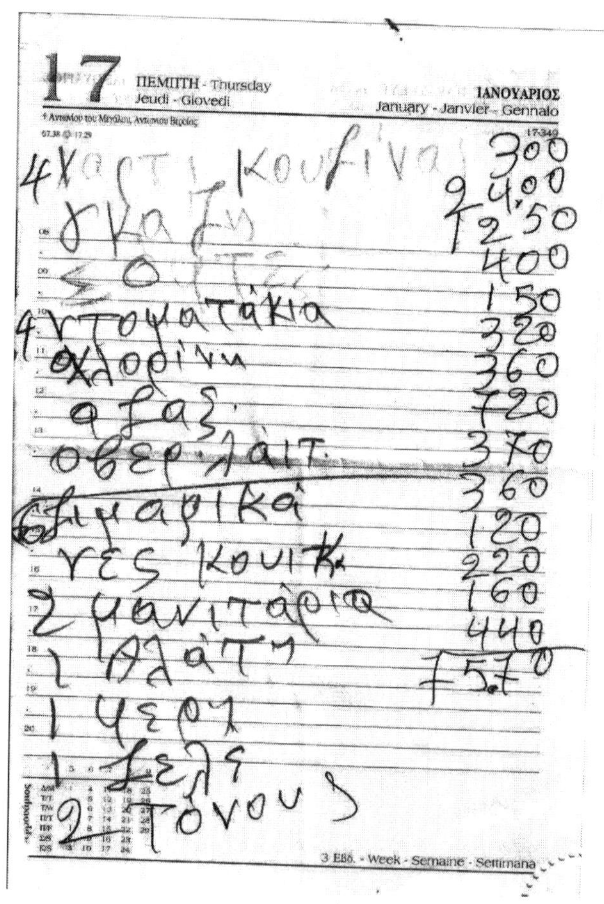

While the contrast in worlds can be unusual for those coming to the island, many people forget that it is at least as confusing for long-term inmates who go abroad.

Those who have dwelled for extended periods on the island have experienced the feeling that they left the planet and a new brand of human exists out there—beings with faster reflexes, a species that has become a cog in some mysterious, larger computerized mechanism.

Okay, we are not so backward that we are going to be awed by automatic doors and punters with shopping trolleys just because they don't exist here (although the contrast is a bit of a shock at first), but the new world is always inventing new ways of making one feel extraterrestrial.

Once after many years on the Rock without parole, I visited the first world and was staying as a guest in a household with small kids. Travel weary and jet-lagged I elected to crash early and bade the family goodnight.

Before retiring, I opted for a stroll in the garden for a breath of fresh air. I was midway through discretely watering a bush when I heard a metallic click. Suddenly a searchlight illuminated my activity. Frantic efforts to terminate-and-tuck inflicted some damage on the way past the zipper, and the entire family witnessed my distress through the lounge's filter blinds.

"Of course you wouldn't think about heat-seeking spotlights. They are all the rage now—everyone has them. There are a few areas where they won't be triggered. I will show you tomorrow. You must have been on the fringe of their radar," my host patted me understandingly on the shoulder. "No worries mate, you get a good night's kip. You'll feel rejuvenated in the morning."

I conked out almost immediately, despite the adrenaline shot.

Drowning from within because of the earlier unfinished business, and disoriented by strange surroundings, I woke up. The luminous dial on my watch said it was just gone four in the morning, and not wishing to disturb the household, I felt my way, brail-like, along the rows of books toward a door in the gloom. Floorboards creaked as I padded in my bare feet.

I decided to get my bearings and gave the light switch behind the door a quick flick—

Orange brilliance began spinning in the hallway, accompanied by the windup wail of an air raid siren. Outside, the strategically situated spotlights turned night into day—a beacon of sound and light in a slumbering suburb.

"Better phone them quick and tell them that it was only our houseguest," my bleary-eyed hostess, cradling a yelling infant, said to her husband, who had appeared, clad in underpants and brandishing a baseball bat.

A rapid reaction force boasting response time in under ten minutes was winging its way to our aid apparently.

"Never hit this red switch." My hostess pointed. "It's called a panic button."

"No shit!" escaped before I remembered the sniffling youth. "An effective way to scare the burglar to death, but is there any way one can alert the cavalry without attracting the attention of the whole region?"

If my pulse was anything to go by, this sort of anti-intruder device could well induce cardiac arrest in the switch flicker too, somewhat defeating the objective.

"Of course, we have a silent alarm button in a couple of discrete places. I will show you in the morning." She grinned at the sight of me, standing scarlet in my jocks.

Such an exciting reveille prevented further kip, and I got to thinking as I lay in the dark once everyone had gone back to bed. In my world keys were superfluous. In this world, once locked *inside*, these beings had standby armies and heat-seeking spots to prevent robbery—and peeing in flowerbeds.

I made my apologies over breakfast, and my host understandingly gave me a few lessons in home security, including code to punch into a calculator on the wall should I wish to go downstairs at night. I immediately vowed that I would not be setting a toe out of bed until daylight for the duration of my stay, and therefore learning secret passwords would not be necessary.

"Don't be silly. Feel free to make yourself at home. You may want to go to the kitchen or watch some late TV," he laughed. This code, he explained, deactivated motion detectors, which were also trained to hit the panic switch and summon SWAT teams.

Shopping sounded like a simple enough chore, and I elected to join my mate on a jaunt to the mall once I had memorized the code and been shown the technological ropes of household devices (a lot of remote controls, each with a lot of buttons).

Not having driven a vehicle for over a decade, I declined the offer to pilot, the idea of city traffic too daunting without a little practice on a quiet country lane first. My host aimed his keys at the car; it chirped good morning and flashed its indicator lights, simultaneously unlocking itself. Astounding stuff for a bloke who still thought electric windows were tops.

The seatbelt slid itself forward for buckling, and the dashboard said something about the hand brake not being released, proving yet again that the new world and the machine were becoming integrated. A friendly symbiosis—providing one knew which buttons to push or what gadget to aim. Automatic gates slid back for our exit.

Apart from inexplicable bustle, the shopping mall appeared on the surface to be much as I remembered: escalators, air conditioning, elevator music, water fountains, and a supermarket the size of a jumbo jet hanger—a world from a previous life.

"Go and get a lettuce," said my mate, pointing to an adjacent isle as his trolley was in gridlock.

Somewhat in awe of the selection, I hesitated before choosing, and as I went to grab, something spat on my hand. I jerked back in surprise, nearly elbowing an elderly lady in the jaw.

It took a couple of seconds to realize that automatic misting system had been introduced to induce freshness, a clever idea someone had come up with in my absence. I had coincidentally reached for the greens just as the timer went off.

Other humans were no longer involved in the fruit-selection process anymore either. One tore a plastic bag from an industrial ream and bunged the intended purchase on a digital gram-o-meter, which evicted a sticky, bar-coded, dated, stamped, officially computerized label—not a wasp in sight.

Another challenging aspect for inmates abroad is dealing with the first-world inhabitants. They have developed a natural suspicion of anything that isn't regulated, including us beings unfamiliar with the workings of their mechanized society.

"You know how to put gas in a car, right?" asked Jesse, whom I'd accompanied to the country to investigate a business opportunity. He tossed me the keys after pulling up to a petrol pump. "Put ten bucks in. I'm just popping across the road for something."

"Of course, I have owned cars before, you know. Put that hose into that hole near the boot," I joked as he headed off.

Simple, I thought. One unlocked the petrol cap, twisted it off, stuck the pump's nozzle into the throat, and pulled the trigger. Nothing happened when I squeezed and jiggled the lever a couple of times.

I replaced it in its cradle and had a glance at some written instructions on the side of the pump, which didn't suggest I was doing anything untoward. Figuring the device was faulty, I unhooked the second hose from the other side of the pump. Behind me a waiting pair of sideburns in a Stetson was leaning against his pickup, impassively chewing a toothpick.

The second pump to didn't respond to agitation either, not a drop.

This was during the first Gulf Rhubarb, and there was talk of oil shortages, so I figured maybe the well was dry, perhaps awaiting fuel from a tanker that stood parked nearby. I replaced the second hose and read the instructions more carefully. A lot of blurb on safety, but it seemed I was on the right track in pump operational procedure.

Other vehicles were now queuing up behind the gyrating toothpick.

"It's finished. Maybe that's got some," I said, I pointed to the tanker. The toothpick moved, though the rest of his face stayed still as stone, so I tried to lighten things.

"Blame that Saddam fellow. Maybe you should try another pump. They seem to be working." Others in the garage appeared to have petroleum access, but I didn't want to risk moving the vehicle.

The toothpick froze in contemplation as it tried to figure out whether I was a loon, taking the piss, or perhaps both.

My host ambled up, looking perturbed by the queue. By then four cars and a truck had assembled in line. I had been on the brink of inviting the toothpick to come and try for himself, if he didn't believe me.

"Did you pay?" asked my host.

"Obviously not. We haven't got our petrol yet, and besides there isn't an attendant to pay." I remembered that in the days when humans dispensed gasoline, an attendant had stood guard, watching, lest the customer overran the requested amount. Self-service still needed an overseer, I thought.

Turns out one pays a bloke in a distant building, who with dexterous button pushing then releases the exact amount to the pump you designate, all monitored from his desk by remote cameras. Fancy stuff and easy to master once one is aware of the procedure.

Not twenty-four hours away from the Rock and I had learned some valuable lessons about living in the first world. Do not push any unidentified button (and there are buttons for everything), and do not expect human beings to be part of commercial transactions. A machine is running the show.

The machine has also developed an additional way of funding itself by constantly emptying its citizen's pockets of their spare coin. Want a supermarket trolley? Feed it some silver. Park the car? More shrapnel. Even taking a leak can cost pennies.

First-worlders are trained to constantly feed the system, even while driving. At regular intervals they throw coins into tollbooth baskets, not even stopping on the way past, the exact coinage ready. Ashtrays have become loose-change trays. Piggy banks are now just ornaments.

Personally, I'll do without a various selection of lettuce and put up with wasps anytime in favor of the human element. When it comes to visiting the grocery store, you can't beat home as far as I am concerned. People can still do business without instruction from machines, and technicians have to wait for parts.

"You know the problem," said Top-Job after a frustrated client had left his laboratory in a huff, muttering something about the punctuality of plumbers back home. "They come here to get away from the city, for something different, but they still want their city life here. If you want Stuttgart scheduling, then go to Stuttgart, I tell him."

I had stopped in to collect a lightbulb, some thing on last week's to-do list, just as Yannis finished with his client. He continued loading Leo with toolboxes, and the little donkey stamped impatiently, bored with standing—keen to go on a plod.

"Of course, he will be back *avrio*. What else can we do? We must wait"—Top-Job started to lead the animal off—"unless of course he wants to go to Stuttgart to get the replacement part himself."

50

OLYMPIC RHUBARBS AND HYDRA'S PARTICIPATION

Never underestimate the Greeks—or the Gods that watch over them. Six weeks before the 2004 Athens Olympics were due to begin, nobody thought it would happen: highways were incomplete; stadium roofs were missing. In fact only the athletes appeared ready. Various committees and international bodies were discussing moving the venue back to Barcelona; some even suggested that the Chinese were almost ready for their 2008 hosting and could probably get it together in time.

Then, in a split second, the whole thing turned around. A miracle, a fluke, the stuff of fairytales—call it what you will, but a friendly Greek god smiled on this nation just in the nick of time. I was there when it happened, and I will never forget it.

I was sitting next to our self-appointed harbormaster, Pan, the moment it occurred. There was a momentary silence, and then chaos erupted. Premature fireworks boomed across the harbor.

Greece, if it could hold out for another quarter hour or so, had done the impossible, scoring a magical goal that promised to carry the country to victory, at odds of a hundred plus to one, in the European Football Cup Final.

When victory was confirmed, it took about two seconds of stunned disbelief for a fever to sweep the nation, a euphoric pride that gave the country the impetus to complete preparations and host one of the most spectacular Olympic games of modern times.

A few weeks after the games ended, Ingeborg and I were sitting on Kamini rocks where she was catching a last minute sunbath before escaping the island. We had been debating the merits of my latest venture, and she appeared to be winning.

It was, after all, a realm she was familiar with—the world of television networks—which she insisted had changed radically from my media days in the early eighties. I was of the view that people were the same even if technology had advanced.

Ingeborg is an energy force unto herself: uninhibited, outspoken, and not to be missed in a crowd—or on a beach. Her opinion is known to be strong, its validity endorsed by the respect she commands as a Dutch journalist.

The night before we had been watching one of Ingeborg's fascinating documentaries from one of her missions abroad, and that morning I had shown her my little contribution to the world of television from that Olympic summer.

"It was a media man's dream, and all the old instincts kicked in," I enthused. With twenty years of local knowledge, I had felt confident I was the man for the job. By "job" I mean the chance to promote our island in a manner that eclipsed all others: showcasing Hydra to the entire world a few hours before the opening ceremony of the 2004 Athens Olympics.

A couple of weeks prior to the event, I had received an e-mail from Mike Bushell, a senior sports presenter from BBC World. He had seen my website for the first edition of *Rhubarbs* and wondered if I could give him any local advice. The BBC was flying in on the Monday night before Friday's opening extravaganza and had exactly one day to shoot "rural" Greece.

Mike explained they were thinking of including Hydra in their report, "just as a backdrop," and to interview a couple of locals about their thoughts on the Olympics, what the Games meant to them, that type of thing.

Presenting the Rock and its inhabitants to a billion people, 350 million households, was the chance of a lifetime, and I grabbed the opportunity. This was something good for the island that could only benefit all of us who lived and worked here.

Mike said they planned to leave Athens and driving to Napflio and Porto Heli for some of the shoot. Perhaps if they could manage it, they would stop in Hydra if they could coordinate hydrofoil schedules from Ermioni just across on the mainland. They thought it would be nice to squeeze an island into their report.

I suggested a water taxi across from Porto Hydra on the main land, which would give them flexibility and save them hassling with tourists and baggage on public transport. Mike said they were thinking of taking a donkey trek to the monastery for a segment but added that as a noncommercial news team, they did not have large budgets to play with.

I wrote back that not only would a donkey to the top of the mountain cost as much as a stretch limo, but the trip would take up just about all of their allocated time. Deploying nineteenth-hole marketing tactics remember from another life, I suggested instead a shorter scenic trip around the cobblestone streets of town, using the saved time to grab a swim and a bit of sun before the grueling schedule of the Games.

Mike is a man of humor, and we spoke the same language. Over a couple of weeks and dozens of e-mail and phone calls, we formulated our plan.

Mike asked if it would be possible to have a "spontaneous" Greek party at a taverna complete with plate throwing. On asking around, locals told me plate throwing was a thing of the past; these days they throw flowers at the dancers.

I relayed these new facts to the BBC. While Mike appreciated the updated info, he said the world in general associated Greece with throwing plates in celebration of anything, and flowers would be too ambiguous. Then he mentioned that tourist places in Athens offered plate-throwing entertainment, which his crew could take in once they returned to Athens in the evening. I immediately said that we could throw a few plates for the purposes of the documentary, so not to worry.

My enthusiasm for this auspicious marketing opportunity was mostly met with perplexion. Nobody seemed to grasp the fact that this was a golden chance to give the island exposure that money couldn't buy.

I spoke to Despina, a taverna owner in Vlichos, who'd agreed to host the plate-throwing event. She did not immediately understand why I insisted that she offer the BBC lunch on the house.

"If you advertised your business on a Greek TV channel, it would cost you about 5,000 euros for thirty seconds. These guys have an audience all around the world. They'll be seen in hundreds of millions of households on the day before the Olympics. You cannot put a value on that. Its priceless promotion compared to a few plates and a lunch for three," I said, referring to Mike, his translator, and his cameraman. "You can even use your older, slightly chipped plates," I said.

I had similar conversations with the water taxi driver and muleteer. All obliged, but I know they were only doing it for me. It stood to reason, I explained, that even though Mike and crew were a news team and would report what they saw, if they were shown hospitality and had a nice day, their report would reflect that mood.

"What if they had arrived unannounced?" I hinted. The week before the Olympics, an extra camera crew wandering about wouldn't be noticed. An American film crew once reportedly asked a port-front taverna for a seafood pasta and was presented with an eighty euro bill for the dish as it contained lobster. Needless to say, the island did not feature favorably on that news channel. I didn't want the lobster experience for the BBC World!

As it turned out, another local attempted to guide a Korean crew around a week after the Games, and one shop owner tried to charge the national news channel 300 euros for the privilege of having his shop filmed. Needless to say, he didn't make it into the Korean spot, and who knows what the documentary ultimately had to say about Hydra.

In negotiations with Mike, I had offered to set up an interview with Mayor Kosta Anastopoulos. I checked with the mayor personally on this matter and explained that as the BBC was on a very tight schedule, we'd need to a set time. Double-checking the day before Mike arrived, I popped my head into a rather chaotic municipal office and asked Martina, Kosta's able secretary, if we were set for the following day.

"*Tea?* I know nothing of this," she shrugged, a phone clamped to her shoulder. "It is not in the book."

She saw my expression and added quickly, "and I cannot disturb him now. The president of Estonia is visiting the island." Visions of turning up with the Mike and his crew, when they had specifically changed their filming venue on my word, and not having any of my promises materialize began to haunt. I threatened to camp in the office until I had an affirmative answer.

The prestigious Olympic medals had also been designed by a local gold shop owner, Elena Votsis, and I set up a shoot with her in her shop. Mike was delighted at the prospect of getting two separate reports out of one day's shoot.

I met Mike off the boat, and we sat down for a complimentary introductory coffee on the port. He did a quick shot of the café's owner and a couple playing *tavli* (backgammon) with the harbor front as a backdrop. The day went smoothly, and Mike even observed that in a split-second a single goal had seemingly transformed Greece.

I explained the varying logistics of organizing the filming to Ingeborg on the rocks in Kamini, then mentioned that my debut as a locations manager had gone almost unnoticed.

"So what did you expect, a thank you?"

"Well, no, just some goodwill and perhaps a few kudos in having shown that the Internet is a multifaceted way of promoting the island, generating spin-offs that are not tangible in hourly rates or bookings."

"You should have been on a salary." She was siding with a lobby of locals and expats who were of the opinion that I should have charged a basic hourly fee for my expertise.

I countered that in the grand scheme of things, a paltry wage would have changed the whole dynamic. I'd have been an employee, told what to do. Instead I had been able to act as a guide, and a good guide was far more beneficial to the whole shoot. I had made sure they didn't encounter any surprises by, say, wandering into a stray taverna and ordering budget-gobbling "crab spaghettis." Or get mistaken for wealthy American filmmakers with large wallets.

Plus we had a really nice day without the embarrassment of exchanging small change as the crew boarded the hydrofoil back to Athens. Mike left in a good mood, and anyone who leaves a place happy is bound to reflect this in his report—hence the glowing and rather extensive piece he did on the island.

The report was an absolute gem and showed Hydra in a glowing light. A most generous allotment of about six minutes in total aired on the BBC several times the day before, during, and after the opening ceremony. Several of the major Greek channels used footage from it on their nightly news broadcasts.

So, I was a little perplexed and even miffed that the grandest thing I had done for the island had gone almost unnoticed. In fact most people simply asked, mystified, why I had bothered since I wasn't getting paid.

"Honey, you live in a different time. This is how it is in the real world. Only now it's caught up with you guys on Hydra," she chastened. "The world has gotten smaller. The old days are gone. Capitalism has caught up with everyone. Get real."

With that an agitating mobile phone emphasized her point. Holland was calling on business—her television network had collared her sunbathing.

"Ask them if they need a location manager. Any reasonable wage will do," I jibbed.

In an ironic twist, twelve months later Mike called me to say he and his crew had loved Hydra so much that the BBC wanted to do a follow-up, a year on from the Games, looking at how they had affected Greece. Ingeborg agreed to put them up gratis in her home for the night.

51

MUCH A-RHUBARB ABOUT NOTHING

Police, lawyers, topographical engineers, electricians, and a various selection of neighbors got into the fray. A rhubarb over nothing, it had half the village taking sides and caused rifts in lifelong friendships. The local grocer kicked his own sister out of his shop and told her that her euros were no longer good in his establishment.

From vast experience I knew the folly of not securing one's boundaries when purchasing property on the Rock, and I thought I had covered the lot. When we bought our little house on the hill, I had triple-checked that all the paperwork was in order. I sent our legal team searching back decades, confirming with the municipal registrar, the tax office in Poros, and notaries that the deeds were in order—not a stone out of place or left unturned in diligent bureaucratic correctness.

The house needed substantial renovation; new electrics, plumbing, and basic refurbishment took place over a period of three months. Among the final touches was the installation of our satellite dish. I had suggested we clamp it to a sturdy metal pole jutting out from the back of the *spitaki* (small home).

"*Oxi*," said Lampis, our buck-eared technician. "That pole is DEH (Greek electricity company), and that is not allowed. We must use our own foundation, and anyway, we wouldn't get a good signal from there."

He scouted the perimeter and looking for the ideal spot to erect our dish. The south-facing wall on the top corner would be the perfect place, he suggested. I pointed out that this overlooked the empty, overgrown plot next door.

"No problem. You have one meter space all around your home. Nobody is allowed to build right up against your wall," he shrugged.

I had inquired because, early in our renovation project, the whitewasher had painted a small door attached to the back of our house. The little door was supposedly in dispute because old photographs proved that it blocked what had originally been an open thoroughfare, and another neighbor had objected.

No sooner had the whitewash dried than we received an angry phone call from the owner of the adjacent plot objecting loudly to the painting of the simple wooden portal. We were obviously encroaching on her land, perhaps angling for a land grab and at the very least infringing on her property rights. We were ordered to sand the door down immediately, or police would be summoned.

The adjoining land, overrun with weeds, was itself said to be in a fourteen-year legal battle with another neighbor over its ownership. So even though we could have argued the point, in the interest of creating good neighbors, we complied, diplomatically letting the fact that the door was attached to our house pass. One learns that getting into rhubarbs with the neighborhood is ill advised and defeats the object of living in a tranquil little village where nothing goes unnoticed. We had the door sanded down to raw plywood.

It was dusk when Lampis duly borrowed a long ladder and set our satellite dish way up, out of the way. We were finally connected and settled in our new home.

At midnight the phone rang. An irate voice claimed we had violated her property rights, and if we didn't remove the dish at once, she would take "steps." The dish projected "almost a meter onto her property," and she was most indignant that we had audaciously placed a stepladder on her land to install it.

"In Greece we don't walk into somebody's house without asking permission," she fumed. "I want to be good neighbor, but—" She left the word hanging in veiled threat.

Her timing and tone did not invoke a polite response.

I pointed out that an empty piece of unkempt land hardly counted as a "house" and that according to the qualified electrician, we were quite within our rights to attach the satellite dish to our wall. I added that calling after midnight was also considered rude, no matter what country one was in.

I said we would look into the matter, but far as we had been informed, we had not broken any law. I somewhat sarcastically apologized, however, for not having had the electrician call to request permission to invade her "house" with a ladder for five minutes. I'm not the best when awoken abruptly under the best of circumstances.

I consulted with another old friend, Jeannette, who owned the house just behind us. I asked if the woman was justified in asking us to remove the dish, at our expense. She assured me that we were well within our rights. In fact, she confirmed that the neighbor in question lived in Athens and had a couple of years earlier illegally erected the garden door between our house and the bottom of Jeannette's garden wall.

"She only comes out for a week or so in mid-summer, and I already have a disagreement with her because she attached a string of klieg lights along my back wall, which she has no permission for; she certainly didn't have the courtesy to ask my permission," confided Jeannette.

"Plus, when she is here, she leaves them burning all night long, making my house look like a lit Christmas tree, and they attract bugs and mosquitoes. If she tells you to take the satellite dish down, then tell her she must remove that gate from your house," she said emphatically. "You must stand up for yourself; you can't let her bully you."

Given the difficulty of getting a technician to turn up, a matter that can take weeks, especially for such a minor job, I decided to ignore the matter. If and when she came back with her complaint, I would plea-bargain with her: in the interest of "good neighborliness," if she let us leave the dish, we wouldn't pursue the matter of the illegal gate attached to our house.

It sounded fairly reasonable to my mind; after all, she didn't even live on the island, and the dish wasn't interfering with her view, space, or serenity. Not giving the matter another thought, I wandered down to our local.

No sooner had I sat down, than a toothless mustache came steaming up with a stream of agitated, almost incomprehensible Greek. From what I could gather, we had broken the law, and we were to remove the offending dish immediately.

I tried to explain our rights and point of view, saying that we were in direct negotiations with the owner of the land and would sort it out ourselves. He went off mumbling, and I turned to our builder, Pavlos, who was looking as me quizzically. I explained what had happened and asked his advice.

He agreed with me and told me not to pay attention to the old fellow, who apparently had a taste for vast quantities of retsina and sometimes interfered in matters he shouldn't.

"He has nothing to do," quipped Pavlos. "He just make nonsense about for nothing."

Forty-eight hours later, at least this time in the early evening, the Athenian plaintiff was back on the line, demanding to know why the dish was still up. Her spies had told her we had done nothing.

I tried introducing the garden-gate bargain but could barely get my point across as it invoked further fury. Heated debate ensued about logic, good neighbors, and reasonableness. What was all the fuss? I asked, especially as I had been reliably informed that we had every right to stick a dish on our wall, and it wasn't interfering with her anyway.

"Apart from this," I added, " it is nearly impossible to get a qualified electrician at such short notice, even if I wanted to. Lampis is very busy, and he's one of two people on the island who knows how to calibrate the dish. The other guy is impossible to find."

At this point she threatened police visitation and court battles involving lawyers. While my indignation tempted me to contest her irrationality, experience and better judgment got the better of me. Years in court and the associated expense, just to prove a point, were more than a moral battle warranted.

I said I would try to get the technician back, but as she should well know, sometimes on the island that can take weeks. She seemed appeased.

I did get hold of Lampis, who said that we had done nothing wrong, but if it would stop the growing dispute, he would come and move the dish.

"No rush, just when you can," I said, knowing that meant he wouldn't be by for at least a fortnight. I hoped that the whole thing would blow over by then and moving the dish wouldn't be necessary.

The following day I popped into our little neighborhood grocery, where a few of the local lads were doing their usual: sitting on empty beer crates, sipping a couple. They had been debating the growing satellite dish war. I was invited to sit and tell our side of the story. Basically the boys concurred with our point: the woman, a wealthy Athenian, supposedly didn't even own the adjacent land outright. One chap said that his uncle, who lived next to the plot, had been in court for nearly a decade and a half because he also had title to the property, so she had no leg to stand on. His uncle was on our side, and he had said we could leave our dish where it was.

This was reassuring news, and I decided I wouldn't go to the expense and hassle of relocating the device. With most of the village on our side, I saw no point in pandering to the unfair whim of some Athenian dragon, especially as she was a comparative outsider.

About a week later the toothless mustache had another go at me in front of the locals seated at our taverna. I informed him of the new status quo, at which point he got quite animated and stormed off.

"Bravo" hooted a few.

That night the Dragon was back on the line, this time with ultimatums. Have the dish down within twenty-four hours, or she would send her lawyers and the police. I couldn't get a word in edgeways before she hung up. This was starting to get ridiculous.

Let them come, I thought in anger. I planned to explain the situation clearly and calmly and, at the same time, to point out the illegal door attached to our wall—which, I would suggest, we would happily continue to put up with if she backed off.

Before I came back from town the next day, I was told an official photographer had been up to the property with a suit in tow. Collecting evidence for court, my informants assumed.

Logic overcame confrontational tendencies. In Greece one is guilty until one proves oneself innocent, so if the Dragon did lay nemesis, no matter how much legal and moral high ground we held, we would be committed to months, possibly years, in court. Factoring in the expense of a lawyer and trips into the Big Olive, I decided to capitulate and tried calling Lampis.

Lampis's wife, it turned out, had fallen suddenly ill, and he had taken her back to Albania, his return date unknown. The only other technician potentially qualified and in possession of the equipment to target and install a satellite dish was Spiros the Specter, and he was probably working for the government TV channel.

I called the Dragon in an attempt to stop the lawsuit and explained the situation. She said that she would arrange for one of her electricians to remove the dish. I said fine, but a technician with specialized skills and tools was needed, not your run-of-the-mill lackey. I emphasized that it was imperative for the dish to be removed and reinstalled at the same time because we needed the satellite connection for our work.

Her technician would be up the next day, she assured, as though to suggest that I had been lying about the difficulty of obtaining said service.

Sure enough, the next morning I heard the clatter of a ladder and went to investigate. Dimitri, a local electrician and old acquaintance, stood looking, hands on hips. I asked if he had a satellite-seeking device.

"*Oxi*," his eyebrows jerked in the negative. "I no can do this work. Only Lampis or Spiros can do this."

I gloated inwardly, knowing the Dragon hadn't been able to find a quick fix. I told Dimitri that the Dragon and I had agreed that the thing wasn't to be removed unless it could be reinstalled during the same project.

"Tell her what we discussed, because maybe she doesn't believe me," I said. "I told her there were only two people qualified for the task, and you can check—Lampis is away indefinitely, and Spiros … well … " I smiled.

"Yes, it could take months for the ghost to appear," Dimitri laughed. He agreed to call the Dragon.

I assumed the matter postponed and relaxed in the belief that an accord had been struck and the legal hounds called off.

Early the next morning I became aware of activity on the plot and went to see what was afoot. Atop a long ladder was a young lad who had already half dismantled our satellite dish. I knew him by sight and also knew that his primary career was donkey boy.

"Do you know how to reinstall it?" I asked suspiciously. "Because if you can't, you have no right to take that down. We need it for our work."

He simply shrugged and said I was to speak to "him." He nodded to where the toothless mustache was sitting among the weeds under a tree, puffing a cigarette. I asked the shadow under the tree what he thought he was doing and how he intended to get our communications back up. He didn't even look my way.

The dish came down, and the donkey boy unceremoniously dumped it over the wall and onto our terrace. They departed; I stewed. This was out of line, and I was tempted to haul the Dragon's gate off our wall. Once again, experience and fear of involved legal wrangling cautioned me against such rash action.

I tried calling the Dragon in Athens but only got an answering machine. Two days without the dish later, we were down at the local. The mustache was sitting inside in his corner, nursing his barrel of wine. I am not a bloke who flies off the handle very often, but there does come a time when one has to speak one's mind.

Making sure not to do it in front of the others, who were sitting outside, so as not to humiliate him, I confronted the old swine. I told him in no uncertain terms that what he had done was illegal and that I had come to an arrangement with the Dragon personally. Now we were without coms and with no visible technician on the horizon. I demanded that he give me the Dragon's mobile phone number and her surname, because I was going to the police myself. He sat looking sheepish.

It was just gone midnight when we got home. The phone was ringing. The dragon, apologetic, explained that the old mustache was her uncle and land manager and had not been authorized to pull our satellite down. If I would give her a day, she would have the matter rectified.

Amazingly, the next day another electrician arrived, presumably from Athens. He started tap-tapping the cabling around to the back of the house, then erected our dish in what appeared to be an appropriate place. But when it came to tuning us in, he looked worried.

"It cannot turn to find the TV because of the roof," he said. "It's too close to the wall."

I realized the poor fellow hadn't a clue about this type of system. I explained that we didn't need to aim at the mast above the monastery on the mountain but at a satellite in the sky somewhere to our south. I must have shown despair; he looked lost.

I could tell whether the dish was pointed in the correct general direction, but finding the exact position usually required some sort of high-tech device.

I judged the approximate angle from memory and went inside to set the dish to signal-detection mode. Our vertical signal was well in the 90 percent range, but our horizontal detection was zero. I shouted through the bathroom window for him to tweak the dish sideways. Within a couple of minutes, we had a clear picture—pure luck.

Much relieved, the electrician took a minimum fee and left with a smile. Later that evening I sent the old mustache a jug of wine. Peace at last—though it seems that sometimes one has to shout to be heard. In any event, I thought the matter closed.

Six months later, on a blustery winter's night, the usual local suspects were huddled in the valley's sole open taverna. In the midst of an important football match on the television, the subject of our resolved satellite dish war resurfaced.

The toothless mustache resurrected his summer coup and his role in the relocation of the dish. He started wagging a crooked finger at our builder, Pavlos, for having suggested to all that we had satellite dish air rights over the empty plot of land. Pavlos told him in no uncertain terms to shut up.

The old gizzard said gloatingly that he had won the day and that our fellow hadn't had the balls to stand up to him. Young bull, old bull stuff.

Pavlos, still working on various projects at the house, recounted the episode the next morning. "Of course I make sure there are no womens in the restaurant first, but I stand up and show him who is a man."

When the mustache had accused him of having no balls, our man, his dignity now under attack, dropped his pants, adding counterinsult to injury. "You think I have no balls? What are these?" Guffaws from the room resulted in the old mustache letting loose a stream of *malakas* and other phrases best not translated.

Life in our village may be many things, but boring it is not. Both Pavlos and the mustache, better known as Dimitris, have since passed on, and both are sorely missed by this little community. After armistice was reached, concluding the satellite dish wars, they shared a table on numerous evenings at one or another of our village tavernas, as they always had done in the past, rhubarbing with the rest of the boys, thick as thieves.

52

DIGITAL DONKEYS AND TANGLED WEBS

Paradise was getting tough. By the mid-nineties I was beginning to think that I had made a huge mistake in choosing the Rock as a permanent home. The influx of a younger, stronger, and cheaper workforce was jeopardizing my livelihood as a carefree jack-of-all. Er, David,* jobs—garden pruning, whitewashing, even lightbulb changing—had dwindled. What's more, the new laborers justifiably enjoyed a sympathy factor, having recently been freed from a poor totalitarian state to the north.

The influx had encouraged me to become a little more responsible about life, and as I've mentioned, I upgraded my activities to include holding house keys. But managing people's homes added hassle to "the simple life" I had chosen, and I began to wonder whether I was destined to spend the rest of my life sitting around waiting for the electrician, plumber, or carpenter.

I loved my island existence, but it was getting more and more expensive; the days of social intercourse on a shoestring were vanishing. One needed funds to participate in port-front joviality on a regular basis, which meant one fell

* See appendix A for an explanation of this honorific.

out of the loop and lost further leads in making ends meet. Catch 22 … a pickle.

The alternative, leaving, was too daunting to contemplate, and I began to wonder if perhaps escaping the rat race landed one in an inevitable rattrap. After a dozen years, the thought of traffic and nine-to-five corporate schedules was terrifying.

Having spent most of my adult life "marooned" on Hydra, I was ill equipped for life in the city, even if I could find gainful employment. What, after all, were the chances of a thirty-eight-year-old bloke, who had spent the last dozen years chasing donkeys and dreams around an island, obtaining a bona fide position in the "real" world?

My ex-marketing and journalist credentials were a bit long in the tooth and certainly wouldn't be sending me to the front of unemployment queues, but I tried my hand at journalism and mailed an article off to the *Greek Times* anyway, thinking that maybe I could get back into writing and still live on the island. I had written a lighthearted piece about the folly of war and advocating peaceful settlement to a brewing rhubarb with neighboring Turkey at the time.

Fully armed naval fleets had been converging in an aggressive manner at the "accidental" hoisting of a Turkish flag on a small, barren Greek rock in the Aegean; national pride was at stake. The article was published, but the locals did not receive my peaceful overtures well and took me to task for my lack of appreciation for historical boundaries.

I was genuinely surprised that my suggestion—that peaceful dialog was preferable to two NATO allies attempting to annihilate each other over a chunk of granite that couldn't support a rabbit—could generate such a negative, almost hostile response. My appetite for reentering the responsible world of journalism abated, and I was no closer to finding a new career. Clearly my skin still wasn't thick enough.

Another very important factor influenced my impasse and planted seeds of doubt about my being able to remain full-time on the Rock. Bachelorhood was loosing its shine, and the chances of meeting Miss Right were looking slim from a solitary bunker (the room I rented). Nobody eligible stayed on the island much longer than a sabbatical, and fearful regiments of protective clan generally dissuaded one from courting local girls. Some would call it a premature midlife crises, but to me it was a conspiracy, a quandary.

Then I "discovered" the Internet while visiting friends in Stockholm during the summer of 1996, and I immediately envisioned its potential on the island: it was the answer to my dreams and my dilemma. By the end of that year I had opened a little Internet cafe and launched a community website. This new invention had me in awe for months. I'd once waited nearly five years for a phone on the island, so the contrast in technology—the ability to send an instantaneous e-mail for a fraction of the cost of a snail mail stamp—was doubly exaggerated from my perspective.

But as folk around the world found Hydra on the Web, I soon found myself back in Er, David, territory. I didn't mind, really, but I was still convinced that we had created the Internet for more than just chitchat about the weather or whether so-and-so was on the island.

This feeling nagged more the longer I wasted time sending, receiving, and browsing on an old analog line in a new digital world. Frustration at the lack of technical support on the island and new diseases called computer viruses wreaked havoc with the HydraNet office and website. Having a shop was seriously responsible stuff.

Still, it was infinitely better than comparatively uncomplicated menial labor, so I persevered. I had the largest library ever compiled at my fingertips; I could talk to the world, listen to music, play solitaire—when not pulling hair out over broken connections and crashing systems.

One afternoon I was at home in my bunker watching President Bill Clinton being grilled on CNN for fiddling with a thong on the Oval desk. On a whim I wrote a letter to *Time* magazine—something whimsical about the Monica Lewinski scandal being nothing more than a "Capitol Hill of Beans" in the global political scheme of things. I saved it to floppy on an old laptop to take down and send from the office the following day.

I sent the sentiment off to *Time* with barely a thought, and having received an automated thank-you and the usual blurb that a human reader would eventually get around to reading it, I dismissed the submission from mind.

A few weeks later Captain Brian called me from Kamini and said that my comment had appeared in *Time* magazine, an edited, condensed version to be sure. Still, I was stunned by the reality; this was proof that one could share one's thoughts with millions of people at the touch of a button. And that one had to be careful what one said, to think before hitting send. What if in an irresponsible flash of irritation I had written that I thought the fellow a twit (which couldn't have been further from the truth)?

Then in late 1998 I read an article in *Time* that changed everything. A passing asteroid had almost had our name on it. It was life-on-earth termination stuff, and yet the news had been relegated to page 82. What's more, the chaps searching for these space rocks were stone broke. An idea formulated: why not use the new global coms to find a solution to an old global concern (asteroids have hit earth before; it really was nothing new). I researched the topic on Internet, and there didn't seem to be any sort of site devoted to researching ways to prevent an actual asteroid-induced Armageddon.

An enthusiastic e-mail about the concept of using the new World Wide Web to generate awareness and raise private-sector funds for the cause of defending our planet from asteroids won me an invitation to Tucson, Arizona, to meet respected astronomer Tom Gehrels to discuss the idea. He confirmed the pauperly state of this science. The long and short was that while some folks I discussed this with saw merit in the concept, when I wanted to pass the idea on, none had the inclination take it up. The proposed scheme required commitment, responsibility, and time they didn't have.

I was already suffering from a case of the "what-ifs" in my past and didn't want to add another. I knew I had to try to put the idea into practice, or I'd go to my grave with "WHAT-IF" stenciled in capital letters on my forehead. Too often I had formulated a plan and merely dipped a toe into the water of enterprise. I decided to follow through with this idea, especially considering the magnitude of the problem, and started the FAIR Society, a charity devoted to future asteroid intervention research.

Then the idea about researching asteroids took a twist I didn't foresee. I met with an instant negative reaction when I mentioned the subject a second time round. Instead of generating further interest in the topic, I faced closed doors and blank expressions. (Not from the scientific community, who are grateful for any assistance.)

I suppose, too, that many suspected I was no longer playing with a full bag of marbles, and it took tenacity to get the project launched.

I was prepared for a little ridicule, but I wasn't expecting such instant turn-offs. I had hoped that by lightening the subject, giving it less gloomy analogies, and building an upbeat site with a difference, people might soften to the project. I approached Scott Alan, a renowned cartoonist from Seattle, about the FAIR charity, with the express intention of giving him ideas to create artwork to accompany articles. I knew from past experience in media marketing that a lighthearted sketch breaks the ice on a serious topic. He graciously joined the antimeteor team, and we created some interesting, humorous, and unusual cartoons under the cleverly named brand Frontispace.

But I was a little over optimistic in my estimation of changing attitudes, and debate rose to epic proportions. For instance, the God question came up. I had blundered ahead, focusing purely on the scientific side of the equation, and not considered a spiritual dimension. Wasn't I defying God's will by trying to prevent an asteroid Armageddon? Who was I to play with the Almighty's Judgment Day. This curve ball took me by surprise because I am not anti-religious, quite the contrary.

The challenge required a responsible answer.

I countered with a comparison to tsunamis. Not so long ago they too were deemed evidence of God's wrath; these days we don't think of a subterranean warning system as interference with God's will. I explained that my asteroid website merely pointed out what science has documented. Asteroids are nonspiritual hunks of rock that exist everywhere, along with planets, suns, moons, and comets; perhaps it was time we started thinking of them as just that, natural phenomena.

If the Great Creator is responsible for everything, including our ability to do science, then how could it be against his will to develop technology to solve problems wherever they arise? Besides, no website society or organization could do anything to alter the divine will anyway; an impact event could happen tomorrow, and we'd need years to develop the technology to intercept a space rock, even if we did know it was coming. I offered these simple pragmatic facts to help uncloud the issue.

I got donations from a number of good friends and sent the funds on to Spaceguard, a global asteroid-detection program, which helped the organization buy a number of important widgets for its telescopes. I posted the news with photos on the website, hoping that once the society was able to prove that funds raised actually did go to the scientists and this wasn't just another cyberscam, it would acquire momentum of its own.

I never intended to make a career out of locating hazardous asteroids. Who, after all, wants to spend the rest of his days dubbed the "Doomsday Man." Life is far more interesting here on earth; so I made my contribution to the cause and got on with life, treating the society as an administrative hobby only.

I turned to writing about life in the donkey lane, happy to turn my mind to more down-to-earth topics. My first book was favorably reviewed on its appearance, and here's the kicker: the companion website guided a note from BBC sports presenter Mike Bushell into my inbox. He figured I could give him some advice about the island, and the ensuing rapport we developed led to Hydra's being filmed exclusively to represent rural Greece in a documentary for the BBC World's opening coverage of the 2004 Athens Games.

While he was here, I asked Mike his opinion about an off-the-wall e-mail I was thinking of submitting to *Click*

Online, a popular weekly BBC World series about innovative technologies that included a section on interesting websites. I asked if he thought they'd consider the FAIR site. Mike's encouraging reply prompted me to hit the send button.

One doesn't really expect one's website to be selected for review out of the millions submitted, and I put the e-mail out of mind. I forgot all about it in fact—until I got an e-mail from a mate in Germany months later saying he was impressed with what the BBC had to say about the website.

That review led me to writing these words, explaining why I seem to ruminate on two totally different subjects, the Rock and space rocks. But really, the two aren't so separate: saving the donkeys from a space rock is my choice of charity. After long efforts to keep the Rock and space rocks apart, it finally dawned on me that writing is writing, whether about donkeys or doomsday. In the end they are just words, and writers are in the business of sharing them. For without words, we cease.

The power of this relatively new mode of correspondence was proved to me absolutely when the best thing to happen in my life arrived in the form of a single, brief e-mail at the exact moment when I least expected anything positive for the future. It was from the Banker's daughter.

"Hello, David," it read. "I don't know if you remember me, but this is Jennifer, Michael Kelland's daughter. We met back in 1994. I googled you and found your book site. I wondered if you could offer some advice. As you probably already know, we are having an ash scattering for my father this summer on Hydra, and I am bringing a friend who has a bad back. Is there a chiropractor on the island?"

Of course I remembered; in fact, I'd never forgotten. She was the one who had gotten away. We had had an innocent flirtation after a long summer's day twelve years earlier, after which her father had threatened to hobble me. I'd hoped for Jennifer's return ever since, but she'd never come back to the island. It was the very first e-mail I received as a freshly single bloke when I reconnected my computer in my new bachelor pad in Kamini. The OTE had taken a mere three days to rehook my coms, possibly a record in telephone and TV transfer time on the island. It felt like fate.

Jennifer came to spend that summer with me, as my "houseguest" and "editor," in my breadbox of an apartment. By October we had bought a house together, and she moved to the island permanently the following spring. Now we live and work together, writing about the island and doing what we can to promote Hydra's tourism.*

And after all the years of flak I took for what others saw as, at best, my quirky notions about an asteroid Armageddon, my fears were sadly confirmed on February 15, 2013, when a meteor strike injured over 1,000 people in Russia. With that event, attitudes have changed. I felt that I had done my part with FAIR. The world is now acutely aware that high-velocity rocks from space can and will find us. Meanwhile, all we can do is enjoy our daily rhubarb.

* We run a noncommercial, humorous, rhubarb-like website called the *Kamini Comet* (www.davidfagan.org) and another devoted to tourism, the Hydra Island Greece website (www.hydraislandgreece.com).

APPENDIX A

THE THIRTY-NINTH PSALM OF DAVID

On the occasion of my thirty-ninth birthday, fellow expat Roger Green wrote this poem. He read it to friends at a gathering held in my honor (any excuse for a party) at the Pirofani, a much-favored Kamini restaurant. I've included it as an example of how my "careers" on Hydra have been the source of amusement!

"Thirty-Ninth Psalm of David"

Oh, David,
Just a minute, please.
The Gore-Booths want some extra keys
For several guests from overseas;
And can you meet them from the Dolphin
And arrange for them to get some golf in?

Er, David,
Leonard Cohen begs your pardon,
But can you tidy up his garden
And paint his house before next week?
(He wants to let it to a Greek
Who has been seriously depressed
And now requires a total rest.)
He hopes your skilled clearing up

Will speed the fellow's cheering up;
Only, he says, the truly jolly
Can give rein to their melancholy.

And, David,
Brian and Julie called
To say they were appalled
To hear you haven't tiled their floors
Or washed their walls or cleaned their doors;
Less in anger than in sorrow,
They want it all done by tomorrow.

Oh, David,
Jacques and Dominique
Are coming with a crew next week
(They don't know when they'll be arriving)
To make a film about pearl-diving
(Yes, you heard right—not sponges, pearls—
They need a dozen sexy girls)
Directed by Dmitri De Clerq
(He's sure he can make it work),
Set on a Caribbean shore,
So please can you lay in a store
Of shoe-polish? With you as back-up
He plans to have the Hydrans black up.

Er, David,
News from Michael Lawrence—
He bumped into Le Goff in Florence;
After some drinks the pair decided
Nevermore to be divided,
And planned a show of Art for All
In the Melina Mercouri Hall.

But, David,
They need your assistance,
They're doing this thing from long distance,
So can you undertake it all

And take ten crates round to the Hall;
Arrange in judicious mixture
Every sculpture, every picture.
Money? No problem. Now you pay,
But you'll be reimbursed one day.
The task itself is pure simplicity.
You organise advance publicity—
Their working title strikes a balance
Between their slightly kinky talents:
They want to call it—a joke quite harmless—
Views of Greece by Legless and Armless

And, David,
Please don't lose your temper,
But Kostis' bitch has caught distemper;
He fears the creature may be dying,
So will you kindly catch a flying—
Convey the doggie to the vet,
He'll be forever in your debt.
And could you pick up, while you're there,
All the school textbooks for next year?

Oh, David,
A bewildered female
Wants you to help her with her e-mail.

Er, David,
Richard Branson needs you soon
To hold the string of his balloon.

And, David,
Can you bring a donkey
To fetch a telly that's gone wonky?

Oh, David,
How long will it take
To round up Gabriella's snake?

Er, David,
Can you mend a light,
Unblock a loo, and book a flight?

And, David,
An Israeli lawyer
Has been making inquires for yer.

But, David,
Tonight you can relax,
Unplug the phone, switch off the fax,
Watch some television, soppy
Enough to make your hard disk floppy.
On this your birthday, we wish you well,
And everyone else can go to—
Spetses, Ermioni, Poros—anywhere but Hydra.

But, David,
Think how life would crawl
If nobody wanted you at all—

Written By Roger Green. © Studio Viriditas Productions 1997

APPENDIX B

ESCAPE FROM THE RAT RACE REDUX

One evening my ex let out a scream from the bathroom.

Convinced a *megalo serrandapothi* could be the only possible wild life to cause such panic, I grabbed a slipper.

While we are not high on the menu, these forty-legged, red-brown creatures pack a sting and are, at the very least, to be evicted from the premises. I have seen one over a foot long—so big it couldn't fit down a shower drain!

I bumped into the highly agitated woman fleeing the loo, making much noise and gesturing with her hands to indicate a three-foot something. The grand daddy of all centipedes, I assumed.

"A giant sewer rat."

"What, where?"

"Climbing out of the toilet!"

I looked at my flimsy slipper. Even if she was only half exaggerating, I was poorly armed, and so headed for the kitchen to find a broom.

"It was standing with its back legs on the back of the bowl—straddled across, front paws on the lip, about to get out. It was black and wet. Imagine if I had been sitting down. It is so big it could barely turn around to escape back down the pipe!" she gushed. "And you think it's funny!"

I explained about the need to change armaments—hence my apparent desertion from the front line.

"If indeed there was a man-eating rodent in our loo, then obviously a featherweight synthetic slipper wasn't going to do the job."

"What if it comes back?"

"We keep the lid down until the hardware store opens." A trap seemed the obvious solution, if only for peace of mind.

"But it can lift the lid."

"Then we'll put a weight on it."

"But what if the kid wants to use the loo in the middle of the night?"

Convinced the rat could return, and finding the battening solution wanting, she resorted to defensive tactics common to many housewives. Chemical warfare!

A large rat was a formidable foe, and Baygon wasn't going to do the trick, so she went to the supermarket before it closed.

"I'll make sure he doesn't fancy coming up my loo again," she muttered as she disappeared straight into the bathroom upon return.

I next heard the most dreadful hacking. She came stumbling out, gasping between coughs. Three bottles of hydrochloric acid, topped up with lashings of bleach, had created a gas strong enough to topple horses.

By this time wafts of noxious vapor had followed her into the lounge; doors and windows flew open. Newly polished brass door handles oxidized green.

Next morning, it didn't take much sleuthing the to find the cause of this rodent invasion.

"Our neighbor, Yannis," tutted the landlady, hands on hips. He had been cleaning out his wine barrels and had poured *petrelio* (petrol) into the communal *vothros* (septic tank). Fumes in the rat's colony had forced an evacuation. The evidence was reinforced the day after by the floating body of a juvenile rat in the toilet of my writing bunker.

The neighborhood smelled less flammable after a couple of days, and I guess the surviving rats went back underground. Yannis promised not to rinse his barrels into the *vothros* the following spring, and we began actively encouraging the local cat population.

At around the same time, our other neighbor's cat had half a dozen kittens, which he'd carried off one night to a distant neighborhood once they were weaned.

The Sprog, my animal-loving, preteenage stepdaughter Harriet, brought them all back under cover of dark the next evening.

The neighbor's wife looked perplexed the following morning, so Harriet decided to help her out.

"See, no matter where you take them, this mother is clever and will bring them home," she explained. She knew that most islanders abhor the murder of animals and that now the returned kittens would at least be fed.

* * *

As I sat in my bunker shortly after this incident, putting together the final draft of the first edition of this book, *Rhubarbs from a Rock: Escape from the Rat Race*, I came across a Photoshopped image I had created of a rat in the bunker's toilet bowl. It reminded me of the larger rat that had played a starring role in the above rhubarb and also reflected my ideas about the rat race in general. In my view, the alternative to days spent in the rat race is life in a rat maze. It's not speed that counts; it's how you get there, and no single way is simple.

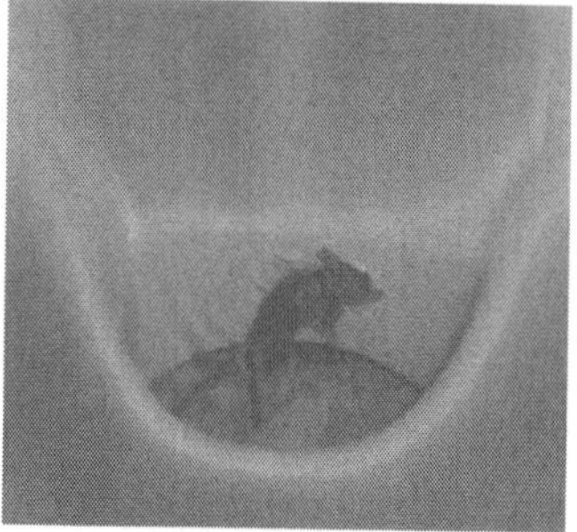

Cover images for Rhubarbs I and II.

In that same bunker I began working on *Rhubarbs Too: A Sucker for a Pretty Place*, now incorporated into this volume. As I was writing away in mid-February I was unfathomably attacked by swarms of mosquitoes. I set fire to spiral coils and lathered myself in repellant, and still they came. Hence the proposed cover image for the second book:

I obviously survived the mozzie war and moved on with life. For those contemplating escaping the rat race, I have this advice: travel light, pack Kevlar, acquire a thick skin and a cast-iron stomach, and develop an immunity to rhubarbs.

GLOSSARY

aerodromio	airport
aeroplano	airplane
Afriki	Africa
aftos eena o David	that is David
amessos	right away
astinomia	police
asvesti	whitewash
avga	eggs
avrio	tomorrow
bazi	rubble
bravo re!/sou!	well done, you!
catastrophia	catastrophe
chlorinei	chlorine
democrasia	democracy
demos	municipality
dimarxhos	the mayor
disscolo	difficult
dora	gift
dromo	road
eemay	I am
eesai endaxi?	are you okay?
efharisto para poli	thank you very much
egho	I have

Eirlandos	Irishman
ella	come here
ena peninta	one fifty
endaxi	alright
etsi	like that
Fahgan Ntevint numero epta	Fagan David number seven
fassaria	commotion
file mou	my friend
glossa	language
glyko	sweet
helicoptero	helicopter
batteria pethane	battery is dead
kai	and
kalamari	squid
kalispera	good afternoon
kalo taxithi	good trip
kanga	pneumatic drill
kathera	clean
keeria/ keerios	missus/mister
ketzup	tomato sauce
klepsie	steal
klistophobia	claustrophobia
kokkinelli	rose wine
kokkoretsi	traditional Greek Pascha dish
komputer	computer
logariasmos	the bill
loulouthi	flower
malaka	wanker
malaka eemay?	I am a wanker?
essai ena malaka!	you are a wanker!
malako	soft
manyana	tomorrow in Spanish
megalo	big/large

meh kati paraxeni	but something strange
methavrio	day after tomorrow
mezes	appetizers
mikro probleema	small problem
moustardo	mustard
mularia enai poli thoulia	mules are a lot of work
musta	nonalcoholic grape juice
neh	yes
nero	water
numero ena	number one
keerios demarxos	mister mayor
octopothie	octopus
olla endaxi	all okay/fine
oraya	lovely
othontaglyffeetha	toothpick
oxi	no
pali	again
palio	old
pappou	grandfather
parakalo	please
mia beira, ke ena boukali pagomeni aspro krasie meh tessera vouteria	one beer please, and a bottle of white wine with four glasses
thelo avga ke baycon	I would like eggs and bacon
malaka	wanker
Pascha	Greek Easter
pethane	he died
petrelio	petrol
phantasmos	ghost
philosophia	philosophy
plakakia	floor tiles
platia	town square
po-po-po	uh-oh

poli paleo	very old
portofoli	wallet
poté	never
póte	when
poutana	call girl
pragmata	things
pseftis	liar
revma	electricity
san	like
Schloss	castle
seismos	earthquake
serrandapothi	centipede
signomee	excuse me
skoopethia	rubbish/garbage
spatoula	spatula
spiti/spitaki	house/little house
tarantoola	tarantula
tavli	back gammon
tee	what
tee echies?	what have you got?
tee kanees me to kokkinelli mou?	what is happening with my rosé wine?
tee kanees/kanete etho?	what are you doing here?
tee nah kanomay?	what can we do?
tee symveni?	what is the matter?
tellyorasie	television
theeskolo	difficult
thekahdes	decades
thelo leego kokkinelli sou!	I want a bit of your rose wine!
thermofisino	hot water heater
tiropita	cheese pie
to xerees?	do you know?
tora	now

vlepete	look, you look
vothros	septic tank
xeni	foreigner
xrimata apo Polandia eetaneh mesa	polish currency was inside
yamas!	cheers!
yassou	hello/goodbye
yaya	grandmother
yia to mellon	for the future

ABOUT THE AUTHOR

David Fagan, born of nomadic Irish parents in 1958, spent his formative years in Africa, confused by circumstances beyond his control. After lunch on a Greek island day trip in 1983, he opted against reboarding the cruise boat. He has lived and worked on Hydra full-time, pursuing its alternative lifestyle by any means that presented itself, since 1984. These days he lives in Kamini, a village in many ways reminiscent of Hydra thirty years ago, the Hydra portrayed in this book. He has a keen interest in astronomy, history, Formula 1 motor racing, and international rugby; he understands the rules of cricket and has mostly forgotten how to drive.

In 2006 his now wife Jennifer joined him in full-time residence on the Rock. Aside from writing and editing, they run three websites about Hydra: the Kamini Comet (www.davidfagan.org); a tourism website (www.hydraisland greece.com); and a website to raise funds for the island's cats (www.hydraark.org). David also runs the Fair Society, a charity to raise funds for future-asteroid-interception research (www.fair-society.org).

Printed in Great Britain
by Amazon.co.uk, Ltd.,
Marston Gate.